Fighting Nature

ANIMAL PUBLICS
Melissa Boyde & Fiona Probyn-Rapsey, Series Editors

Other titles in the series:

Animal death
Ed. Jay Johnston & Fiona Probyn-Rapsey

Animals in the Anthropocene: critical perspectives on non-human futures
Ed. The Human Animal Research Network Editorial Collective

Cane toads: a tale of sugar, politics and flawed science
Nigel Turvey

Engaging with animals: interpretations of a shared existence
Ed. Georgette Leah Burns & Mandy Paterson

Fighting nature

Travelling menageries, animal acts and war shows

Peta Tait

SYDNEY UNIVERSITY PRESS

First published by Sydney University Press
© Peta Tait 2016
© Sydney University Press 2016

Reproduction and Communication for other purposes
Except as permitted under the Act, no part of this edition may be reproduced, stored in a retrieval system, or communicated in any form or by any means without prior written permission. All requests for reproduction or communication should be made to Sydney University Press at the address below:

Sydney University Press
Fisher Library F03
University of Sydney NSW 2006
AUSTRALIA
Email: sup.info@sydney.edu.au
sydney.edu.au/sup

National Library of Australia Cataloguing-in-Publication Data

Creator:	Tait, Peta, 1953– author.
Title:	Fighting nature: travelling menageries, animal acts and war shows / Peta Tait.
ISBN:	9781743324301 (paperback)
	9781743324318 (ebook: epub)
	9781743324325 (ebook: mobipocket)
Series	Animal Publics.
Notes:	Includes bibliographical references and index.
Subjects:	Human-animal relationships--19th century.
	Animals in the performing arts--Social aspects.
	Animals and civilization--19th century.
	Exotic animals--Social aspects.
	Animal welfare--Social aspects--19th century.
Dewey Number:	304.27

Cover image: Detail from *Claire Heliot*, poster by Adolph Friedländer (1903), Circusarchief Jaap Best Collection, circusmuseum.nl
Cover design by Miguel Yamin

Contents

Acknowledgements	vii
Introduction	ix
1 Ferocious lion acts	1
2 War with animals	37
3 Imperial hunting show legends	67
4 Mobs and hooligans, crowds and fans	103
Plates	135
5 Head in the colonial lion's mouth	145
6 War arts about elephantine military empires	179
7 Nature's beauties and scientific specimen contests	221
Conclusion	249
Works cited	255
Index	271

Acknowledgements

This book about 19th-century menageries and animal acts emerged out of research into trained elephant and big cat acts in the 20th century, and I continue to be very grateful for the support of friends and colleagues who made it possible for these histories of animal performance to be published. I am in your debt. I want to sincerely thank Annie McGuigan for all those countless big and small ways in which she encourages and thoughtfully supports my work, and for her invaluable comments on the early draft.

Thank you to Dr Rosemary Farrell for her research assistance on this project, and to others who assisted with earlier archival research projects on circus, and a big thank you as always to Dr Diane Carlyle. *Fighting nature* has been directly supported by La Trobe University's (LTU) English and Theatre and Drama DPR research funding, and indirectly by LTU Faculty of Humanities and Social Sciences study leave awarded in 2011. Thanks to my LTU colleagues and special thanks to Professor Sue Thomas, Dr Kim Baston, and my collaborators on the Circus Oz living archive project. As well, I would like to acknowledge the animal studies reading group in Melbourne until recently convened by Dr Siobhan O'Sullivan, because it provides ongoing and invaluable discussion of the socio-political frameworks surrounding non-human animals. Thanks to Dr Melissa Boyde and Dr Fiona Probyn-Rapsey for seeing the potential of this work for their series and thanks to Dr Agata Mrva-Montoya and Susan Murray at Sydney University Press.

Earlier versions of the chapters on Van Amburgh's act and on Fillis' circus lion act appear in Tait 2009 and 2011, and on Seeth's, Morelli's, Pianka's and Heliot's acts in Tait (forthcoming).

Introduction

Crowbar in hand, Isaac Van Amburgh became famous for confronting lions in the confined space of a cage in a new type of public entertainment. His look alone was believed to subdue lions although in performance he manhandled them forcefully. Sensationalist handling acts proliferated and the feat that came to typify 19th-century travelling menageries involved tamers, including lion queen Ellen Chapman, putting their heads into a lion's mouth. Shows in which captive animals submitted to humans proved extremely popular, and Van Amburgh also appeared fighting tigers and lions in elaborate theatrical pantomimes about imperial wars. By the mid-19th century, lion tamer acts were emulating African safari hunts with pistols fired into the air. Similarly war re-enactments with animals and nationalistic sentiments not only increased in number but greatly increased in scale, reproducing realistic effects with the latest cannons, gunpowder and trained horse actors lying dead.

Fighting nature: travelling menageries, animal acts and war shows reveals how animals were integrated into staged scenarios of confrontation throughout the 19th century, ranging from lion acts in small cages to large-scale re-enactments of war.[1] Public demand for animal shows ensured their expansion. The coercive treatment of,

---

1   'Animal' is used throughout for 'non-human animal' and 'human' refers to 'human animal'. The species names used follow common usage.

and fraught interaction with, travelling animals in such fighting scenarios infiltrated every aspect of cultural activity: from theatrical performance to visual art, from adventure books to scientific pursuits. Initially presenting a handful of exotic animals, travelling menageries grew to contain multiple species in their many thousands, and these animals in captivity were indirectly or directly caught up in simulations, and actual incidents, arising from the violent actions of humans. *Fighting nature* describes how a range of human fighting practices coincided with animal exhibition and animal presence in public entertainment that spread globally. From staged enactments of power and nationhood to spontaneous offstage physical fights in menageries, animals were surrounded by notions of fighting that were formal and informal, orchestrated and accidental.

I propose that while the theatrical mimicry of fighting reflected cultural fascination with ideas of conflict, acts with animals emerged from, and converged with, social and species processes of actual confrontation, conflict and violence and overwhelmed any narrative of reciprocated human–animal kindness. While staged battles with animals pandered to national hubris, far less glorious were numerous offstage fights that erupted between humans in and around menagerie cages. An atmosphere of threat and hostility permeated the 19th-century travelling menagerie and first-hand accounts reveal that members of the public attacked animals. The concept of fighting additionally denotes the human effort to subdue struggling animals but keep them alive, while emphasising how animals fought back; animals were not passive in this process or in lives lived in captivity. Animal shows repeatedly demonstrated emotionally conflicted human–animal and human–social relations. Yet, conversely, theatrical rhetoric about reciprocated kindness and pantomime narratives delivered a false impression of affection and harmonious friendship between humans and other animal species. The contention of this book is that since aggression and violence underpinned the exhibition of animals and manifested overtly in the very popular fighting acts and war shows, aggressive violence towards animals shaped public experience. The travelling menagerie and the war re-enactment in circus were thereby contributing to the militarisation of society and its values rather than merely reflecting them. A precept of fighting nature, even war with nature or 'nature to war against', haunted 19th-century animal exhibition.[2]

Introduction

Travelling shows presenting exotic wild animal species increased in parallel with the expansion of the process of hunting to obtain them and this book details how it reached an almost incomprehensible scale in the 19th century – actual total numbers are difficult to estimate.[3] Animals were caught up in a chain of economic transactions that were emblematic of a 19th-century determination to exploit nature, often through force. An immeasurable number of animals were hunted, trapped, transported and traded for profit to European and North American menageries and zoos, and those bought by travelling menageries continued to be transported and moved from place to place. Menageries proliferated in Britain and the rest of Europe in the first half of the 19th century and, as an exported entertainment form, expanded greatly in the USA after the mid-century and in the far reaches of the British Empire in southern Africa, Australia and New Zealand towards the end of that century. The exotic animals deployed in performance were initially transported from colonial homelands to imperial centres, but through the century they were also moved around colonial regions. Menageries grew into auxiliary businesses accompanying the largest circuses after the 1870s, touring geographically diverse regions and travelling back to Britain and Europe with circuses towards the end of the century.

Fighting nature investigates the significance of what was being enacted through menagerie acts, spectacles and theatrical performances that highlighted animals between the 1820s and 1910s. It asks: what ideas of nature did touring menageries, animal acts and war shows manifest?[4] It appears that animals embodied broad concepts of nature, though it was fearful expectations of attack that proved particularly popular with 19th-century audiences. While ideas of a fearful nature were being challenged by social thinking – for example, by Thomas Carlyle and John Stuart Mill, and David Hume and Charles Darwin – the public attended menageries in large numbers. Although themes

---

2   Carnegie 1898, ix. This idea was expressly picked up in commentaries about the extremes of colonial environments and expressed as 'Nature to war against'; it was also said that 'nature everywhere demands his toil'.
3   The common usage of 'species' as a generic term is retained and 'exotic' refers to imported animals and 'wild' refers to exotic animals captured from the wild.
4   For a seminal history of British ideas of nature, see Thomas 1984.

of aggressive interaction were juxtaposed with displays of what Harriet Ritvo summarises as an 'ordered creation' with animals 'sedately marshaled' in the Victorian zoo menagerie,[5] orchestrated performances of conflict attracted attention and even notoriety as they reinforced belief in a need for human dominance. Fighting acts were the lead exhibits in the travelling menagerie and circus pantomime was dominated by war re-enactments with horses. In comparison, where a quality of timidity was accorded to an exotic wild species, the species was invariably relegated to a subsidiary tier of menagerie exhibition.

Animals were caught up in human wars everywhere and the advent of 19th-century war re-enactments with animals made this deployment publicly visible, if not war's deadly consequences.[6] As imperialist ventures came to be embodied by exotic animals, they became covertly indicative of an imperialism of the human species towards other species. Animals were part of the official technology of war, but they were also scapegoats for human social and personal frustration. As Kathleen Kete points out, anti-animal cruelty legislation was overtly connected to fears of social revolution and mob violence, and the protection of animals involved modelling 'restraint of angry impulses'.[7]

During the process of researching 19th-century animal acts, I found recurring descriptions of bad behaviour by spectators, and descriptions of menagerie workers fighting each other and the townspeople. A common thread of fights and fighting emerged from first-hand accounts of 19th-century menagerie and circus menagerie life in Britain, and in the USA and in other parts of the world. This suggested continuity with behaviour patterns identified in the 18th century. Louise Robbins specifies deceptive businesses, staged animal fights, bloodshed, and human fights at fairs in 18th-century France, and that fighting activity was common despite 'a widespread trend in Europe away from public displays of the suffering and death of both animals and humans'.[8] This aspect suggests an ongoing carnivalesque dimension to the public fair that Mikhail Bakhtin points to in medieval gatherings in which social status could be temporarily reversed and social propriety ignored. In an investigation

---

5 Ritvo 1987, 243.
6 Cooper 1983; Hediger 2012.
7 Kete 2007b, 3.
8 Robbins 2002, 93.

Introduction

of the sensory responses to animals and utility among 18th-century spectators, Christopher Plumb outlines how exhibited 'animals are fed, teased and beaten by both proprietors and spectators, and these animals would evoke feelings of empathy, disgust or fear'.[9] Such tendencies did not disappear in the 19th century, and actually expanded with an increased scale of exhibition.

Audiences for touring menageries were largely local. The arrival of a touring menagerie show with staged cage acts frequently coincided with incidents of local conflict and fighting in the attendant crowd. I suggest that exotic animal exhibition implicitly aligned incidents of misbehaviour in the local social environment of the impermanent menagerie with the distant processes of aggressive acquisition in a remote colonial location often at war. Violence surrounded exhibited animals, from the circumstances of their acquisition and trade to their inclusion in staged acts that simulated aggression or depicted official war history, and to the ad hoc bad behaviour among menagerie spectator throngs. Exotic animals in the 19th century became a metaphoric part of narratives of overt and covert human violence that implicated the overarching politics of nationalist and military conquest and economic exploitation as well as local disturbance and unrest indicative of social turmoil. The menagerie exposed social schisms and anxieties within the larger political context.

This book offers a history of how the range of public performances expanded as travelling menageries grew in scale throughout the 19th century and reached audiences everywhere. It focuses on travelling menageries, including those menageries that travelled with circuses, and it seeks to add to the recent analysis of the history of the zoo and of the menagerie.[10] The selective focus is on animals that toured, rather than on menagerie zoos with permanent sites that may have also staged performances. This is an investigation of staged acts[11] that accompanied exhibited animals managed in businesses called menageries.[12] It

---

9   Plumb 2010b, 273.
10   See, for example: Hoage & Deiss 1996; Hancocks 2001; Hanson 2002; Rothfels 2002a; Baratay & Hardouin-Fugier 2002; Simons 2012. Also see Bennett 1995.
11   Robbins 2002, 265, note 71, explains that further investigation of staged acts is needed.
12   For a definition, see Veltre 1996, 19.

also considers accounts of how humans and animals in 19th-century travelling menageries were regularly threatened, which may parallel similar incidents involving circus performers; this aspect of circus history is generalised rather than particularised.

The open space in which the travelling menagerie was located acquired significance through the temporary presence of the animals and it became a socially ambiguous space, one perceived as unordered. Reflecting on 19th-century distinctions, Ellen Velvin explains that '[i]n all zoological gardens the animals are mainly kept for purposes of science, but in the animal shows they are kept for amusement and profit, and the environment is totally different'.[13] While such a division of purpose may have been less manifest in practice, it was this different atmosphere that was an inducement to spectator responses. The anecdotal accounts of showmen suggest that an unsettled local situation became heightened by the arrival of the show. Travelling menagerie tent shows encountered unruly spectators and confrontational mobs as they moved from town to town. In the mid-19th century, William Coup explains how the spaces occupied by touring shows in the USA:

> appeared to be the favourite arena for the settlement of the neighborhood feuds that were then characteristic of backwoods communities. Weapons of every sort, from fists to pistols, were employed and bloodshed was the rule rather than the exception.[14]

For spectators, the menagerie seemed to have fewer restrictions and less status than other travelling shows such as circuses that were graded according to the standard of equestrian skill. Menageries were at the outer limit of socially acceptable entertainment and in part because of expectations of trouble. George Conklin claims that where 1870s tenting circuses also had accompanying menagerie tents, this meant that '[t]he menagerie was a sort of catch-all in the show' as it included 'men and animals not definitely connected with some other part of the aggregation'.[15] A perception of a disparate grouping may have inadvertently influenced spectator attitudes.

---

13   Velvin 1906, 24–25.
14   Coup 1901, 10–11.
15   Conklin 1921, 148.

Introduction

An undercurrent of defensive hostility remained palpable. Abuse and fights were regular occurrences in an environment founded on the physical dominance and submission of animals. A social realm of hostile behaviour towards animals and fights among humans was connected by animal species and individual animals to the staging of battle spectacles with horses and menagerie animals that depicted conflicts played out in foreign lands. At the same time, a contradictory ideal of animal–human kindness appears in pantomime narratives about human conflict in foreign places with sympathetic animals aligned with one side. Rhetoric about kindness diverted attention from violent treatment and fighting practices.

Ritvo's foundational investigation of attitudes to domesticated and imported animals within 19th-century British culture reveals how social notions of compassion and kindness in animal care also became indicative of national pride, and this identification became important to the development and acceptance of anti-cruelty values.[16] Principles encouraging the wellbeing of working animals were only erratically and spasmodically extended to the care of travelling menagerie animals. Proclamations of kindness towards animals reflected human ideals, and the struggle for the moral improvement of humanity was also played out in rhetoric about animals in menageries. Simplistic beliefs and injurious practices in animal care often occurred because of inadequate knowledge about the behaviour of specific animal species. Though several enterprising menagerie owners and animal keepers championed kindness to appeal to public sentiments and possibly to offset spectator criticism, it also seemed to be a source of dispute among them. Expectations of kindness were more indicative of broader patterns of belief circulating in the British Empire than actual menagerie practices. There were persistent claims that kindness shown towards large captive animals would be reciprocated, but kindness was ineffectual and unreliable for the menagerie management of caged and roped animals. Behind the scenes, the treatment of travelling exotic animals could be brutal, so the atmosphere surrounding captive animals remained volatile.

Throughout the 19th century, exotic animal acts in the Anglo-American menagerie were expressly linked to religious stories that

---

16 Ritvo 1987. For the history of UK campaigns against animal performance, see Wilson 2015.

reiterated human moral triumph and animal benevolence, adventurous journeys of exploration and conquest, mythic Herculean acts, and historical and national socio-political events of battles and wars. These were delivered through short descriptors on the sides of cages, promotional handbills and long theatrical narratives; an animal tamer's costume, props, gestures and movements also conveyed specific narrative impressions. Other 19th-century narratives with human–animal tableaus, however, evoked fantasy worlds in which humans either befriended, or were befriended by, a number of different animal species. Although menagerie animal acts might seem removed from a literary domain, there was continuous exchange with other spheres of culture, and influential books also included the memoirs of big-game safari hunters, one written by the leading circus showman, GA Farini.

The demand for shows that staged aggression was unmistakable, for while timidity in animals may have been endearing it remained less exciting and less marketable. At the same time controversy about 19th-century touring menageries reflected social unease about the risks in staged acts, since they magnified the possibility of violent death from animal attacks. Paradoxically, the possibility of witnessing such an attack attracted spectators. The potential for accidents became a source of compelling anxiety, particularly since accidents featured in newspapers. Concern for animal welfare, however, was less apparent. At least in response to public displays of carnivore feeding, some members of the public expressed disgust that this was on show.

Menagerie acts, like other performance forms, were cultural inventions created by imaginative performers[17] and industrious entrepreneurs who forged a number of precedents, and these were imitated and proliferated in lucrative ventures, large and small. Animal exhibition proved profitable, encouraging competitive practices among owners and fostering criminal activities, with competition among businesses becoming a feature of menagerie enterprise.

---

17 'Performer' is used throughout to refer to the 'human performer' but the term 'animal performer' is only applied here to trained acts in which a set routine was rehearsed and had involved a degree of agency from the animals (see Chapters 6 and 7). Handling acts coerced responses out of animals in public view; individual animals did become familiar with the situation and learnt to respond accordingly when handled.

Introduction

Fighting nature presents well-known acts and shows created by individuals who made menagerie history; these individuals were both human and non-human animals.[18] This history of menagerie animal shows brings to the fore the centrality of animals in all popular performances that depicted war, battles, confrontation and fighting. Their inclusion may have had a normalising effect on social attitudes to animals in situations of violence. Certainly some 19th-century observers indicate conflicted responses and possibly species discomfort with animal inclusion in displays of fighting. Nevertheless the animal shows probably made the co-option of different animal species in war seem acceptable to the 19th-century public. Anti-cruelty campaigns did not prevent human war practices being extended to an ever-increasing number of animals, or the hunting of animals by military men becoming an extension of war.

Approaches to colonised animals

The contribution of 19th-century popular culture to ideologies of colonisation and empire has been investigated in historical analysis since the 1980s,[19] encompassing animal studies more recently. Public zoos and menageries encapsulated the prevailing attitudes towards nature in the 19th century, as animal exhibition explicitly responded to curiosity about the regions in colonial empires, and their growth and proliferation became indicative of imperialist triumph and conquest. Menagerie animals were a visible part of a wider national ethos of British and European colonial rule and the shows drew spectators from across the social spectrum, including politicians, members of the royal families and the military. Animal acts reinforced state authority. The appeal of shows with exotic animals additionally came from their capacity to enhance public displays of nationhood and nationalistic evocation of warring empires.

Fighting nature draws on analysis of popular culture and its social and political influence, including in relation to science and natural history,[20] since travelling menageries and animal shows also bridged these

---

18 Alberti 2011a; the volume presents animal biographies.
19 MacKenzie 1986a.

concepts. The topicality of 19th-century theatre in Britain and its depiction of political events and wars has been well recognised within theatre history.[21] The capacity of circus in Victorian England to espouse patriotism and nationalism has been convincingly investigated following similar analysis of American circus history.[22] The cultural significance of touring menageries and the use of menagerie animals in pantomimes is shown in *Fighting nature* to have perpetuated similar social meaning. In addition, newspapers disseminated aspects of British and European culture, including sport in the colonies,[23] and it can be added, informed the public about animal shows. In acknowledging a proliferation of histories of popular culture, Billie Melman argues for 'the circulation of history between its images and the forms and social lives and meanings given to these images through procedures and practices of usage and, when possible, through the imagination and fantasy', in order to interpret the dynamism of cultural representation and materiality.[24] Popular histories of animals demand comparable approaches and interdisciplinary corollaries but also recognition of ethical boundaries in human–animal relations.[25]

Investigations of 19th-century British social practices, including colonial hunting and imperialism, prove invaluable sources.[26] A history of 19th-century travelling menagerie animal shows is a considerable challenge – not least because each distinctive species warrants a history – since archival records are limited, irregular and are frequently generalised. Further, as David Lambert and Alan Lester explain, there was a 'longstanding problem' for historians about 'how to write about such vastly different places, processes and people as those contained within the ever-changing 19th-century British Empire at the same time – how to link the local and particular (metropolitan *and* colonial) with the general and the universal (imperialism)'.[27] Animals could be added to 'places, processes and people'. Given that there was no singular

---

20 For example, see, MacKenzie 1990a; Goodall 2002.
21 Bratton 1980, 119–37; MacKenzie 1986b, 2–3.
22 Assael 2005; Davis 2002.
23 Baker & Mangan 1987.
24 Melman 2006, 4.
25 Fudge 2002, 3–18.
26 Ritvo 1987, 4; MacKenzie 1988.
27 Lambert & Lester 2006b, 4–5.

colonial discourse, Lambert and Lester suggest that individuals might be able to effectively reflect the dispersed and layered nuances of colonial diversity. This approach also makes a history of menagerie animal acts feasible, since individuals illustrated local settings and precedents as well as showing how the specific circumstances of a menagerie can point to the wider set of practices and power relations. It should be pointed out again that the individual lives that encompass and illustrate discursive frameworks were also non-human ones. The activities of individual humans and animals whose acts became indicative of types of performances with travelling shows, were forged in specific localities, but these spread globally.

Histories of imperialism and colonialism expose how cultural dominance manifested conflict and armed confrontation. Catherine Hall's summary of studies in 19th-century British imperialism delineates approaches in postcolonial studies, maps the progressive expansion of the British Empire in the 19th century, and defines terms.[28] While this imperial dominance was achieved through strategies of overt war and violence – more evident in military histories – it is also in historical studies of gender and colonial identity where the impact of an unfolding spectrum of socio-political violence is exposed.[29] Here individual lives encapsulate larger forces. Hall specifies that the postcolonial histories of indigenous peoples incorporate the history of human torture, and in relation to the persecution of the racial Other,[30] and point to larger patterns of human–to–human violence. But she focuses on how colonialisms were produced by different social groups who comprised ideas of the European,[31] and her categorisation of workers in the colonies might be extended to include menagerie workers and operators and hunters. There are insights about human violence scattered throughout a range of colonial histories.[32]

---

28 Hall 2000b.
29 For example, see Levine 2004a; Woollacott 2006. Rob Nixon (2013) proposes that there is ongoing 'slow violence' towards the environment within social structures.
30 Hall 2000b, 12–13.
31 Hall 2000b, 16: 'Travellers, merchants, traders, soldiers and sailors, farmers, prostitutes, teachers, officials and missionaries – all were engaged in colonial relations with their own particular dynamics'; 25: in addition, there were scientists.

Relevant to approaches in this book is Melman's extended analysis of the popular appeal of depictions of social and historical violence in literature and entertainment, which was also a historical consuming of history. Popular enthusiasm for imperial Britain during the 19th century even spread within North America, fuelled by public displays that encompassed entertainment, and this made manifest a psychology of 'popular imperialism' that was indicative of the dynamic between government and society.[33] In broadly defining 'popular' as something beyond a pseudonym for working class, Melman criticises the 'comfortable and secure' and 'orderly' view of history, and considers the influence of Michel Foucault's *Discipline and punish* on studies of spectacles and ideas of 'crowd-policing' as well as, it should be noted, modes of surveillance and striving for order.[34] Melman argues for a history of, and history as, a space of social danger. The point is that popular depictions did expose the material consequences of state violence; in this instance, for animal lives.

A history encompassing practices ranging from hunting in the colonies to touring colonising countries provides one way of exploring the bodily impact of social forces of human violence. While definitions of human violence remain contested, it is evident that animals were completely caught up in an all-pervasive conflict that underpinned land acquisition and cultural dominance and the enforcement of colonial rule. Summarising a process of unrestrained violence in colonial territory, Ritvo writes that '[k]illing large exotic animals emerged as both the quintessential activity and symbol of imperialism'.[35] While indigenous populations fought wars to retain their culture and land, colonial enterprise additionally encompassed eliminating roaming animals

---

32 Jock McCulloch contends that interdisciplinary investigations offer useful explorations in relation to indirect manifestations of state power. See McCulloch 2004, 220–21, 223, 224. McCulloch cites Hannah Arendt's *On Violence*, arguing that the state perpetuates political violence, and Norbert Elias in *The Civilizing Process*, arguing that modern European states developed instrumental forms of state violence.
33 MacKenzie 1986b, 6–7.
34 Melman 2006. For a theoretical discussion of animals and Foucault, see Tester 1991. For the influence of Foucault on ideas of looking and seeing, see Flint 2000, 13–16.
35 Ritvo 2002, 34.

Introduction

from large tracts of land that could be cultivated and repopulated with European domestic species. Only some of these displaced indigenous animals survived to be sold into menageries.

British government officials and other professionals made their imperial careers in the 19th century by moving between positions in different colonies, and Lambert and Lester explain that 'each colonial life provides insight not only into the heterogeneity of the empire ... but how ideas, practices and identities developed *trans-imperially* as they moved from one imperial site to another'.[36] Contemporary historians recognise 'the networked nature of imperial space'.[37] Lambert and Lester broadly chart the development of approaches within the discipline of history from an acknowledgement of political resistance within what was termed the 'periphery' of the empire – which necessitated government intervention and military involvement in former trade outposts and ensured that economic and political motivations became caught up in recognition of the function of geographical space – to the subsequent explicit critique of ideas of centre and periphery. Such histories highlight the influence of interconnected ventures by individuals within the context of official interventionist policies, in ways that are also pertinent to menagerie history.

The official discourse of empires camouflaged the violence of occupation and wars of resistance. Lester outlines the stereotyping of indigenous peoples within three broad overlapping British colonial discourses – 'governmentality, humanitarianism and settler capitalism' – seeking to produce 'orderly, well-regulated behaviour'.[38] He continues that discourses were 'made and remade' as dispersed places were 'knitted together within a global cultural and political fabric'. While ports connected by ships linked the colonies and Britain, these material links and the economic practices were effectively served by discourses of the British and colonial press. News about colonial wars, however, did not necessarily reflect an official position and instead could reveal diverse interests.[39]

---

36 Lambert & Lester 2006b, 2, italics in original.
37 Lambert & Lester 2006b, 3, 14, also 4.
38 Lester 2001, 4–5.
39 Potter 2003, 43.

Certainly the 'geographical imagination' of historians in relation to the significance of geographical place and space has become part of analysis and this can be usefully extended to animal histories.[40] But perhaps a historian's effort to reflect order when faced with profuse materials with complex intersections means that the prevalence of periodic incidents of social disorder escapes closer scrutiny. Incidents of disorder may need to be considered for their links to larger patterns. The ways in which socially sanctioned violence and fighting led to darker, covert consequences and repercussions and infiltrated all facets of personal and professional experience becomes explicit in accounts of individual lives in colonial regions. For example, one commissioner in South Africa was educated in an atmosphere of competitive sport and flogging, developed a reputation as a game hunter, and served in the cavalry in wartime before he took up official government and policing positions that included restricting the mobility of local indigenous women and ensuring the migration of male workers.[41] This imposition of force on indigenous people exists within a continuum that also crosses the species divide. The significance of this example is that it cuts across different histories. Developments in sport, war, education, employment and colonial life might constitute discrete histories, but these became unified in the lived experience of individuals so that incidents of violence that seem contained might be located within widespread connected patterns of social violence perpetuated through multiple social spheres inclusive of the treatment of animals.

While accounts by, and of, the individuals who made use of colonial networks to hunt and exploit animals are a prelude to a history of travelling menagerie acts, it is menagerie owners, performers, workers and animals who are the focus of *Fighting nature*. Individual situations can link local circumstances to the larger realm of imperialism and the discursive frameworks are encapsulated by the individuals caught up in all types of fighting acts. Traces of these acts can be found in advertisements, posters and newspaper reviews but the gaps in the documented record mean that further explanation about animals and acts has to be sought in memoirs of showmen, which also function as primary source material. Although they must be read critically, they do

---

40 Lambert & Lester 2006b, 4, citing J Callagher and R Robinson.
41 Hayes 2000, 329, 332–34.

Introduction

provide extended accounts of individual animals and acts. Some circus histories and biographies of human performers helpfully reproduce primary documents. Animal act histories must draw on a combination of sources, and it can be presumed that more than one listing or description in documentation might imply significance.

Since each animal species was historically traded and exhibited under distinctive circumstances that varied from country to country, this account of 19th-century wild animal acts in travelling menageries in Britain and the rest of Europe, the USA, southern Africa, Australia and New Zealand must present selected examples and precedents. The usage of the terms 'animal' for non-human animal, 'species' for genera, and 'wild' to distinguish captured exotic species from domesticated ones follows common practice. My earlier investigations of circus acrobatic and trapeze history made it possible to track social advancement through innovations that pioneered major social developments and progression in, for example, athleticism, female fashions and body training.[42] It might be argued, however, that the spread of menagerie acts and exhibition was socially regressive, rather than progressive.

The following chapters focus on the staging of different ideas about fighting nature. In a staged triumph of courage, lion king Isaac Van Amburgh confirmed early 19th-century ideas about overcoming fear of nature as he aggressively entered a small cage with lions and tigers and bodily handled them (Chapter 1). Lion tamers were emulated by lion queens such as Ellen Chapman from the late 1840s, and exotic animals were also taken out of menageries to join well-trained horses in circus war re-enactments. The new genres expanded existing artistic depictions of species antagonism and hierarchical nature (Chapter 2). A gulf developed between menagerie practices of physical dominance and the inclusion of animals in quasi state ceremonies and sentimental pantomimes about 'the gentle children' of nature showing loyalty to humans. From the 1850s, performers such as Maccomo, in the costume of an African hunter, simulated the conquering of a hostile nature in staged hunting acts. Those acts reflected how show proprietors, including PT Barnum, were assisted to greatly enlarge their travelling

---

42 Tait 2005. A history of trapeze acts in theatres and circuses after the 1859 invention of flying action reveals that aerial gymnasts pioneered physical culture and body-fitting clothing for males and females and were socially influential.

menageries by British and other European hunters who journeyed to Africa and other remote geographical places (Chapter 3). Meanwhile, individual spectators attacked animals and menagerie crowds included aggressive hooligan and criminal elements. In contrast there were the loyal spectators who rallied in defence of national favourites such as the elephant Jumbo, in Britain, after Barnum bought him for the American public (Chapter 4). In another example, audiences were willingly duped by the hoax of a whitewashed elephant billed as nature's mysterious sacred elephant while they rejected one obtained from an Eastern temple by Barnum. Menagerie businesses travelling with tenting circuses expanded noticeably in the USA after the 1870s, delivering large spectacles of a boundless nature. They toured internationally and were emulated in southern Africa, Australia and New Zealand by shows that additionally contained re-enactments of indigenous wars in southern Africa (Chapters 5 and 6). By then the menagerie tamer routinely put his or her head into the lion's mouth in acts staged alongside demonstrations of carnivores being fed raw meat; perceived as displays of primitive nature, these proved particularly controversial in the colonies, where acts with female tamers were banned (Chapter 5). By the turn of the 20th century, as tamer handling was superseded by Hagenbeck's and Bostock's animal training with minimal bodily contact, male performers, dressed as soldiers, demonstrated physical discipline and dominance over nature while female performers like Claire Heliot (see cover) were attributed older, 19th-century ideals of kindly care for nature (Chapters 6 and 7). The training of exotic animals was viewed as an aspect of the expanding natural sciences alongside the safari hunt for museum specimens – and both captivated the American president, Theodore Roosevelt, who went on safari (Chapter 7). By the early 20th century, staged spectacles brought together all the 19th-century modes of displaying nature in fighting scenarios to accompany one gigantic battle re-enactment with war veterans and horses playing dead while the business of trading animals underpinned European war preparation. Practices related to fighting and war between humans relied on the human hunting of animals. This made human treatment of other species unmistakably war-like.

1
Ferocious lion acts

Travelling menageries exhibited groups of lions and/or tigers in small cages along with other animals throughout Britain during the 19th century. These travelling exhibitions began to include a demonstration of bravery by a lion keeper entering the small cage, and by the late 1830s well-known tamer acts included displays of force against lions. Isaac Van Amburgh rose to prominence among 'brute-tamers' for his capacity to subdue so-called wild beasts.

This chapter outlines how menagerie handling acts by male and female lion and tiger tamers developed in Britain between the 1820s and the 1860s, and considers these acts of confrontation and staged conquest in relation to 19th-century concepts of nature and fear. Early cage acts were underpinned by biblical and Roman notions that were soon enlarged with the fantasy narratives and geographical adventure stories of theatrical pantomimes.

Early exhibiting

The public exhibition of exotic animals such as big cats and elephants was intermittent until the 19th century. The Romans traded and exhibited numerous wild animals from Africa and staged them in public entertainments,[1] but exhibiting remained small-scale over the ensuing centuries in Europe with most of these rare animals destined for private collections. Exotic animals remained the possession of wealthy individuals, albeit in ways that pre-empted later menageries, and they also became a type of currency in international diplomacy.[2] For example, the Tower of London menagerie collection received a gift of three leopards from the Holy Roman Emperor Frederick II to Henry III in 1235, and this Royal Menagerie expanded through the centuries.[3] The antecedents of travelling menageries in Britain might be traced back to travelling exhibits with a single exotic animal; an elephant was exhibited after 1254, and lions were touring around Britain by 1585, and another elephant toured in 1623.[4] Lions, in particular, became the perennial favourites and in 1654 John Evelyn records how he watched a lion play with a lamb, and put his hand into a lion's mouth to feel its rough tongue.[5] Samuel Pepys describes several visits to lions on public display.[6] Three elephants were on display in Britain in 1675, 1683 and 1720 as live exhibits but did not survive long, although their bodies remained of scientific and cultural interest, and by 1803 elephants were noted as attracting the most attention.[7] Following the pattern of individual animal exhibits in Britain, a lion reached the USA in 1716, and the first tigers in 1789.[8]

Animal fights with domesticated animals were staged historically. Social resistance to animal entertainments and, in particular, the staging of animal fights gained momentum in 17th-century Britain when the Puritan leaders successfully campaigned to close London's Southwark theatres, and especially those venues involving bear-baiting

---

1   Robinson 1996, ix, republished diagram; Hoage, Roskell & Mansour 1996, 8–18, survey historical development from the ancient world to 19th-century zoos. Also see Hancocks 2001, 6–10.
2   Bedini 1997, 29–30. There were records of elephants reaching Europe in 797, 1477 and after 1510 and of an effort by Cosimo Medici to unsuccessfully stage a fight between ten lions and domesticated animals. Pope Leo X created a menagerie with lions, leopards, bears and other animals in cages. One elephant, Hanno, was sent on as a gift from Portugal to the menagerie and was depicted in visual art. Hanno was considered a white elephant and a rhinoceros was also sent, 81, 115.
3   Hahn 2003, 12–17.
4   Blunt 1976, 16–17; Hahn 2003, 107; Speaight 1980, 14.
5   Evelyn 1908, 173. The lion may have been young or toothless.
6   Jackson 2008, 77.
7   Plumb 2010a, 525–43.
8   Joys 1983, 2–3.

with dogs.[9] The human theatre was eventually reinstated under licence with the restoration of the British monarchy. Staged animal fighting, too, continued and, as might be expected, with attempts to pit an exotic animal against a domesticated breed. In 1825 George Wombwell, with Wombwell's menagerie, was aware of the fight history and gained notoriety for staging a fight between a lion and six mastiffs.[10] But such animal fighting entertainments were uncommon public practices in part because of the costs of replacing exotic animals. In entertainments for the aristocracy in Europe, however, in 'spectacular eruptions of violence . . . [t]hese fights would be played out in an abundance of brutality and blood.'[11]

The advent of menageries presenting exotic animals to the public in the 18th century expanded on the trade in exotic animals for the private menagerie collections in royal and aristocratic gardens.[12] Public menageries in Britain that travelled and presented a variety of animals, including exotic animals, developed in conjunction with the entertainments of the fair. Gilbert Pidcock's 'Exhibition of Wild Beasts' existed from 1708 as a small-scale exhibit; Pidcock travelled to fairs and through the British countryside with exotic animals in a caravan.[13] Pidcock's subsequently merged with Polito's, and later under Edward Cross it developed into the salubrious indoor Exeter Change in a permanent venue located in the centre of London.[14] By the late 18th century, travelling menageries in Britain had acquired sufficient numbers of individual exotic species to allow comparisons between members of the species. Public animal exhibition might have satisfied curiosity and provided sensory stimulation, but there was also aggression towards the animals from both exhibitors and spectators.[15]

The exhibiting of exotic animals to the paying public proved profitable and grew in scale. An 1805 advertisement for Polito's read: 'The largest travelling collection in the known world, to be seen in six safe

---

9 See Wickham 2002, Vol 2, 84–86, 165.
10 Blunt 1976, 20.
11 Baratay & Hardouin-Fugier 2002, 24–25.
12 Festing 1988, 104–17.
13 Plumb 2010a; Bostock 1972 [1927], 8; Hone 1838, 1245.
14 Altick 1978, 308–10; Ritvo 1987, 208–09.
15 Plumb 2010b, 273.

and commodious caravans, built for the purpose and all united (which altogether provides one of the noblest views of the wonderful productions of Nature ever beheld) in the Market-place.'[16] This advertisement reveals that for sixpence, members of the labouring classes and children could see the diversity of nature embodied by: 'a noble lion', 'Royal Tigers', kangaroos, panthers, a beaver, leopards, wolves, a wolverine, a 'civet', a 'muscovy cat', a 'satyr', an 'ichneumon', a possum, a 'wanderoo and upwards of fifty other quadrupeds'. Wealthier spectators were charged a shilling.

The growth of 18th-century trade networks and 19th-century colonial land acquisition facilitated the expansion of the range of animals on display. As Harriet Ritvo explains, animal trading developed within the pattern of Britain's extension of imperialist control of the colonies in Africa and Asia and followed the trade routes.[17] Since some animals, like lions and tigers, did breed in captivity, there were species-specific circumstances that should be noted in this ongoing process of menagerie expansion. The trading and exhibiting of live animals involved financial resources, and exotic animals came to be valued according to scarcity and the cost of their acquisition.

The number of travelling menageries in Britain expanded in the early 19th century with George Wombwell starting to tour Wombwell's menagerie from 1805, in competition with, for example, Ballard's, Atkins' and Hilton's.[18] Wombwell's descendants would eventually operate three touring menageries with female family members in charge at different times.[19] Travelling menageries bought from traders; John Simons presents a history of one of London's key trading businesses, run by Charles Jamrach and his sons, which also exhibited animals.[20] Public interest in animal exhibits can also be attributed to publicity, and in Britain, a lioness who escaped from Ballard's became

---

16 Bostock 1972 [1927], 8, citing advertisement in *Nottingham Journal*, 1805, 28 September.
17 Ritvo 1987.
18 Frost 1875, 74–77; Bostock 1972 [1927], 8–10.
19 Bostock 1972 [1927], 72. Wombwell's, Bostock and Wombwell's and Edmond's Royal Windsor Castle and Crystal Palace Menagerie. From the 1880s, both Frank Bostock and Edward Bostock operated major animal shows that toured internationally. Also see Alberti 2011b, 39.
20 Simons 2012, 21–50.

famous for attacking a mail delivery horse in 1817.[21] Ballard's menagerie was at Salisbury Fair when the lioness escaped from her cage into nearby fields. At one point she was mistaken for a donkey, but later emerged on the road to attack the horse pulling the Exeter mail coach. During efforts to recapture her, she killed a menagerie dog, and the publicity surrounding the episode meant that increased numbers visited the menagerie to see the lioness. In response, Ballard raised the admission fee.

Animal exhibiting grew in response to demand, and popular interest was stimulated by publicity. A menagerie would also take advantage of an animal's cleverness; for example, the elephant at Wombwell's would unbolt a door. It was the larger animals that could attract the most publicity, but since even Asian elephants were still rare by the turn of the 19th century, there was a publicity contest in Newcastle to attract spectators to view Atkins' living elephant versus Wombwell's dead one. Apparently Wombwell's dead elephant attracted larger crowds.[22]

In a significant historical development, wild animal displays expanded in longstanding public leisure garden attractions, and London's Zoological Society in Regent Park, which included animals from the Royal Tower menagerie, opened its collection to the public after 1827.[23] David Hancocks explains that animal exhibiting catered for increased numbers of the 'idly curious', at a time when untamed nature was acquiring increased value.[24] Private and public collections were understood to provide opportunities for scientific observation of exotic animals, in line with the 18th-century pursuit of knowledge. Zoological curiosity corresponded with progressive social change and even political upheaval. Walter Putnam explains that in the turmoil of political change in France, the two Indian elephants in the French royal family menagerie became 'objects of immense scientific and public curiosity' for the citizenry within the new republic because they 'served to measure the contours of the geographic world'.[25]

---

21 *Manchester Times* 1891, Menageries and lion tamers, 27 March: 4; Bostock, 1972 [1927], 9–10.
22 Frost 1875, 76.
23 Wroth & Wroth 1896; Scherren 1955.
24 Hancocks 2001, 6, 31.
25 Putnam 2007, 154.

As the numbers expanded, exhibited animals became integral to displays of nature within the wider social practices of leisure and travel and were often framed by convoluted anthropomorphic emotions. An English visitor in Paris in 1814 and 1817, who twice visited the Muséum d'Histoire Naturelle, noted seeing living lions, an elephant and Monsieur Martin Brown, the bear.[26] The personified profile of the bear was raised after he was accused of murder in 1820 when a man who fell into the bear pit was killed. Although this was not the first death, there was an investigation to alleviate public anxieties, popularly satirised as a trial in which a lion and other animals presided in judgement. It was the possibility that the victim was eaten by the bear that aroused public fears of cannibalism arising from Martin's anthropomorphised identity, but that event also coincided with social unease about wider events in the French colonies, including slave uprisings. Paula Young Lee finds that the satirical trial defended the bear with rhetoric comparable to that used in defence of human insurgents, and the prevailing counter discourse was that 'nature' needed to be displayed in ways that reflected all its divisions.[27] Physical barriers in menageries also needed to reflect beliefs about the differences between species in nature.

The problems of containment and control did inhibit menagerie expansion and this was most apparent with the travelling circus. Circus managers recognised the value of exotic animal attractions for decades before these attractions could be routinely integrated into each performance in the circus ring program. For example, a zebra was first walked around the perimeter of Astley's Circus ring in 1780, although zebras did not seem to appear again until 1832.[28] Circus was dominated by acts with horses, and a small range of menagerie cage exhibits did accompany some circuses from the 1840s. Circus was invented by Philip Astley and, for 100 years after 1768, despite increasingly complex human acrobatic feats, clowning and rope acts, the program in the circus ring was principally a display of equestrian prowess with the rider's mastery and acrobatic skills impressing spectators accustomed

---

26   Young Lee 2010, 619.
27   Young Lee 2010, 625.
28   Speaight 1980, 80; Andrew Ducrow staged two new spectacles on 24 September 1832, one of which was *The wild zebra hunt* with either four or five zebras and fireworks, see Saxon 1978, 249.

1 Ferocious lion acts

to horses and horseriding. Astley's was licensed to present equestrian shows and had both male and female riders – clown horse acts were particularly popular.[29] Under Andrew Ducrow's management, Astley's long evening programs with human acrobatic interludes and rope-dancing acts expanded the pantomimes to include spectacular melodramas expressly written to feature groups of fast-moving horses, often in war re-enactments (see Chapter 2). Some early British and European circus programs included domesticated animals from street, fair and garden performances,[30] and these were added to an evening's entertainment in the interludes between the appearances of the horses. Dogs performed from the earliest years, and trained farm animals like pigs, cows, geese, rams and goats were added periodically – there was a 'learned' pig act at Astley's by 1784.[31] Circus spectators could applaud the surprising capacity of species from familiar domestic worlds and the animals could be easily and cheaply acquired for performance.

Most bred and imported exotic animals, however, remained in the more controlled confinement of zoological gardens, public menagerie ventures and private collections. The latter included those commonly kept by scientists in the 19th century. For example, in the mid-century, as a surgical student at Oxford University, Frank Buckland kept a private menagerie of living specimens including a bear together with his dead zoological specimens; later he worked in the natural sciences.[32] An animal in a public menagerie was usually billed as being from a general geographical region and, because the public associated exotic species with faraway places, a visit to see an animal became like encountering a foreign world. A kangaroo from the Botany Bay colony (not yet unified with the other colonies as Australia) was first exhibited for a costly one shilling entry fee in London's Haymarket in 1791, to a curious public who had previously only seen the elfin-like image first drawn by Sydney Parkinson and copied by George Stubbs. Live kangaroos would subsequently become common in private and public

---

29   Saxon 1968; Kwint 2002a; 2002b.
30   Altick 1978, 40–41; see Wykes 1977, drawn images of 'tutored animals' from the Middle Ages with a bear, a monkey and a hare, 48.
31   Speaight 1980, 78–79.
32   Bompas 1886, Buckland kept a bear, a monkey called Jacko, an eagle, a jackal, marmots, guinea-pigs, squirrels, snakes and so on.

menageries, widely recognised as harmless.[33] In the first decades of the 19th century, England exported its convict prisoners to the Australian colonies, and imported fauna curiosities.[34]

Wombwell's became the best known of the travelling public menageries in Britain, and by 1840 the scale of exhibited captive animals was extensive. The public promenaded at their own pace amid the exhibited 13 lions, lionesses with cubs, eight tigers and one tigress and cubs, leopards, a puma, a jaguar, a panther, an ocelot, a sloth, bears, striped and spotted hyenas, wolves and jackals.[35] The bears included a polar bear and black and brown bears and there were three elephants, a rhinoceros, white antelope and three giraffes transported from northern Africa by Monsieur Reboulet. The giraffes were the most recent acquisition and were among the first of their kind to appear in a menagerie.

Touring public menageries provided extensive opportunities to view exotic animals and, like other entertainments, stimulated imaginative responses. As Edward Ziter explains about 19th-century entertainment spectacles, these popularised a geographical imagination with their implicit power relations.[36] Such imagining was enhanced by the sight of exhibited exotic animals.

Handling feats and fights

In 1825 an unnamed keeper at Atkins' Royal Menagerie in Britain entered a partitioned cage which held a lion and tigress and their offspring and interacted with them.[37] William Hone observes how:

> the man then took a short whip, and after a smart lash or two upon his back, the lion rose with a yawn . . . [and] by coaxing, and pushing him about, he caused the lion to sit down, and while in that position

---

33 Younger 1988, 53, 55–56; Jackson & Vernes 2010, 65.
34 Simons 2012, provides lists with prices for these imports.
35 Sturtevant 1925, 76. There were also a serval, two genets, coati-mindis, raccoons, porcupines, a pair of gnus, a Brahmin cow, and white antelope.
36 Ziter 2003, 3.
37 Winney was named on bills as the Atkins' lion tamer with Astley's by 1832, see Frost 1875, 79; Saxon 1978. George Speaight claims that the unnamed first handler was Winney, see Speaight 1980, 126.

opened the animal's ponderous jaws with his hands, and thrust his face down into the lion's throat, wherein he shouted, and there held his head nearly a minute.[38]

This feat was subsequently claimed for Isaac Van Amburgh, clearly not the first handler to undertake it.[39] Next the Atkins' keeper had the tigress jump numerous times through a two-foot (61 cm) diameter hoop. After some perseverance, the lion reluctantly followed. At the end of the act, the keeper lay on the floor sandwiched between both animals.[40] Regardless of moments of playful interaction and the act of pretending to sleep designed to display the keeper's compatibility with the lion and tiger, from the earliest menagerie acts, there was physical coercion with varying degrees of force used to bodily move lions and tigers. Pushing and handling came to typify menagerie human–animal big cat acts and underpinned the progression towards compliance and tameness by the end of the act.

Hone writes that the temperament of the tiger is 'fierce', 'cruel' and that he or she often reacts without a reason and is a species capable of 'uniform rage, a blind fury'.[41] The whole species was judged as hostile, and comparisons between leopards, lions and tigers were indicative of a 19th-century tendency to classification. The comparative scarcity of elephants in touring menageries in the first part of the 19th century was apparent in Hone's comment that Atkins claimed to have the only elephant on tour at that time.

The record of which handler was first to undertake taming and basic stunts in the menagerie cage or den was complicated by publicity that routinely laid claim to presenting a 'first'. The keeper from Atkins' was entering the cage in 1825 and possibly handling the lion's jaws, although Frank Bostock credits George Wombwell with the idea of putting on display two sick cubs alongside the keeper who nursed them to health. Wombwell had the keeper sitting with the cubs, billing him as a 'lion-tamer'.[42] Fifty years later there was acknowledgement of an

---

38　Hone 1838, 1180–81.
39　*Operative* (London) 1839, Literature, 6 January: 11.
40　Hone 1838, 1181.
41　Hone 1838, 1178.
42　Bostock 1903, 28–29.

unnamed Wombwell's keeper in the 1820s to 1830s who sat like a rider on a lion's back and opened the animal's mouth.[43] As a boy in the mid-1830s in Britain, Thomas Frost remembers seeing the Wombwell's menagerie keeper, Manchester Jack, enter the lion, Nero's, cage 'and sit on the animal's back, open his mouth'.[44] In emulation of the devout Daniel, who emerged unscathed after a night spent in the lions' cave or den, menagerie acts represented a triumph of faith over fear.[45] 'Den' was the widely used 19th-century word for 'cage' in the menagerie, providing direct biblical associations with the early Christian era in Rome, and the stories of Daniel and Androcles. But despite the legitimacy acquired through this biblical framing, even the earliest of acts with wild animals attracted critics. A journalistic account found Winney's act at Atkins' with his poses as Daniel and Hercules 'passing strange' and in poor taste.[46] Spectator responses were mixed from the outset.

There was also a quite different account of Wombwell's first fighting act. George Wombwell presented a fight between a lion and six mastiffs at Wombwell's menagerie – no keeper was mentioned. George had been told a story about lion and dog fights in the Tower of London during the reign of King James I, and he had staged a dog and lion fight in Warwick on 26 July 1825.[47] In a report recalled some years later, George Wombwell's business was poor due to competition from an increased number of menageries. George usually exhibited two lions, younger Wallace and older Nero, and he decided to put the placid Wallace on show together with six mastiff dogs for an entry price ranging from one to five guineas. All seats were sold but the fight disappointed spectators because, while the lion would scratch a dog and take a lump of skin, and the dogs looked like they would attack the lion, the performance did not become a 'serious fight'.[48] George, who made a sizable amount of money, claimed that he could not make them fight. It seems likely that this lion-baiting did take place because it was recalled as

---

43   *New York Clipper* 1872, Lions and lion tamers. 13 April: 12.
44   Frost 1875, 89.
45   See Daniel 6:23.
46   Quoted in Speaight 1980, 80–81.
47   Bostock 1972 [1927], 4; Blunt 1976, 20; Hahn 2003, 218. In December 1830 there was an inadvertently fatal fight at the Tower between a lion and two tigers. Ritvo 1987, 27 and note 92.
48   *New York Clipper* 1872, Lions and lion tamers, 13 April: 12.

part of the Wombwell family annals. Edward Bostock writes disingenuously in later years: 'Such a fight, of course, would not be allowed in these enlightened times, but in those days all sorts of animal fights were encouraged, and heavy stakes were lost and won on the results.'[49] Certainly these 'wicked sports', such as fights with domesticated animals, were prohibited by British law in 1835 and subsequently in other countries.[50] As Edward indicated, the fighting act between animals was also a gambling act.

Human-animal proximity and tamer handling also carried the misconception of compatibility between humans and wild animals. Menagerie demonstrations by tamers were periodically integrated into pantomime spectacles in the circus and the theatre from the 1830s and within narratives in which even friendship between humans and lions was possible in a faraway land. The circumstances of interaction in a theatricalised spectacle were more nuanced than that of the menagerie cage act, and therefore possibly more misleading regarding human-animal relations. Henri Martin, who made menagerie appearances in Europe from the 1820s, was an equestrian who acquired a menagerie through marriage, and he developed a reputation even among naturalists for his zoological study of animals.[51] At the Cirque Olympique in 1831, Martin performed behind a wire screen in a mimed melodrama with an orientalist narrative written especially for his group of lions. In *Hyder Ali, or the lions of Mysore*, he played the nabob Sadhusing persecuted by sultan Hyder Ali. In the show, Martin's character was eventually imprisoned in the lions' cage, and he exhibited his ease with the lions by appearing to lie down to sleep with them in a forest. This forest was home to llamas, a buffalo, a monkey, two boa constrictors and a kangaroo gathered together in a fantasy of a geographical place.[52] After Martin appeared at the Drury Lane theatre in 1831 in a version of this pantomime, the keeper Winney from Atkins' emulated the character by appearing at Astley's in 1832 billed as Zoomkantorah from India.[53]

---

49 Bostock 1972 [1927], 4.
50 Assael 2005, Appendix, 160. See Thomas 1984, 159–60, 185, about cockfighting and horseracing.
51 Saxon 1978, 82, 239–40; Thétard 1947, Vol. 2, 228.
52 Saxon 1978, 239–41. Martin retired in 1840 to run a zoo.
53 Saxon 1978, 251; Speaight 1980, 80.

Presumably this was intended to theatrically heighten the lions, now-familiar hoop-jumping display in the den, and such acts set precedents for orientalist costumes in lion and tiger acts. By the mid-1830s, Martin, who had pioneered exotic animal acts in mainland Europe, and Van Amburgh, who had done the same in the USA and Britain, had established reputations as the leading tamers, known as 'lion kings' in the UK and 'lion tamers' in the USA.

'Lion kings' proved particularly popular attractions and were soon widely copied, coming to dominate travelling menageries by the mid-19th century. The act in the cage revealed the human performer gaining control over the lion, and the title of 'king' or 'lord' was promoted for the human trainer although, in species hierarchies, the lion with his majestic mane and control of the pride was also considered a king among animals. While the handling methods were highly questionable, and possibly exaggerated in contemporary accounts, nonetheless an impression of force was a deliberate strategy to enhance the theatrical spectacle. One performer came to dominate lion king handling acts – Isaac Van Amburgh.

Lion king

Isaac A Van Amburgh rose to prominence among 19th-century menagerie performers first in the USA, and then in Britain. The claims about his achievements, however, probably exaggerated his feats. For example, '[s]ince the year 1834, the public of both hemispheres has looked upon him as the greatest lion-tamer in the world.'[54] Whether or not he was 'the greatest', Van Amburgh was certainly the best known of the tamers not least because he was a clever showman and an astute business manager who leased his performance spaces including theatres.

---

54   Ferguson 1861, 14. I am using OJ Ferguson (c.1861) because of the section 'Manner of taming elephants' although there is a very similar version of the same text by H Frost who is named as a manager, presumably of the Van Amburgh menagerie in the USA when there is an OJ Ferguson as press agent. I wish to thank Steve Gossard and the Milner Library Special Collections librarians at the Illinois State University for their assistance and clarification about the differences between the two books.

1 Ferocious lion acts

Significantly, Van Amburgh pandered to audience interest in confrontation and yet encouraged impressions of his mysterious effect on animals. He was probably entering cages with a mix of lions, tigers and leopards in the USA by 1833, and in Britain at Astley's by 1838, where he acquired the label of the 'American Lion King'. His confrontational act demonstrated the 'great moral drama of nature'.[55] In doing so, however, it implicitly confirmed the triumph of humankind over nature.

While entry to the cage aroused spectators' fear for the handler's safety, there was also some compassion expressed for the animals since they were handled and appeared to some spectators to be physically subdued by Van Amburgh in his act. His theatrical style and accompanying rhetoric reinforced his capacity to tame animals, a process that his act demonstrated in front of spectators, and he became much better known than a reported seven predecessors who pioneered this type of act and were probably milder in their handling techniques. Apparently Van Amburgh's performance involved displays of aggressive bravado to confirm his dominance of the animals and it was his reputation for forceful action that came to typify human–lion exhibitions. His taming act staged an impression of confrontation, followed by animal submission.

Claims that reiterated the effect of Van Amburgh's mere presence on wild animals and on spectators were contradicted by other accounts of his striking and hitting animals during the act. A claim that Van Amburgh tamed animals through his magnetic presence seemed to spread as his reputation grew, and it was possibly promoted to offset criticism. The effectiveness of Van Amburgh's taming was vividly illustrated through the act's use of a lamb. In one drawing, Van Amburgh confronts a lion, and in another he kneels, his arm raised in a triumphant gesture, with a child standing and straddling his knee beside the prone body of a lion, while Van Amburgh holds a lamb, an unmistakable symbol of innocence.[56] The proximity of these figures that were emblematic of vulnerability confirmed that the wild animal had been rendered harmless.

---

55 Ferguson 1861, 13.
56 Drawing reproduced in Verney 1978, 120.

Born in July 1811, Van Amburgh started out in the early 1820s as a boy attendant who cleaned the cages of a travelling menagerie.[57] The contemporary biographical details about how Van Amburgh came to work with lions and tigers vary, and it is likely that these accounts were embellished after Van Amburgh became well known. RH Horne, writing as Ephraim Watts, met with Van Amburgh and claims that he 'distinguished himself' after a head keeper was killed when trying to move a lioness into another cage, and Van Amburgh 'offered to tame her spirit' and entered her cage 'with his crow-bar'.[58] The crowbar remained a prop in his act.

Watts' description of Van Amburgh's physique is intriguing. He was five foot ten-and-a-half inches (1.79 m) and handsome, although his body was 'steep-looking', 'narrow-sided', 'long-backed' and, while he was exceptionally strong, he was not muscular.[59] In contradiction, however, was the admiration expressed by another observer for his 'Herculean caste' and 'extraordinary muscle power'.[60] Van Amburgh's physique attracted interest, as if the lion king was on show among the animal bodies. His facial features were 'especially delicate, almost female' with 'extraordinary' eyes: 'the balls project exceedingly, and it seems as if he could look all round him without turning his head' but, while 'bright' and 'shining', they were also 'cold, whitish' as if like 'a dead ghost's'.[61] Watts claims that it was the power of Van Amburgh's eyes which made wild beasts fear him – rather than his crowbar.

Watts' account also states that Van Amburgh's grandfather was a Native American named 'Great King of the Forests', and that his mother dreamt of roaring beasts during her pregnancy.[62] Typically 19th-century descriptions located wild animals in forests.[63] Van Amburgh

---

57 Saxon 1978, 321. Saxon says that Van Amburgh started out with Rufus Welch and the New York Zoological Institute, Bowery, and that he performed in 1833 and became an overnight success. Watts 1838, 27, Watts calls the menagerie owner Titus; Ferguson 1861; Mizelle 2012, 264–69 and images.
58 Watts 1838, 27–28.
59 Watts 1838, 14.
60 *Times* (London) 1838, 11 September: 5, quoted.
61 Watts 1838, 14. See the sketch of Van Amburgh in Ferguson 1861, ix.
62 Watts 1838, 14–16.
63 For example, see *The Hull Packet* (Hull) 1840, Carter and his lions, 18 December: 8, 'wildest and most savage creatures of the forest'.

1 Ferocious lion acts

was described as having the power to subdue 'man-eating' lions and tigers through his presence. This was traced back to a childhood love of animals and naturalist study that led to his capacity to exert control over smaller animals. Apparently '[h]e not only tamed all those he had an opportunity of meeting a few times, but also acquired a surprising influence over them'.[64] Similar comments circulated in newspapers and potentially influenced public opinion and the reception of the act, as this report reveals.[65]

> The Lion halted and stood transfixed – the Tiger crouched – the Panther, with a suppressed growl of rage and fear sprang back, while the leopard receded gradually from its master. The assembled spectators were overwhelmed with wonder ... Van Amburgh had triumphed over both men and beasts.[66]

There were approving shouts from spectators.

Contemporary comic verse engaged with public fears about his potential death, enhancing the act's appeal. Van Amburgh was depicted as fearless when confronting the lions.

> Wonderful Fact ...
> He entered the cage with his whip in his hand,
> And dauntless amidst the fierce crew did he stand;
> Then played with their mouths, without terror or dread –
> But the lion waxed wrathful and snapped off his head.
> The actors they screamed, and the audience ran out ...
> – Van Amburgh arose![67]

Van Amburgh was acknowledged in this stanza playing with the mouth of the lion, if not putting his head near the jaw. The satirical poem implied that the act involved a lion fighting back and a theatrical

---

64 Watts 1838, 20.
65 See *Freeman's Journal and Daily Commercial Advertiser* (Dublin, Ireland) 1838, 26 September, np; *Aberdeen Journal* 1838, 10 October, np (British Library Newspapers database [BLN]).
66 Ferguson 1861, 12.
67 *Operative* (London) 1839, Literature, 6 January: 11.

embellishment suggested the demise of Van Amburgh that was subsequently reversed when he stood up – the poetic humour claims that he had been restored to life with an ointment. Deliberately or inadvertently staged in the action, there was a Christian refrain to the tamer's survival in a lion act.

Apparently Van Amburgh countered criticism that animal acts caused moral ruin and religious offence by quoting Genesis about how humans are accorded dominion over other animals.[68] It had a circular effect, with descriptions of animal submission in his act interpreted as almost a biblical miracle: 'The Lion licked the hand that overcame him, and knelt at his conqueror's feet; the Leopard fondled as playful as a domestic tabby; the Tiger rolled on his sides.'[69] Ferguson continues that Van Amburgh created a tableau in which he called animals to come to him; he was 'the proud King of the animal creation. It was a striking exhibition of love and confidence reigning where fear and power could only be supposed.' The process of overcoming animal aggression in Van Amburgh's act had been assumed to have been achieved through love.

While commentators were concerned to represent the capacity of animals to submit to Van Amburgh as their master, in keeping with a triumph of human love and biblical idealism, descriptions of his act hint that he used some force to keep them obedient. One reviewer specifies that Van Amburgh 'cuffed and struck at the lion and tiger, pinched their ears, and slapped them right and left'.[70] This account makes it clear that he handled the lions forcefully.

The contradictions were perpetuated in pantomimes about overcoming aggression. Van Amburgh's act was integrated into a pantomime with confrontational associations, in contrast to Martin's earlier pantomime with its impression of peaceful co-existence. Van Amburgh appeared at Astley's between 27 August and 20 October 1838, dressed as a Roman, Malerius, in *The brute of Pompeii, or the living lions of the jungle*, in which he was cast in among lions, tigers and leopards in two cages in the arena at Pompeii.[71] Malerius befriended these lions and tigers and diverted their attack. A business collaboration

---

68   Watts 1838, 36.
69   Ferguson 1861, 12.
70   *Aberdeen Journal* 1843, Issue 4989, 23 August, np (BLN).
71   Saxon 1978, 323–24.

between Andrew Ducrow and Van Amburgh transferred this theatrical display of interspecies friendship to Drury Lane theatre but in a different incomprehensible melodrama about a hero cast among the lions and tigers. The partnership ended abruptly when, for an unknown reason, Ducrow and Van Amburgh came to blows behind the scenes.

Van Amburgh continued to present his act at Drury Lane, including in a Christmas pantomime. Early in 1839, Queen Victoria went to see it six times and made a backstage visit to watch the animals being fed, in defiance of the outrage expressed in newspapers about this type of display in a London theatre.[72] Apparently on the Queen's second visit, the Drury Lane box office took over £712, the largest amount in its history.[73]

There was an effort to bring together the act by Wombwell's keeper, probably Manchester Jack, and Van Amburgh's act to create a competitive trial of daring at Southampton.[74] The contest did not eventuate, perhaps because Van Amburgh's reputation had gained pre-eminence, and Wombwell's was trying to gain some advantage by this association. Competition among acts was intensifying.

With regard to the staging, there were probably physical barriers or partitions between the animals in the cage, although most images do not confirm that spatial arrangement. It is likely that the barriers could be removed and reinserted at different times during the act. In an illustration of the pantomime stage arrangements in 1843, Van Amburgh is at one end of a cage and there are two lions, two leopards and a tiger at the other, suggesting that they were only close at certain moments during the act.[75] In Edwin Landseer's well-known 1847 painting, *Portrait of Mr Van Amburgh as he appeared with his animals in London theatres*, Van Amburgh stands forcefully centre stage with arm out, pointing, as the animals seemed to cower to avoid him (Plate 1; see also Chapter 2). The image suggests that his commanding presence alone tamed animals.

---

72 Saxon 1978, 324–25; Rothfels 2002a, 158–59, citing Van Amburgh.
73 Ferguson 1861, 17.
74 *New York Clipper* 1872, Lions and lion tamers, 13 April: 12.
75 *Illustrated London News* 1843, Mr Van Amburgh and his lions at the English Opera House, 21 January: 44.

Van Amburgh's menagerie act toured British theatre venues, and an Edinburgh review gives a more detailed account of the interaction with the animal performers:

> The den containing the wild beasts occupies the whole breadth of the stage, and is divided by a partition in the middle. The occupants of the one section are a lion, two tigers, and three leopards, and of the other, a lion and lioness, and three leopards. There must have been few of the spectators who did not feel a shudder, when the intrepid man stepped into the first den, and stood calmly amid the monsters ... [as a] lion crouched ... tigers lay ... [and a] leopard prowled ... At a signal they spring upon his shoulders and rest upon his head, or spread themselves on the ground to make a pillow for him. They box with him, and growl, and snarl, and snap with their long fangs when he indulges them in a playful combat; but though he may irritate them by knocking their heads on the ground, or cuffing their ears, yet a hint is sufficient to still the angry growl, and to bring them crouching to his feet. He distended the jaws of the lion while it roared, and then shut and opened them rapidly, breaking the roar ... [the lion] pressed its nuzzle lovingly against his cheek.[76]

But when a lioness snapped, Van Amburgh came closer to look at her, and apparently she shrank away. The act involved handling animals and even wrestling one, and he clearly handled the lion's jaw. But there was minimal mention of even rudimentary tamer feats; for example, the basic trick of hoop-jumping that was performed elsewhere. This may indicate that there was a turnover of animals in Van Amburgh's act.

A later newspaper description of Van Amburgh's touring performance confirmed the enormous public appeal of the act and described how he put his face near to the lion's mouth. Van Amburgh could attract 2000 spectators to a show, including 'distinguished members' of Oxford University.[77] It was a large audience for a 19th-century provincial performance. By 1843, he displayed a giraffe, a novelty at that time, before entering the lion and tiger cages as a character, Rollo, whip in hand. He was:

---

76 *A Concise Account* 1841, 10.
77 *Jackson's Oxford Journal* (Oxford) 1843, 13 May: 3.

1 Ferocious lion acts

> saluted by a savage growl from the tiger, who stood erect on his hind legs against the bars of the cage, while the lion maintained a dignified appearance and the leopards continued to gambol around the den . . . [Van Amburgh] actually put his face into a lion's mouth: during all of which the spectators could scarce repress a shudder of horror.[78]

The public willingly attended to be shocked. The 1843 account offers one indisputable description of Van Amburgh putting his head into the lion's mouth, as well as pushing the animals.

The act confirmed a hierarchical arrangement of species by presenting Van Amburgh facing danger and exercising dominance, sometimes through physical handling contact with the animals. This was interpreted as a display of human courage and fearlessness and Van Amburgh was promoted as being without fear. He showed no obvious physical signs of fear and at some point in the act, possibly at the finale, a lion may have licked his hand and he may have caressed a leopard or another animal. Watts was at pains to point out that instead of being fearful of the animals, Van Amburgh 'looks upon himself as an object for them to fear' because they are 'cowards at heart', and their 'terribleness' can be overcome.[79] Van Amburgh was accorded boldness, modesty and a 'kind, communicative' temperament.[80] The tamer who effected submission was demonstrating largesse to a less deserving species, aggressive by inclination; the act verified the forbearance of humankind.

In a report of a conversation with Britain's best-known military veteran, the Duke of Wellington, Van Amburgh apparently denied that he was ever afraid: '"The first time I am afraid, your grace," replied the lion king, "or that I fancy my pupils are no longer afraid of me, I shall retire, I shall retire from the wild beast line."'[81] While this meeting suggested an effort to associate the nation's leading military battle hero and a fearless lion tamer in public perception – an association with heroism often repeated in the 19th century – it also confirmed Van Amburgh's status as the leading tamer and that the act was regarded as comparable to going into battle.

---

78 Jamieson & Davidson 1980, 39, citing *Nairnshire Telegraph*.
79 Watts 1838, 36, 42.
80 Watts 1838, 36, 42.
81 Cited in *New York Clipper* 1872, Lions and lion tamers, 13 April: 12.

The act's costumes conveyed historical references and alluded to the Judaeo-Christian stories that were central to the meaning of the acts. Landseer's painting showed Van Amburgh in a simple Roman-style tunic, and other illustrations showed him in a more decorative costume suggestive of a soldier or gladiator.[82] But his bare arms and legs would have conveyed some vulnerability, offsetting the impression of an invincible fighting persona. One illustration of Henri Martin with a lion shows him standing above a lion in a Roman-style tunic and about to attack, his knife hovering above the lion; in a second he wears an animal skin suggestive of a prehistoric hunter; in a third he is dressed in a white shirt and trousers.[83]

If a number of circus historians have claimed a performance heritage back to the Greco-Roman era for the foundational circus skills such as acrobatics and rope-walking, the 19th-century circus historian, Thomas Frost, also makes a connection between menagerie animal performances that he saw and animals in Roman spectacles.[84] The association was no doubt reinforced by mid-century theatrical menagerie demonstrations like those of Van Amburgh, whose costumes and rhetoric deliberately alluded to ancient Rome, with animal fights and duels between gladiators and animals as entertainment. But menagerie cage acts were 19th-century inventions and unlike the actual fighting acts of ancient Rome, which had often ended in animal and human death.

Cage acts were theatrical presentations, and integrated into orientalist narratives about geographical exploration that had been widely presented in theatre from the late 18th century. Pictures of stories could be put on the sides of cages and later in the USA the Van Amburgh menagerie cages depicted 'scenes, incidents and accidents in the life of

---

82 Speaight 1980, 82; Coxe 1980a, 136.
83 Coxe 1980a, 129; Thétard 1947, Vol. 2, 228.
84 Frost 1875, 88; Circus historians disagree about claims like these made by 19th-century historian Thomas Frost. Circus histories for general readers sometimes contain a section about the human skills commonly used in acts that were performed for centuries before their integration into a circus program in the ring from 1768, and these do not necessarily encompass animal acts. For example, see Durant & Durant 1957, 2–8; or Hoh & Rough 1990, 23. Displays of acrobatic and rope-walking skills, fully integrated into the early modern circus, had been practised in festival, holy day and fair entertainments over millennia.

1 Ferocious lion acts

Dr Livingstone, while hunting in the African deserts'.[85] Van Amburgh toured Britain in 1841 in a pantomime in which he played Karfa, an Arab slave accompanying Mungo Park as he discovers the source of the Niger. In this stage production a tiger enters without a cage. '[T]he dramatic effect of this feline actor's *entrée* is most powerful – indeed several ladies screamed'.[86] Van Amburgh's character rolls over with the tiger, saving his (Christian) master – an army officer and a naturalist – from the wild animals and Moor enemies. Karfa's later encounters are in a den at the behest of the Moor leader; he leaves triumphant. The inclusion of wild animals in the dramatised spectacle might have been popular for its realistic effect, but with physical contact it was also sensational.

Van Amburgh's successor and competitor at Astley's was James [John] Carter, who followed in Van Amburgh's wake in 1839, adopting his style but without his impact, even though Carter is depicted unusually in one illustration as bare-chested.[87] Carter performed in Britain, other countries in Europe and briefly in the USA. In a ten feet square cage, he stopped fights and was the 'master of the wildest and savage creatures' who 'trembled with fear at his presence'.[88] He may not have instigated his own act and instead may have been groomed by George Wombwell.[89] Carter was hired in 1839 by Ducrow to work with the whole menagerie in *Afghan*, billed as an 'Egyptico-Hindu-Arabian Spectacle'.[90] He worked on Astley's stage behind a wire screen with horses, zebras, crocodiles, ostriches, lions, tigers and leopards, and at one point even drove a harnessed lion like a chariot horse. But Carter's act at Astley's was criticised because the lions and tigers seemed too tame. Maurice Willson Disher quotes critics who said that the lions did not display the 'savageness, an uneasiness, an air of offended dignity' or 'growls' to provide spectators with 'the satisfactory feeling that the life of a fellow creature was in danger'. The public expected acts with

---

85   Ferguson 1861, 78.
86   *Preston Chronicle and Lancaster Advertiser* 1841, 23 January: 2, a reprinted review from the *Manchester Guardian* (BLN).
87   Thétard 1947, Vol. 2, 228.
88   *Hull Packet* (Hull) 1840, 18 December: 8.
89   Slout 1998, 45, explains that there are conflicting accounts of James Carter, who died at the age of 34 on 11 May 1847.
90   Disher 1937, 146, and cites critics.

menagerie animals to deliver confrontation, or at least a sense of excitement, and fear for human safety through risk-taking.

Carter and Van Amburgh appeared together in an orientalist theatre fantasy, *Aslar and Ozines, or the lion hunters of the burning Zaara*, in 1843, but not to acclaim, as the critics decried the lack of plot and poor acting of the 'brute-tamers'.[91] These pantomimes relied on vague knowledge of animals, often in a misleading association with a foreign geography. Carter worked with an animal called a 'Brazilian tiger', who was probably a jaguar.[92] In 1848, Van Amburgh performed in *Morok the beast tamer* at Astley's, in a drama based on the story of the Wandering Jew, and was billed with a 'black tiger' that was probably a panther.[93]

Van Amburgh's crowbar and Carter's encounters with hostile animals were possibly not indicative of all the acts of their contemporaries; Henri Martin was thought to be considerate of the animals in his act, as was Manchester Jack. Van Amburgh was understood to have used a crowbar to achieve submission and for protection, and he was also reputed to beat and to starve the lions and tigers to make them react during performance. Joanne Joys writes that it is hard to separate such accusations from promotional hype, especially as it was offset by creationist claims that the animals knelt in submission, according to religious expectations.[94] Certainly tamers lay down with the animals in handling stunts. Whether they used theatrical effects to deliver an impression of forcefulness or not, they may have used ruses to make the caged animals react.[95] This happened with other animals. For example, piano wires were used to lift the arms of chimpanzees tied to their seats on stage.[96] An increasing number of acts involving 'lion tamers'

---

91   *Illustrated London News* 1843, Mr Van Amburgh and his lions at the English Opera House, 21 January: 44. In 1845, Astley's, under William Batty's management, hired a presenter named White for a time.
92   Frost 1875, 90–91.
93   Speaight 1980, 82.
94   Joys 1983, 7.
95   Culhane 1990, 21. Nathaniel Hawthorne, in his account of seeing a lion and tiger act in the USA in 1838, found the animals 'torpid' and the attentiveness of the audience more impressive than the showman putting his arm and head in a lion's mouth. This tamer may not have been Van Amburgh as Culhane claims he was.
96   Cooper 1928, 9–10.

1 Ferocious lion acts

meant that comparisons were made between them. A contemporary account, however, dismissed claims of 'furious attacks', explaining that Van Amburgh controlled the animals with commands, and 'he has no occasion to use any peculiar violence' or to subject even a tiger to 'severe corporal punishment with a large horsewhip'.[97] But this defence suggests persistent accusations. While the crowbar was possibly a prop and/or the protective device of last resort and the whip provided sound effects, even if the animals were accustomed to these acts, they were physically forced into position through handling that was at least intrusive and, at worst, brutal. Therefore a perception of the tamer's special abilities belied the use of human strength.

The tamer act represented a display that was scarcely thought possible. There was disbelief that the lions did not devour the tamer, given that they had 'power' and the 'physical strength'.[98] A tamer act was considered extraordinary because the perception of danger induced excitement and amazement. Van Amburgh met these expectations with his heightened delivery.

It was clear, however, that Van Amburgh was a 'shrewd and able showman'.[99] He returned to the USA in 1845 and worked with the newly established Van Amburgh & Co. menagerie for the next decade, building up two touring menageries. Although he retired from presenting the act in 1853, he continued to accompany the touring show managed by Hyatt Frost.[100] When Van Amburgh died on 29 November 1865 at the Sam Miller's Hotel, Philadelphia, he was synonymous with lion acts in menagerie entertainment. Isaac Van Amburgh's animal-handling act exemplified the taming of a fearful nature.

---

97 *Times* (London) 1838, 11 September: 5.
98 *Illustrated London News* 1843, Mr Van Amburgh and his lions at the English Opera House, 21 January: 44. Retrieved 10 May 2011 from online Historical Archive.
99 Sturtevant 1925, 76.
100 The Van Amburgh menagerie continued until 1895. Slout 1998, 309. *New York Clipper* 1872, Lions and lion tamers, 13 April: 12. There are numerous newspaper accounts of his death and injury which are not accurate.

Fearful nature

An animal was an undifferentiated representative of a species and was framed within a human idea of an amorphous nature that needed to be ordered and in which aggressive animals threatened and yet cooperated with humans. The confrontation with lions and tigers in 19th-century menagerie acts was considered to curtail a naturally 'fierce disposition' so that animals were tamed.[101] In the confined space of a small cage, the costumed handler posed in a tableau that emulated familiar Christian themes and historical stories or even the myth of Hercules wrestling a lion, which, in turn, legitimised the act. The elephant is not included in the Bible, giving lion acts in particular pre-eminence, and by the mid-19th century, some were incited to roar loudly, as if about to attack the human performer, accentuating his or her bravery. The reputation of the animal for fierceness attracted spectators, but the act needed to demonstrate Christian authority over the natural world.

In demonstrating the human handler's capacity to overcome his or her fear in approaching and in handling an animal deemed physically dangerous, menagerie acts drew on pre-existing preconceptions of hostility. Yet the idea that humanity should at least give animals a sporting chance instead of staging an unfair fight was evident,[102] and anti-cruelty advocates hinted at kindness to wild animals. At the height of Van Amburgh's popularity in Britain, veterinary surgeon to the Society for the Prevention of Cruelty to Animals, W Youatt, recounts how school boys were told the story of a lion remembering a runaway slave who had once hidden in the lions' den, and had extracted a thorn from his foot. The lion had been hunted and trapped and was 'half-starved' when he encountered the slave again. Youatt writes that:

> with mane erect and fearful roar he darted towards his victim. But ere he had half traversed the arena he slackened his pace, and, creeping towards the man, looked wistfully in his face and licked his feet.

---

101 Bostock 1903, 183. Menagerie animals were considered untrained by comparison with later approaches after the 1880s.
102 Boddice 2008. For some relevant anti-cruelty propositions and sporting fair play, 211.

1 Ferocious lion acts

They were the companions of the desert; and the noble beast had not forgotten his benefactor.[103]

The lion had the capacity to return kindness and to be a loyal friend. But this anecdote was recounted alongside Youatt's stories about the loyalty of dogs, suggesting slippage in distinguishing species attributes. Youatt is explaining general principles against cruelty towards domesticated and 'inferior animals' and he makes an argument that their welfare and rights should come out of comparable human values in the society. He argues that humanity stands to benefit when it prohibits cruelty to animals and extends sympathy and affection, and that this cannot be fully achieved by legal means and requires public support.

Concern about the mistreatment of animals in 19th-century menageries coincided with the questioning of prevalent assumptions about nature, fear and courage. When John Stuart Mill considered the concept of nature and its cruelty in the 1850s, he discerned that an experience of wildness arose out of fear, but that this fear could be overcome through courage. While acknowledging some ambiguity in his use of terms, Mill finds that nature 'denotes the entire system of things' or things 'apart from human intervention', but that humans are inseparable from the spontaneous process of 'nature's physical or mental laws', with their actions either altering or improving nature.[104] Significantly, the natural world was widely understood to be cruel and harsh, full of conflict and killing. Mill explains that the human is like a particularly crafty wild animal until tamed by culture. Civilised culture brought about improvements in the behaviour of nature, including human nature.[105] Mill disagrees with the view that courage, then, was considered to be part of an untamed natural state, and therefore the overcoming of the natural condition of fear was understood as a virtue. Instead he argues that courage, too, was socially produced rather than natural, and accompanying emotions were evident so that humans may be 'naturally pugnacious, or irascible, or enthusiastic, and these passions when strongly excited may render them insensible to fear'.[106] In

---

103 Youatt 1839, 45. also 35, 33, 106.
104 Mill 1969, 401–2.
105 See Thomas 1983, 24–27.
106 Mill 1969, 393.

Mill's analysis, before the publication of Darwin on emotions, social imperatives could facilitate courageous behaviour.

Handlers in menagerie acts were probably more pugnacious than courageous. Wild animals in cages or in chains showed nature's wildness, albeit safely contained. The conflation of animals with fearful nature allowed a menagerie handler to mimic notions of nature's courage in humans and the imposition of order on nature. But the staging of these acts also entrenched beliefs in the lion's and tiger's innate aggression and extreme hostility to humans. If dominance of nature came to exemplify human progress, a menagerie act that enacted a shift from fearful confrontation to calm relations with animals confirmed the triumph of civilisation over untamed nature.

By the 1850s, the tamer entering the lion's cage had become a standard feature of menageries, although there was disquiet over the proliferation of these acts in Britain. Accidents also meant that the worth of the exhibition was questioned. In providing useful publicity, the occasional bloody spectacle of tamers being mauled, and their off-stage reputation for drinking heavily, fuelled social opposition.[107] Accidents may have happened because of alcohol use by presenters, but it is also possible that some reports of injuries were exaggerated. The courage of menagerie tamers was part theatrical, since the risk of attack was promoted as part of an act's calculated appeal. The emotional impact was contrived and crucial.

Menagerie cage acts staged familiar narratives to elicit predictable emotional responses and by presenting different species in close proximity. Alexander Bain gives a biblical example of the lion and the lamb lying peacefully together as an extreme juxtaposition resulting in the strongest emotional impact on viewers. Bain's example also relates to menagerie acts with this combination that replicated existing symbolism and utilised social beliefs about specific species. Bain gives a further example with the use of monkeys in artificial action to create humour, although he notes that an artist working with animals could not be a zoologist or a geographer. He specifies: 'the monkey, from its being a creature so much more filthy, mean, and groveling, and which therefore in performing human actions, presents a wider contrast of dignity and

---

107 Bostock 1903, 203. Frank Bostock claims that animals will reject a presenter who is drunk, incorporating animals into the prevailing morality.

debasement'.[108] In his reasoning, the greater a contrast between animals and humans, the greater the emotional effect.

In a distinctive example of animal performance, monkeys, long relegated to comedy acts, became part of acts with a more earnest tone in response to social fears in the 1860s. Trained monkeys – recognised as performers in Elizabethan England – were also part of circus equestrian acts, and were at Astley's Circus in the 1830s, trained to ride as jockeys on horses in comic imitation of humans.[109] This juxtaposition of horses and monkey jockeys was a popular performance often called a 'Dandy Jack act', and one claim names the monkey as Jocko.[110] A widely presented circus pantomime of the time, *The Brazilian ape or Jocko*, however, had a human performer dressed up as Jocko the ape. In the 1860s, there was growing social anxiety that feared the animal in the human. An imitation of human behaviour in monkey performance that was not particularly comic was effected for quasi-scientific purposes and public fascination.

Jane R Goodall writes: '[T]heatre and performance not only provided entertainment for the widest spectrum of the public during this period, but were also a major form of general communication about topical issues', including evolution.[111] From the 1860s menagerie exhibitors opportunistically responded to social Darwinist ideas of evolution by claiming to present a living link between humans and apes. Accuracy was not at stake and there was a tightrope-walking sensation in 1869 billed, misleadingly, as a 'gorilla monkey'.[112]

Yet relations with individual animals were not uniform, despite those animals being considered indicative of a generic species, and emotional bonds developed between human and animal performers. A sentimental account of a monkey trainer, desperately trying to save his beloved fellow performer who had caught a chill during winter, reveals mutual dependency as the despondent trainer becomes unable to perform or to make a living after the monkey dies.[113] While a

---

108 Bain 1875, 255, 261. Bain critiques Hobbes and Spencer on humour.
109 Kwint 2002a, 56.
110 Ferguson 1861, 69; Saxon 1978, 139. Also, see Young Lee 2010, 626, performed in Paris in 1825.
111 Goodall 2002, 5, 59–61.
112 Van Hare 1893, 296–97.

monkey riding a horse mimicked human performance and was applauded for cleverness, this routine additionally generated an artificial pattern of compatible relations between other species. Whether presented with serious or comic intent, a particular animal species was staged in extreme contrasts for theatrical effect. If human-like behaviour by monkeys denoted integration into human worlds, conversely acts with apparently fierce lions and tigers compounded notions of species distinctiveness based on emotional temperament, and confirmed humanity's separation from a harsh and fearful nature.

Lion queen

Female tamers increased the appeal of the cage act through the fear of attacks because of their feminine vulnerability. Thomas Frost names Miss (Polly) Hilton from the Hilton's menagerie as the first woman to enter a cage in Britain as a lion queen, appearing around the mid-1840s.[114] She was part of a family menagerie business, the usual way that women became tamers at that time. Wombwell's soon copied Hilton's precedent, and there is a Mrs King mentioned presenting in Glasgow with Wombwell's by 1845.[115] The most well-known 'lion queen' was Ellen Chapman, who was performing by 1847 as Madame Pauline de Vere, probably with tigers and leopards as well as lions, in handling stunts that included opening the lion's jaw.[116] Chapman, known as Nellie, later married 'Lord' George Sanger, who became Britain's leading circus entrepreneur and menagerie proprietor in the 1870s.[117]

The advent of women tamers in the mid-1840s in England added novelty value to the tamer act and suggests that, by then, cage demonstrations needed an additional gimmick. In the USA, Charles

---

113   JCD 1888, 22.
114   Frost 1875, 131; *New York Clipper* 1872, Lions and lion tamers, 13 April: 12.
115   *Newcastle Courant* 1847, 13 August: 3. *Manchester Times and Gazette* 1845, 9 August: 3.
116   Frost 1875, 132; Sanger 1927 [1910], 142. The stage name of Madame Pauline de Vere is attributed to Chapman, notably by George Sanger (Turner 1995, 68), although in one instance it is also attributed to Polly Hilton (*Daily News* [London] 1872, 6 January: 5). Lukens 1956, 85.
117   Turner 1995, 116, Sanger accorded himself the title of 'Lord'.

1 Ferocious lion acts

Wright entered a lions' cage in 1829, and Stuart Thayer identifies women entering lions' cages in the USA from 1848 including two who had their own acts, Mademoiselle Troppecourt and Eugenie Delarme.[118] Handlers displayed fearlessness in simply entering the menagerie cages and this was complicated by women tamers, who elicited a greater degree of horrified reaction from the public. The female tamer implicitly challenged the idea that feminine fearfulness was natural.

Women tamers attracted large crowds. In Britain, Chapman's popularity was greatly enhanced by Wombwell's visit to the royal family at Windsor where Queen Victoria and the Prince Consort, Albert, and their household watched from a vantage point overlooking a courtyard where Chapman's cage had been pulled up under a window. Queen Victoria waited to meet Chapman, the lion queen, who recounted that the Queen gave her a gold watch and chain, and said, 'Oh, my dear, are you not afraid? I do hope you will not get hurt. I felt so terrified when I saw you open the lion's mouth and put your head in its jaws.'[119] If the claim of the Sanger family that Chapman did this handling feat were accurate, and given that it was not standard in tamer acts with women, it certainly would have had novelty value. Chapman replied that she was more nervous about meeting the Queen than entering the lions' cage, to which the Queen added she would pray that Chapman did not get hurt.

Chapman quickly rose to prominence. She may have been directing the animals to move around the cage without touching them but she also did handling feats. George Sanger said that Chapman came to see his act at the Stepney Green Easter Fair in 1848 where he was performing as a conjuror dressed in what he called his 'Hamlet costume': a white shirt with linen cuffs, black velvet tunic and a hat with ostrich feathers. He claims: 'I knew that Nellie was the only girl in the world for me.'[120] Whatever the sequence of events and whether Sanger or Chapman first saw the other's act in 1848, they had met when they were children as both came from travelling show families. Sanger acknowledged that

---

118   Thayer 2005, 129, 132. There were two other women who assisted males, Miss Randolph with Mr Shimer and Miss Calhoun with Thomas Brooks in 1848. A child of six went into a leopard cage in 1849 for eight seasons.
119   Sanger 1927 [1910], 142–44.
120   Sanger 1927 [1910], 143, 144.

when they met again in 1848 Chapman was an attractive young woman, and they talked together at length. But as an ambitious young showman, he probably noted an extra dimension that might have added to her personal appeal. She was George Wombwell's star, earning him more than £100 a day as the lion queen.

When Chapman left Wombwell's menagerie to marry Sanger in 1849, her cousin, Ellen Eliza Blight (also known as Helen Bright) apparently took over the position of lion queen star. A musician's daughter, 17-year-old Blight's career at Wombwell's was brief. Blight died from a tiger attack 11 January 1850 at Greenwich Fair, when a tiger who had not previously shown 'animosity', sprang at her during an additional performance and bit into her face and throat.[121] Frost heightens his description of the event with his choice of emotive language claiming that the tiger 'exhibited some sullenness or waywardness, for which Blight imprudently struck it with a riding whip which she carried'.[122] Subsequently a stuffed tiger was exhibited with a label claiming that he was the tiger who had killed Blight.

Disbelief in a female capacity for courage was revealed by an alternative version from an eyewitness claim that Blight died of 'fright'.[123] No doubt the accident increased condemnation of women handlers and the controversy meant that there were renewed efforts to ban women tamers in Britain.[124] Somewhat later a circus person pondered: 'It certainly does not seem to be a woman's work, though I suppose it wouldn't do to stop 'em at it, or some ladies might feel they were done out of their "rights".'[125] The appeal of the lion cage act was greatly enhanced by young female performers. Female presence also contained eroticised implications and lion queens in Europe later entered the cage with bare arms and necks.

---

121   Turner 1995, 15; Frost 1875, 132; JA 1872, 2. I am using Blight because Frost uses this surname and Turner contends that Bright is a misspelling of Blight, although Sanger and numerous other sources use Bright. A keeper at Astley's died in 1861 and there are other serious attacks, including Macarte losing an arm. Lucas was killed in Paris in 1867 and Rice in Berlin in 1881; see *Manchester Times* 1884, Lion taming, 23 August: 5.
122   Frost 1872, 132. *Era* 1872, Provincial theatricals, 14 January: 5.
123   *Derby Mercury* (Derby) 1872, Lion-taming exhibitions, 17 January: 6.
124   Frost 1875, 132.
125   JCD 1888, 24.

1 Ferocious lion acts

Apparently Chapman was shocked about Blight's death, since Blight was mauled by a tiger who had not been troublesome for Chapman. She was reported as being critical of how Blight worked with the lions and tigers, which indicates that the two women may have been appearing at Wombwell's menageries at the same time during 1848 and 1849. Sanger recounts that Blight was repeatedly urged by Chapman not to hit the animals with the riding whip. Chapman reportedly says that Blight:

> thought it made them smart in their movements. There was no necessity for this flicking at them; all that was needed was to move the whip left or right, as the case might be, and the animals would follow it. But Miss Bright [Blight] preferred to give them sharp little stinging cuts, with the result that the tiger became angry and made her his victim.[126]

This description suggested that Chapman moved the animals around the cage by pointing, and possibly in other ways that suggested reflex actions in response to her movements: the animals moved around the cage as she came closer or reacted if she moved a whip high or low. The deliberate use of such practices was not specified elsewhere, although this insider knowledge would become central to training from the 1880s, and therefore Sanger may have recounted the earlier events informed by knowledge obtained in later years. Importantly, Sanger claimed that if the tamer did not mistreat the animals with unkindness, they would not attack. This claim elaborated on rhetoric about friendship with lions that had been present from the 1820s. It was discussed as a protective strategy. Although an ideal of kindness implies its demonstrative expression, here it was interpreted as not being physically cruel. A belief that 'unkindness', torment and ill-use were the main cause of attacks persisted even though accidental attacks could also be explained as a keeper's inexperience or drinking on the job.[127]

Significantly, Sanger omitted mention of Chapman being clawed on her back and head, in an accident that had long-term health

---

126   Sanger 1927 [1910], 168–69.
127   Sanger 1927 [1910], 164–65. Sanger also gave the example of William Wombwell who was killed by Old Jimmy, the elephant, when trying to stop two elephants fighting. Bostock 1972 [1927], 36.

effects.[128] Chapman's kindly treatment towards the animals had not afforded her protection during that encounter. The evidence about the defensive benefits of kindness was highly selective.

Attitudes to animal handlers were also underpinned by preconceptions about gender identity that cut across national boundaries. *Haney's art of training animals* specifies the value of kindness in training horses by using an example of a woman rider from Europe who found that temperamental Arabian horses responded to her because they had been 'tenderly' reared and fed by Arab women.[129] There was a presumption that certain types of emotional attitudes and behaviours were more commonly expressed by women, and thus transcended even national pride.

Sanger claimed to be relieved that Chapman had given up her lion queen act when they married, although she remained a performer in Sanger's numerous variety shows.[130] In 1856, however, he added six lions to his successful equestrian circus and a troupe of performers dressed up as Native Americans to compete with the touring Howes and Cushing's American Show. He bought the lions from William Jamrach in London and put them into a pantomime called *The condemned preserved*, about a young African man (played by Sanger) who falls in love with the daughter of a rajah.[131] The rajah throws the male lover into the lion's den.[132] The daughter, played by Chapman, follows her lover into the den. When the rajah cries out for someone to save her, it is her African lover who does so. Sanger stated that this act proved popular with the audience. In a concession to social values, the daughter had to be rescued although, as a performer, Chapman probably did the rescuing herself.

The lion king in Sanger's circus by 1858 was James Crockett, a musician who had reportedly developed lung problems and could not play his wind instrument so shifted into lion taming; this may not be the full explanation since he married into the Sanger family, marrying George's sister, Sarah.[133] The inexperienced Crockett was chosen

---

128 Lukens 1956, 85.
129 *Haney's Art* 1869, 21.
130 Sanger 1927 [1910], 175. She played Columbine and performed in fake hypnosis acts.
131 Sanger 1927 [1910], 210.
132 Sanger 1927 [1910], 210.

1 Ferocious lion acts

to be the lion king because he was tall with a long beard, and looked the part. Crockett remained with the act when Sanger's six lions were sold, and became well known in Britain, Ireland and mainland Europe for an act similar to Van Amburgh's, earning £20 a week. His act was deemed to have scientific value, although at Astley's in 1861 Crockett was billed as presenting four lions in a 'thrilling oriental spectacle' as 'the Lion Conqueror' in a plot in which he rescues the story's heroine and her son.[134] He received a ring from Queen Victoria and was eventually hired to work in the USA in 1864, where he died a year later, apparently from heat exhaustion or illness.

Menagerie cage confrontation was only surpassed in popularity by a display of majestic triumph and docility in the presence of royalty. Sanger's had an African lion 'impersonate' a British one for the 1871 royal procession to give thanks for the Prince of Wales' recovery from illness, and Sanger organised with the police superintendent for his carriage with the lion to join the procession making its way slowly through London's very crowded streets to St Paul's Cathedral.[135] Chapman, dressed as Britannia holding a shield and trident, stood beside a lion lying on top of a horse-drawn carriage. The lion was pulled up from his cage on a ramp. An eyewitness recounted that it was very risky, although some spectators thought the lion was stuffed.

Sanger provides details of how he spent £7,000 on his carriage for the procession:

> Our show drew forth tremendous cheering, for its tinsel finery had a great deal more glitter about it than the solid grandeur of the Royal procession. We had our Britannia, Mrs George Sanger, with

---

133 Frost 1875, 128–30. *Daily News* (London) 1872, Lions and lion taming, 6 January: 5. Frost presents this information. Turner 1995, 33, presents a biography of Crockett as being born in 1820 into a show family and becoming the band leader at Sanger's, and there is an anecdote about how Crockett was called to Astley's in 1861 to deal with lions who had escaped or had been let out by a disgruntled groom. Slout 1998, 65. Slout has Crockett hired by Seth Howes. Lukens 1956, 94, claims that the lions were sold to Howes and Cushing, as was the Sanger name, for £2000.
134 *Illustrated London News* 1861, Lions at Astley's, 2 February: 90, an illustration of Crockett.
135 Sanger 1927 [1910], 214; Lukens 1956, 51; JCD 1888, 24.

her living lion on the top to typify the nation and its strength. The Queen, too, was impersonated, in her crown and robes, surrounded by representatives of her dominions all in correct costume.[136]

In the days that followed, Sanger claimed that his Queen's Tableau and colonial entourage and the carriage were seen by 80,000 spectators the first day, and 96,000 the following day. An ex-lion queen as Britannia standing in a tableau symbolising the nation, complete with a lion proved a crowd-attracting spectacle. Even Queen Victoria was pleased with the impersonation and tribute to her sovereignty that brought together imperial triumph and human triumph over other species. The Queen's Tableau wagon continued to be part of Sanger's parades for years, with Chapman later replaced by their daughter, Georgina. (Chapman died on 29 April 1899, aged 67.)

In 1871 George Sanger divided up the family's equestrian circus business with his brother, John Sanger – the siblings thus becoming competitive rivals – and George bought Astley's Amphitheatre in the Westminster Road for £11,000 from the widowed Mrs William Batty. '[T]he menagerie was an integral part of the establishment', the largest in Britain.[137] Sanger emulated Van Amburgh's menagerie act and added a lamb to the carriage roof alongside the lion, and Sanger describes the lion as 'kindly tempered'.[138] Since the description of the first tableau does not mention a lamb, its composition seemed to have changed over time. Sanger's grandson, George Sanger Coleman, claimed that a lion cub, Georgie, and lamb, Billy, grew up together in the same cage and were 'firm friends'. When they were fully grown the lion continued to lick the ram, who would butt the lion. There were also two dogs raised with a lion for a playful act. The Queen's Tableau that Coleman saw was three-tiered, with Britannia seated on the top tier with the lamb and the lion on her lap; there was also a soldier beside her, dressed in a white-plumed helmet with a drawn sword. Perhaps it is not surprising, given these depictions of Britannia side by side with a placid lion, that Queen Victoria became Sanger's most celebrated spectator, and there were command performances on 8 January 1885 and 17 June

---

136   Sanger 1927 [1910], 213, 214–15; Lukens 1956, 50–51; Turner 1995, 116.
137   Sanger 1927 [1910], 210.
138   Sanger 1927 [1910], 243; Lukens 1956, 50–51, 64.

1898.[139] Royal interest and approval conferred prestige on acts with exotic animals.

Lion-taming acts showed animals being subdued during the performance in a transformation intended to elicit thrills, excitement, wonder, and even amazement. It could have been this public admiration that placed these animals largely outside anti-cruelty concerns, and distinctions between the regulatory protection of animal species continued in the 19th century. As Ritvo explains, once 19th-century British society questioned the punishment of domesticated animals, and proposed the moral worth of kindness, these values accorded national pre-eminence to some animal species. Yet exotic animals were the property of humans, who were held responsible as such animals became integrated into imaginative displays. The displays promoted greater control to dispel fear, and to make nature seem benign. Leaving aside Sanger's sentimental tableau of nationhood, those efforts and values did not seem to apply to lion- and tiger-tamers' acts since it suited business that they remained emblematic of a fearful nature. A lion handler might be presumed responsible for the circumstances of the animals, but the claim that exotic animals could be managed offstage with kindness reflected unsubstantiated optimism. Instead the theatrical style of menagerie cage acts showed men and women physically handling the lions in confronting ways, and acts of aggression expanded in style and continued to dominate 19th-century menagerie entertainment.

---

139 Turner 1995, 116.

2
War with animals

This chapter explores how horses, elephants and other animals were integrated into performance about war between the 1820s and 1870s. This new genre of battle re-enactments involving live animals enlarged on late 18th-century military drama and on long-established depictions of war and predator attack in visual art. Military battles came to be staged in the English circus with horses, and the geographical setting of a war in the theatre could be changed with the addition of an elephant. An elephant with a walk-on role lent an aura of authenticity to 19th-century orientalist pantomimes.

If horse 'actors' in the circus made staged battles seem realistic,[1] off stage they embodied an ideal of gentler treatment. But the presence of an elephant on the British stage implicitly reinforced ideas of colonial rule and sovereignty, even in melodrama that contradictorily framed them as the loyal rescuers of humans. Heart-warming sentiments prevailed in attitudes to elephants. Yet behind the scenes, human gentleness towards elephants was limited and unpredictable; elephants were often shot, and on occasion by a firing squad. In public, however, an elephant body in particular straddled royal empire, military skirmishes and romantic fantasies of reciprocated kindness.

---

1   Saxon 1968, 7; horses were considered more reliable actors than other animals and some plays included actions for the horses.

Battle horses

Nineteenth-century circus with depictions of cavalry expanded on military dramas in the British theatre[2] by staging actual battle re-enactments with horses and other animals. The 18th-century origin of the modern circus is inseparably linked to the horsemanship of the cavalry through Philip Astley, who had served in the English army and in war against France (1757–63) before, in 1768, bringing his considerable skill with horses to an equestrian entertainment in Lambeth, London that became known as Astley's Circus.[3] Military training provided foundational equestrian skill for circus entertainment and enhanced its reputation wherever Astley's toured, including to Paris. Top billing went to a star horse that could execute complex movement and tricks like those associated with military parades. It was this horse training and rider control that was initially on show.[4]

Interludes in the 18th-century circus equestrian program evolved into extended dramatic narratives involving horses, hunting, orientalist themes and, above all, military dramas.[5] The latter were increasingly popular in London theatres in the first half of the 19th century; more than 100 military dramas were staged about the Napoleonic wars.[6] Importantly, the representation of battles could be most credibly staged with circus performers on horseback. In 1801 circuses staged depictions of the British in Egypt, with Astley's boasting 'Real cavalry and infantry', and in 1807 Philip's son, John Astley, staged galloping horses followed by a realistic tableau of the battlefield complete with horses that appeared dead.[7] Philip Astley pioneered this trick of teaching a horse to lie down that could be put to use in battle scenes. At Astley's

---

2 Russell 1995.
3 Saxon 1968; Kwint 2002b, 72–115. For a summary of the horse in circus, see Bouissac 2012, 74–91.
4 Wykes 1977, 74. A published Astley family handbill lists an act 'By the Little Learned Military Horse'. Tait 2015.
5 Coxe 1980b, 111. Astley's equestrian scenes included *The Chinese enchanter, The Indian hunter, The Greek chieftain, The Yorkshire foxhunter, The carnival of Venice* and *The courier of St Petersburg*. For an extended analysis of cultural applications of orientalism in art, see MacKenzie 1995.
6 Assael 2005, 46.
7 Cited in Saxon 1968, 46–47.

under Andrew Ducrow from the mid-1820s, 30 or more horses were deployed in the simulation of warfare in the circus, and it was performers in soldier costumes who distinguished the opposing identities in a fight between national armies. The staging of political events, battles and historical sagas with animals added to the increasing appeal of 19th-century circus performance.

Equestrian acts dominated the circus program throughout the 19th century, and horses galloping around a 42-foot (12.8 m) circus ring made it possible to deliver shows with action-based sequences, including cavalry charges. Brenda Assael explains that in Britain, 'the equestrian military spectacle contributed to an important process of national mythmaking, one that did not originate with the state but arose within the unofficial, popular culture'.[8] In her analysis of British theatre and its plays about war in Georgian 18th-century society, Gillian Russell explains that greater public interest arose with a rapid increase in the numbers of soldiers and men with direct experience of war at that time, leading to a 'militarization of British society'.[9] She argues that even away from the theatre, the military delivered a theatricalised spectacle through its uniforms and exhibitions of military life that became like a form of entertainment. The libertine world of the military camp was soon represented in popular drama. Jacqueline S Bratton explains: 'The stage, therefore, offered a framed and bracketed space in which licence, violence, irresponsibility, physicality and other such enjoyable but antisocial acts or sensations could be savoured.'[10]

Enterprising managers increasingly presented major military campaigns as visual spectacles. Visual entertainment included the circular panorama from 1799, a continuous painted canvas that was used to depict major battles in Africa and India, and there was an 1815 panorama of the Mughal Emperor's Durbar Procession in Delhi.[11] Madame Tussaud's Museum of wax figures was started in 1802 as a museum of the French Revolution and was part of a larger domain that reflected 'the centrality and enormous appeal of violence and crime in the democratized and highly commercialized'

---

8   Assael 2005, 61.
9   Russell 1995, 13.
10 Bratton 1991a, 5.
11 MacKenzie 1995, 189–90.

depictions of history.[12] While an expansion in the availability of newspaper and other print accounts of wars and politics increased social awareness, the spectacle with painted scenery conveyed a vivid impression of political events to spectators from all social classes.

Circus re-enactments followed the historical events, although it should be noted that the theatre was dominated by orientalist or escapist drama during the actual years of the Napoleonic wars.[13] These wars, however, provided the most popular 19th-century war re-enactment event in circus, *The battle of Waterloo* by JH Amherst, first presented at Astley's in 1824, which also marked the debut of Andrew Ducrow in Britain. Ducrow had come from Paris where he had been copying Mazurier's popular impersonation of a monkey, but on horseback. The staging of *The battle of Waterloo* involved loud noises, flames and limelight to simulate cannon fire, and each of the three acts finished with a military skirmish on horseback.[14] Maurice Willson Disher outlines how the production included Prussian soldiers pulling a French soldier off his horse and dragging him away, while a peasant woman complained of French violence. Then Corporal Standfast and his true love, Mary, in Scottish disguise, sang a duet, followed by the Duke of Wellington's inspection of the troops before the battle that left the British and Prussians triumphant. In a comic interlude, Standfast was rescued by the comic character, Molly Maloney. In the end, the hero and heroine, Standfast and Mary, were reunited. Illustrations of the Waterloo production named the characters and showed soldiers on horseback engaged in battle as well as infantry men on foot with their rifles ready to fire, and a wagon carrying wooden casks. Soldier costumes dominated the visual impact, with performers playing political figures such as the Duke of Wellington and Napoleon Bonaparte, and these re-creations no doubt helped to glorify historical events among the general public. Assael notes that *The battle of Waterloo* was performed 144 times to 250,000 spectators, and even spectators from the military were impressed with the accuracy of the battles on horseback.[15] In a chapter called 'Napoleon's circus wars', Disher compares the

---

12   Melman 2006, 30–31.
13   MacKenzie 1995, 183.
14   Disher 1937, 92–93, illustration; Marra 2015; Tait 2015.
15   Assael 2005, 51, 52, 53.

staging of Britain and France's military battles in London and Paris. The staging of events in France had made Bonaparte into a stage hero in numerous pantomimes after 1830, often using genuine soldiers. However, the British circus did not present a durable hero of the same status. Instead a military drama with horses at Astley's in London was significant for its depiction of an ordinary soldier as a central character amid the battle. In addition spectators could pay extra for the opportunity to participate on stage in the reconstructed fight on horseback.

Disher points out that circus was a performance form in which the horses functioned like actors in the spectacle.[16] The actions of horse performers in emotionally expressive narratives served both theatrical and national interests and myths – not to mention species interests – in diverse ways. Such realistic military re-enactment generated sympathy and made a dramatic hero of the nameless soldier and potentially contributed to the public's acceptance of war.[17] The characterisation and the action could make war seem benignly familiar to the audience. In turn, circus was well attended by the military.

Ducrow's horsemanship was exceptional and he was especially admired for a feat of wild riding strapped to the back of a galloping horse that appeared to be moving out of control. Disher writes that he 'transformed feats of activity into visions of romance, and on the stage the old horseback spectacles into "grand military and equestrian melodramas"'.[18] The spectacle also pandered to royal interests and ceremonial pomp. In 1834, Queen Adelaide attended a horse pageant about King Arthur that was transferred from Astley's Amphitheatre to the smaller Drury Lane theatre. The theatre version of *King Arthur and the Knights of the Round Table* crowded together the horses and male performers on the stage, so that the view of the painted backdrop was blocked by 'knights caracoling, banners waving, trumpets blaring'.[19] The Queen was so delighted with the fantastical spectacle about the founding myth of the British monarchy that she gave £100 to be distributed among the company.

---

16   Disher 1937, 73.
17   For a discussion of heroism in 19th-century theatre and ideology, see Bratton 1991b, 18–61.
18   Disher 1937, 92.
19   Frost 1875, 86.

Some military melodramas proved more popular than others with the public. A revival of *The battle of Waterloo* in 1853 at Astley's followed the comparatively unsuccessful season of *Amakosa! or, scenes of Kaffir warfare* in which the romantic couple escaped a burning forest on horseback. Following a less successful program Astley's often revived a previous hit, such as *The battle of Waterloo*, or the perennial *Shakespeare on horseback*. Bratton points out that between 1854 and 1855 there were 25 plays licensed about the war with Russia.[20] In 1854 the Crimean War was dramatised at Astley's in *The battle of the Alma*, which staged 100 British soldiers fighting the Russians led by Menschikoff and involved the firing of shotguns at close range, so that the theatrical re-enactment caused actual injuries.[21] The guns were not stage props and caused at least one fatality.

In the surreptitious exchange between popular entertainment forms and the arts, circus co-opted familiar cultural figures and practices from theatre. The soldier figure's appearance in popular entertainment followed a pattern established in late 18th-century theatrical melodramas, which had depicted sailors reaching far-flung regions and, specifically, a hero type, Jack Tar, who became a stock character in naval battles in which cannons and smoke effects were often used.[22] The character of Jack Tar appeared in early equestrian drama at Astley's in *The sailor's return or the British tar*, and Ducrow appeared on horseback in the costume of a sailor. Bratton explains about the mid-century drama depicting the war in Crimea: 'Reciprocity between the press, the stage and the public mood resulted in the creation of a myth of the war' that was 'anti-heroic' in relation to the convention of an aristocratic leader and yet reflected a legacy of older heroic populist prototypes such as Jack Tar.[23] The appearance of an ordinary soldier as a popular character in 19th-century performance was indicative of the military's expanding profile within British society, and within ideas of nationalism. The dramatic narratives in circus reinforced the state's military and

---

20 Bratton 1980, 120.
21 Disher 1937, 99, 211; Bratton 1980, 129–33.
22 Summerfield 1986, 31, citing Willson Disher and Michael Booth. Bratton 1991b, 36–59. Also see Russell 1995, 98–106, 'Jolly Jack Tar' character. Coxe 1980b, 110, 111 see illustration of Ducrow.
23 Bratton 1980, 135.

2 War with animals

political authority, but the entertainment form itself was also unofficially testing the limits of state licensing law, which originally allowed only two spoken-word theatres but permitted riding schools.[24]

The figure of a fighter, if not the institutionalised soldier, reflected mid-century political concerns and possibly those of popular interest, and was evoked in the defence of social rights and liberties. In his examination of 19th-century society and its history published in 1843, Thomas Carlyle makes a link between working and fighting when he writes of the 'Fight of Life' in his critique of poverty caused by laissez faire law and 'Captain[s] of Industry'. Fighting carried both literal and metaphorical significances in Carlyle's analyses of business competition, and of triumph achieved through the submission of others and the plunder and negation of the 'Law of Nature'. While Carlyle condemns fighting with horses and spears, and later guns, as ignoble and murderous, it was seemingly inescapable as the means by which a righteous cause could be supported and achieved, and so fighting also metaphorically encapsulated the social struggle for survival and freedom. He writes:

> Man is created to fight; he is perhaps best of all definable as a born soldier; his life 'a battle and a march', under the right General . . . All fighting as we noticed long ago, is the dusty conflict of strengths each thinking itself the strongest, or, in other words the justest.[25]

The notion of a struggle to survive against scarcity, the environment and the delusions of others in the newly industrialised 19th-century society is personified by Carlyle's fighter, who additionally fought for citizens' rights. But this figure is somewhat at odds with a soldier type who appeared in popular entertainment upholding state authority and fighting in offshore and far-flung foreign wars to defend his nation and his monarch. Richard Altick points out that Carlyle's writings are also heavily ironic and, while his remedy for social ills involves revaluing Christian values, his exposé nonetheless influences social reformers and writers, including Charles Dickens.[26] Carlyle

---

24 Kwint 2002b.
25 Carlyle 1965 [1843], 191, also 186, 193.
26 Altick 1965, xvii.

outlines metaphoric social battles in which he envisages individuals fighting power structures and resisting business practices that seemed to involve combative, warlike strategies. Clearly fighting was a fundamental 19th-century precept.

The celebration of military heroism in circus performance additionally confirmed the central place of horses and other animals in 19th-century conflicts – invariably viewed from an anthropocentric perspective. In the circus, as elsewhere in society, horses were a crucial part of its socio-economic development and, even though circus horse performers were working animals, they may have received fairer treatment ahead of broader social changes in the treatment of other species. The appraisal of horses was influenced by 18th-century Enlightenment values and included the elevation of Eastern horses for their nobility. There were arguments that horses needed to be trained gently, rather than have to suffer brutish treatment from their human riders, who should not dig their heels into the horses.[27] While society was gradually recognising that an owner might be held responsible for the pain and suffering of a working horse, a well-trained working horse in the circus could be billed by name and was valuable. The circus horse needed to have a good appearance and was therefore less likely to be ill-treated.

As well as dramatic plots depending on horse performers, circus provided displays of horsemanship that were deemed educational for the public. Significantly, Philip Astley wrote two manuals on horsemanship and techniques for training horses, sharing specialised knowledge about horse care and techniques for training without violence; these were widely read including in the USA.[28] Trainers required 'Judgment, Temperance and Perseverance' 'to bring brute creation to a proper sense of duty', and he iterates how Christian values should extend to the animal world. Longstanding styles of horse training and presentation were adapted to the circus ring and these were eventually grouped into bareback, liberty, high school (*haute école*), and novelty act types.[29] Each presented a particular air or cadence. The non-comic high school

---

27   Landry 2011.
28   Tait 2015; Astley 1826; Astley 1802. Verney 1978, 80–81, reproduces a historical bill summary of Astley's *System of equestrian education*.
29   Fox 1960; Coxe 1980a, 47–60, 93–104, 171–82. Nineteenth-century circus families became well known for successive generations of equestrian performers.

involved highly choreographed movement derived from European training methods that had originated with horses on parade. Arabian horses proved most imposing in the ring because of their height. In contrast, the freer movement of liberty acts pioneered in the circus by Astley and Ducrow, which involved groups of riderless horses, generated and sustained more dynamic wild action. Each style carried an expectation of a horse's movement that might be described as training for a timbre, and conveyed impressions that ranged from grandeur to exciting galloping. The dominance of equestrian acts in the circus only declined in the early 1900s as Western society gradually shifted away from economic and social reliance on horse power.

Horse performers underpinned staged conflict. Conversely, however, the circus ethos promoted expectations for the nonconfrontational management of horses offstage, although this did not apply to other animals, including elephants.

Elephant solos

Dramatic narratives of historical and national achievement staged with horses in the first half of the 19th century were sometimes further enhanced with the addition of an exotic animal. In particular, a saga set in a colonial region became credible to audiences with the addition of an elephant, even if that animal's appearance made all the other performers nervous. From menageries to zoological societies, members of the world's largest animal species attracted public attention because of their impressive size and their comparative scarcity in Britain and the rest of Europe (they came mostly from Asia until the mid-century). Thus an elephant made a spectacular addition to a performance or a pageant and to a battle scene. But the care of the elephant was haphazard and the biographical accounts of individual menagerie animals reveal that if they became too difficult to manage in captivity, they were liable to be shot.

In London, Astley's rival, the Royal Circus, had initially instigated appearances by exotic animals, putting leopards and tigers together

---

For example, the British Cookes and Clarkes, and the German Schumanns and Italian Cristianis have descendants still performing.

with the horses passing across the stage, to represent the geographical regions of the world. It subsequently staged wordless melodramas about battles and sieges in the pit, using printed scrolls to explain the action and to name the enemy.[30] Astley's adopted this orientalist aesthetic, but had elephants and camels appear in *The siege and storming of Seringapatam; or, the death of Tippo Sahib* that followed a 1791 stage play on this topic.[31] Under John Astley, Astley's staged melodramas and presented a 'Sagacious Elephant or other animal to keep the interest alive', setting precedents for English entertainment.[32] An elephant reportedly first appeared in New York in 1808 in the story of *Blue Beard*.[33]

Two individual elephants, Chuny (Chunee) and Mademoiselle Djeck (D'jeck), helped to make elephants popular attractions early in 19th-century Britain. Chuny, in particular, became the object of public interest and later of childhood memories and social mythology. An Indian elephant, Chuny, arrived in England in 1809; he was exhibited in menageries including the Exeter Change[34] and reportedly seemed calm and gentle. This encouraged his addition in 1811 to a Covent Garden fantasy pantomime, *Harlequin and Padmanaba*, although he took fright at the initial performance, stopped, and eventually stood in a pool of blood after being repeatedly pricked with an 'iron goad'.[35]

Chuny was eventually executed by firing squad after it was feared by his keepers that his wooden menagerie enclosure would not hold him during his 'musth' (or must) mating season. He was killed (with difficulty) in 1826 on the second floor of the Exeter building. As a boy, AD Bartlett, who was later the superintendent at the London Zoological Gardens and responsible for the acquisition and sale of the legendary elephant called Jumbo, observed Chuny's execution first-hand. He writes: 'Being so young I was much alarmed, more on account

---

30   Disher 1937, 75–76.
31   MacKenzie 1995, 182. There was also JH Amherst's *The Burmese war; or, our victories in the east* in 1826, see Holder 1991, 129.
32   Disher 1937, 80.
33   Saxon 1978, 216, citing Vail. For the order of arrivals in the USA, see Flint 1996, 98; Nance 2013.
34   Altick 1978, 310–11; Saxon 1978, 216, citing *Mirror of Literature*, 11 March 1826.
35   Le Roux & Garnier 1890, 124, citing Charles Young.

2 War with animals

of the fury of the charges he made on the front of the den than at the firing of the soldiers.'[36] Bartlett's anxiety was caused by his fear that Chuny's charging would cause the floor to collapse, rather than by any concern for the plight of the animal. After his death, Chuny was depicted in sentimental eulogies that posthumously increased the public profile of this impressive animal.[37] Chuny had not become aggressive in public view, and sentiment increased after his regrettable death; the manner of his death made him seem like a martyr. The name 'Chuny' was revived by Bartlett when he renamed another Asian elephant, Chunee, at London's Zoological Gardens.[38] After their deaths, the bodies of both Chunys were dissected by curious scientists.

Djeck was far more compliant than Chuny and, conditioned to perform by menagerie-owner Huguet de Massilia, she appeared in Paris at Cirque Olympique in 1829, and then with Astley's in Liverpool in a drama about the King of Siam's elephant.[39] The pantomime, *L'Eléphant du roi de Siam*, was created especially for Djeck, who appeared in a sequence of scenes rescuing the legitimate king from usurpers and from prison, carrying him into battle, and, in a crowd-pleasing gesture, holding the king's crown. She also sat at a banquet, ringing a bell. The English version, *The royal elephant of Siam or the fire-fiend*, was followed by *The triumph of Zorilda, or the elephant of the Black Sea*, in which Djeck rescued the heroine and her son from the sea, staged with an impression of moving waves. Appearances in rescue scenarios showing devotion to deserving individuals made the elephant seem heroic. After performing at London's Adelphi Theatre in 1830, and subsequently touring England, Djeck travelled to New York to appear in the Bowery Theatre, before returning to England in 1831. This type of pantomime narrative also travelled and spread the reassuring impression that the elephant could serve humankind.

There were practical challenges in staging elephant performances. The stage had to be reinforced and, as AH Saxon points out, the size of an elephant made other performers and nearby spectators uneasy. The elephant had to be prevented from drinking before the show, otherwise

---

36 Bartlett 1898, 44.
37 Altick 1978, 312–16.
38 Chambers 2008, 64.
39 Saxon 1978, 216–19.

a stream of urine could drench the stage, actors and musicians, although this event, and the effort to put down sawdust if it happened, became an entertaining comic interlude for those out of range; there was at least one such recorded incident with Djeck.[40]

Travelling menageries in England gradually acquired and presented a single elephant, with one appearing at Hilton's from 1833, one at Batty's from 1836, and one travelling in Van Amburgh's menagerie around England from 1838 to the 1840s.[41] An elephant was becoming a more regular attraction.

An elephant in a menagerie or deployed on stage might simply signify a foreign locality, but an elephant in a pantomime also helped to deflect political realities within narratives that decentred the cause of human conflicts. While European war triumphs were re-enacted, the battles taking place elsewhere remained in the background of an exotic saga; these seemed intended to divert public concern about violence in distant settlements. Shortly after the Napoleonic wars, British rule encompassed about one-quarter of the world's population.[42] Indigenous habitants did not accept the increasing impositions of colonial rule without fighting back. Military responses were justified by a distinctive pattern of imperial defensive rhetoric in relation to the protection of settler women from what was deemed to be the threatening violence of indigenous men. This type of demarcation emerged, for example, in responses to the Sepoy Rebellion in India in 1857.[43] Conflict in colonial regions revealed a clash of cultures and this manifested in Britain with rumours about sexual assault and rape. In 1865, after the Governor of Jamaica, Edward John Eyre, violently suppressed a riot in Morant Bay in which 439 people were killed, the debate in Britain, led by Thomas Carlyle, defended Eyre's actions as necessary for the protection of Englishmen and importantly, women. This defence was opposed by John Stuart Mill, who attacked Eyre's decision as being against the rule of law.

In his analysis of reviews of CA Somerset's informative play about the Sepoy Rebellion, *The storming and capture of Delhi*, staged at

---

40   Saxon 1978, 218.
41   Speaight 1980, 85.
42   Hall 2000, 7.
43   Woollacott 2006, 44–46.

Astley's in 1857 with a violent conclusion, Marty Gould finds that reviewers considered the British retaliation justified. He explains: 'Violence which might in another context be deemed shocking or offensive "suits" this theatrical presentation of a naturalized, militaristic, imperial order.'[44] Most exotic entertainment spectacles, however, avoided enactments of overt violence. Popular melodrama elevated British law over indigenous custom, and despite the biases in the narrative and 'fantastic action', some productions aimed at realistic effects and accuracy in the spectacle,[45] with the addition of animals. A colonial battle could reveal female vulnerability through a rescue scenario without necessarily re-enacting brutality. Instead melodramatic pantomimes featuring elephants reinforced the romance of life in exotic locations in an overt embodiment of cultural myths and faraway origins. The presence of elephants on an English stage legitimised acquisitive political authority and, like horses, they were co-opted into the dominant narrative of nationhood and imperial expansion.

An elephant, framed as heroically rescuing deserving individual humans, fostered illusions about relations between species, and reinforced a gulf between public awareness of exotic animals and the elephant's actual physical treatment. An elephant seemed compliant and endearing when he or she undertook a trick such as removing a kettle from a fire or laying down on command.[46] The elephant's public appeal was enhanced by fictional narratives about an elephant nature that was loyal to humans.

Gentle nature and hierarchies

The training of animals without force was recommended by Philip Astley in his late 18th-century training manuals on horsemanship and subsequent manuals by others, including the 1869 *Haney's art of training animals*. It proposed managing horses by 'The Power of Gentleness' and 'kindness'; it even mentioned taming lions and tigers with 'mild measures', and somewhat unrealistically relying on a lion's affections.[47]

---

44   Gould 2011, 162.
45   Holder 1991, 133, 130–34.
46   Coxe 1980a, 128.

Sympathetic approaches to horses, other working animals and domesticated pets reinforced the possibility of human partnerships with larger wild animals. A disjunction existed, however, between disparate practices and professed human ideals.

In her exploration of 'the meaning of kindness' in England, and of sentiments such as compassion, Harriet Ritvo explains how, through decades, the English developed pride in the nation's values towards animals.[48] Public attitudes to animals became integrated into competitive rivalry among nations. By the 1830s the English anti-cruelty movement was associating foreigners with cruelty. While campaigns for anti-cruelty legislation entailed numerous defeats,[49] the belief in an ideal of Britishness and kindness developed these early campaigns. But Ritvo outlines how it was a moral issue of self-discipline and middle-class respectability, so animal abuse came to be associated with lower classes. This meant that prosecutions for cruelty to working animals such as horses had a class bias. As Keith Thomas explains, 'Kindness to animals was a luxury which not everyone had learnt to afford.'[50]

The claim that sentiment and the passions were common to humans and to animals was advanced by the 18th-century philosopher David Hume, in his influential works on human nature, examining the reason, instinct and emotions of humans and animals within attitudes to others and to the surrounding world. He argues: 'Nature may certainly produce whatever can arise from habit.'[51] Yet 'love and hatred are common to the whole of sensitive creation' and 'love in animals, has not for its only object animals of the same species' and '*sympathy*, or the communication of passions takes place among animals'.[52]

---

47   *Haney's art* 1869, 20, 125. In relation to elephants, see Nance 2013, 83–87.
48   Ritvo 1987, 126.
49   Ritvo 1987, 125, 127, 129, 137, 160. If an 1800 anti-bull-baiting law passed through the English Parliament with minimal interest, parliamentarians could not ignore widening public support by 1821 to 1822 when legislation against cruelty to cattle was passed, leading to successive bills in 1835, 1849, 1854, 1876. Neither could they ignore that the Society for the Prevention of Cruelty to Animals, founded in 1824, gained Royal Assent in 1840. Also, see Guither 1998; Chronology in Bekoff & Meaney 1998, xvii–xxi.
50   Thomas 1984, 186.
51   Hume 1896, 179.
52   Hume 1896, 397, 398.

2 War with animals

Nonetheless imagination and will belonged to humans, who should overcome the baser passions that led to cruelty. When Thomas outlines the advent of such new 18th-century sensibilities related to feeling, he notes that Hume identifies a 'blind nature'.[53] Jeremy Bentham's formative moral ideas on suffering emerged to counteract an indifferent natural order, although social values and practices trailed behind; John Stuart Mill would later argue that human suffering took precedence over that of animals.[54]

In the 19th century, a more conventional thinker, Alexander Bain, brought together a range of commentaries that delineated how emotions originated in the senses and sensation, but emphasised how these belonged within a hierarchical arrangement from higher to lower emotions derived from social values. Adhering to orthodoxy through the ordering of the emotions in which love and affection were more valued over anger and fear, Bain explains that higher emotions need to triumph over baser ones; kindness is an emotion of a higher order, while anger is of a lower order. Irrespective of Hume's ideas, Bain delineates how emotions such as love and kindness differentiated humans from other animals, although Bain's writing from the 1870s did grapple with the influence of major thinkers, including Charles Darwin and Herbert Spencer. But Bain's ordering of the emotions contains moral underpinnings and judgements indicative of the prevailing social, rather than scientific, values and upheld belief in a human destiny to achieve a higher position through exercising willpower to conquer a lower order of the emotions. As well as outlining the function of human will, these ideas supported belief in consciousness as uniquely human[55] – this continues today. Even where Bain's descriptions are intended to be neutral, his purpose was the instructive use of human willpower in relation to maintaining an overarching emotional order.

Higher-order emotions like kindness and gentleness were unquestionably indicative of human pre-eminence and species rank. Thus animals displayed animal fear within a lower order, which also included dread and terror, and these arose from either surprise or avoidance of

---

53 Thomas 1984, 170.
54 Rowlands 2007, 135–52.
55 Carus 1989 [1846], 76, with human consciousness under God, but above animal life, in a pyramid formation.

physical pain in their environment. Such responses constituted weakness because they led to panic and loss of control. Bain explains that

> the opposite of fear is Composure or Coolness in the presence of danger . . . not truly expressed by Courage, a noble quality containing an element of self-sacrifice, in opposition to Cowardice, which has in it an element of meanness.[56]

At the same time an even or joyful temperament can be achieved by the 'Power of Will' and knowledge that counteracts a strong imagination. While individuals have a set disposition, they can nonetheless use the will to exercise control, and accumulative acts of control set a social example. In Bain's approach, emotional control is a demeanour, and while a link between attitudes and consciousness is explained, any behavioural consequences seem largely assumed.

Yet kindness was also widely believed to be a natural female attribute. In her examination of emotions and animals in visual art from the mid-18th century, Diana Donald discerns how contemporary social guidance and explanations prescribed that women should show kindness but men should not, lest they seem effeminate.[57] Her analysis of human emotions as depicted in genres of painting argues that beliefs about emotions were reflected and were disseminated through painted tableaux that reinforced female tenderness towards selective animal species. But if emotional displays were a feminine attribute in these circumstances, inexpressiveness typified masculine identity. As Bain summarises: 'A man that towers above his fellow in force, will, endurance, courage, self-denial, strikes the spectator with an exalted idea of power.'[58] There were differences in expectations about the social expression of emotions and kindness, since a capacity for emotional impassivity demarcated a higher order of manliness. Kindness and other higher-order emotions that were evident in observable expression and tender behaviour did not line up with ideas of manly self-restraint that meant instead an absence of physical cruelty.

---

56 Bain 1875, 167, also 168, 160.
57 Donald 2007, 22.
58 Bain 1875, 248.

2 War with animals

Bain agrees that the ordering of emotional attitudes emerges from social imperatives and governed intentions towards others. Expanding Spencer's notion of sympathy, Bain questions a solely biological origin for the most important human emotion of love and protectiveness. In a human-centric approach, he argues that these also transcend sensory causes and sexual drives and parenting, and belong to social exchange. Yet Bain agrees with Darwin's law of antithesis, outlining that in fighting and predatory behaviour the 'dangerously strong rival would inspire anger and fear', but that the opposite situation produces love and manifests a (human) 'species of tender emotion'.[59] Benevolence is a manifestation of feeling pity and/or compassion and could become conjoined with the satisfaction gained from helping others, so that the lower animals could benefit.

Thomas claims that '[p]ity, compassion and a reluctance to inflict pain, whether on men or beasts, were identified as distinctively civilized emotions'.[60] But such emotional idealism needed economic justification. The guidance about unresponsive or uncooperative animal behaviour was not clear – especially if animals were considered to lack the willpower to override their lower emotions. Bain suggests that the whip, used for training horses, means that once a horse associated the sight or sound of the whip with pain, his or her fear produced compliance. Larger animals were selectively and bodily conditioned for obedience, but there was an expectation of reciprocal gratitude for kindness and sympathy, or at least some recognisable emotional response from a social inferior, including an animal.

The hierarchical ordering of the emotions corresponded with the ordering of the species. Bain managed to incorporate some aspects of Darwin's ideas while maintaining the prevailing view that humans are special. In 1872, Darwin challenged the human–animal divide and outlined how fear and terror were evident in both animals and humans through bodily and facial signs.[61] Darwin's understanding of emotions as being interconnected physiological processes in humans and

---

59   Bain 1875, 125, 131, also 142, 145, 333–34.
60   Thomas 1984, 188. 190.
61   Darwin 1999 [1872]. Darwin's study of expressed emotions in animals and humans preceded a major shift into training menagerie animals such as lions, tigers and elephants, from the 1880s. The training of wild animals for the

animals, and with links between, for example, astonishment and fear, and anger and disgust, undermined earlier simplistic interpretations and 19th-century hierarchies of nature's emotions, and even assumptions about the sameness of a whole species; that is, 19th-century emotional determinism. Importantly, similarities were pertinent to the management of exotic animals. For example, a handler's supposed fear of a wild animal could be balanced by a greater appreciation that an animal's aggression towards humans could be motivated by fright. But this created a conundrum. Ideas that animals and humans had similar emotional capacity and therefore physiology impinged on the widespread belief that a wild brute with base emotions needed to be civilised by human emotions, especially those of kindness and gentleness. Darwin's work undermined a species hierarchy in which animals constitute the lower order. He suggested animals had the capacity for a full range of human-like emotions, including supposedly higher-order emotions.

At the same time, however, Darwin's ideas had the potential to allow belief about kindness and comparable emotions in other animals to gain greater momentum. Animals that seemed to demonstrate loyalty in their behaviour or animals that seemed to reciprocate kindness could be integrated into human society. It was advantageous to claim that large-bodied animals would be responsive to displays of kindness.

Benevolence in the menagerie remained conditional. In 1872, JA asked of menageries: 'Can the performing animals in these travelling collections be made secure of receiving unvarying kindness?'[62] The author continued, claiming to have witnessed the 'reckless violence' of keepers losing tempers, and beating them with 'iron rakes' or 'rods'. Even if the rhetoric surrounding animals in menageries did not match their treatment, a public expectation gradually developed that kind attitudes should prevail. The gap between the actual treatment of animals and emotional attitudes towards them was reinforced by the way individual animals were celebrated in performances about kindness to humans, which regularly attracted royal attention.

20th-century circus developed claims for understanding and interpreting the psychology and emotions of wild animals as individuals, see Tait 2012.
62   JA 1872, 2.

2 War with animals

Royal kindness

While the young Queen Victoria was clearly fascinated by Van Amburgh's lion act, which she attended six times in 1839, George Sanger considered that the older Queen was more interested in elephants.[63] Certainly elephants came to dominate Sanger's spectacles, but they were always a longstanding interest of the British royal family and their menagerie, and this was a politicised subject of 17th- and 18th-century satire, in which an elephant was substituted for the monarch.[64] A 19th-century cartoon elaborates on this satirical usage by showing politicians in the zoological gardens, clambering up to ride on a seated crown-wearing elephant, and failing (Plate 3). Sanger, however, was possibly seeking confirmation of widespread social assumptions. If kindness was of a higher order, then in a hierarchical society it needed to be evident at the highest level. Thus Queen Victoria should model kindness even to animals and especially to the dominant large-bodied species such as elephants with a reputation for loyalty. In 1899 she finally and unmistakably obliged in writing when she inquired about an individual elephant.

Whether Sanger was right or not, Queen Victoria was interested in exotic animals that were part of the British Empire, and British royals regularly visited 19th-century menageries and circuses. As a princess, Victoria and her mother, the Duchess of Kent, first visited Wombwell's menagerie on 3 May 1830.[65] Victoria also rode around the arena when the Brighton riding school was being converted to a circus, and part of Wombwell's menagerie was presented at Windsor Castle on 1 November 1834 to King William and Queen Adelaide, and again by Royal Command in 1842, 1847 and 1854.[66] Victoria and Albert first attended Astley's together on 20 May 1841.[67] But Queen Victoria was curious about a wide range of popular entertainments of the time, especially those attracting a high degree of public attention. On 23 March 1844, a little person, the so-named General Tom Thumb (Charles Stratton) under PT Barnum's

---

63 Sanger 1927 [1910], 255.
64 Plumb 2010a, 531.
65 Bostock 1972 [1927], 5.
66 Disher 1937, 131
67 Saxon 1978, 339.

management, was invited to Buckingham Palace; the performance included his imitation of Bonaparte. The aristocracy and the public went to see Stratton perform at the Egyptian Hall in London. Two more invitations to the palace followed and greatly assisted Barnum with his promotion, although later 'there were so many visits to members of the Royal Family that the showman soon felt it necessary to expend nearly one hundred pounds on a court costume for Tom Thumb'.[68]

By the 1840s Astley's staging of royal pageantry and military battles was legendary, and after her life was threatened in a thwarted attack, the Queen was given a special afternoon Royal Command performance at Astley's in April 1846 to see 'A Grand Equestrian Day Representation', and the royal party watched from a box that had been thoroughly searched in an otherwise empty auditorium.[69] The performance included the tableau of *The Rajah of Nagpore*, with more than one elephant. No doubt elephants delivered an authentic aura for foreign royal characters, but the elephant's presence in an English performance, in front of the monarch, would have seemed like quasi-official confirmation of royal dominion over all the inhabitants of their foreign territory. A living elephant in a special royal performance had considerable symbolic value.

As well as special access to living exotic animals, the royal household received animal skins and other dead specimens as state tributes from the empire in an era when stuffed birds under glass were becoming common in the Victorian household with the increasing availability of taxidermy.[70] There is an arresting image of the then Prince of Wales as a young boy in acrobatic tights and a leopard-skin-like shift; he is sitting on a wine barrel, his foot resting on the head of a leopard skin.[71] In an odd reference to Dionysian practice and ancient Greece, he wore a headpiece of grapes and held up a goblet. This was part of a tableau performance by the royal children in 1854, on the occasion of the royal marriage anniversary. It suggests that a trophy skin was available for use as a theatrical prop and such utility of a tribute item confirmed royal prerogative.

---

68 Saxon 1989, 131–32, 133.
69 Disher 1937, 196–99.
70 Poliquin 2012, 68–69; Madden 2011; Turner 2013.
71 Callaway 2000, 105, photograph by Roger Fenton, 103.

2 War with animals

The royals viewed living animals in menageries through the decades when elephants were increasing in number and in parades. After 1871 Astley's menagerie animals, especially the renowned elephants, were used by Sanger to present the largest spectacles in England, including one called 'The Congress of Nations'. The large number of elephants in particular was invaluable to the impact of the spectacle. In 1846 a single elephant was billed at Astley's for two weeks walking along an elevated 'tightrope' that was probably a plank.[72] By 1852 Astley's had the leading act, with four elephants moving together around the ring like horses, and in 1853 an act with one balancing on two front legs. A line-up of exotic animals in routine appearances gradually increased and enhanced the impact of a fantasy spectacle. Sanger's addition of a troupe of 11 elephants to the *Aladdin* Boxing Day pantomime in 1874 outdid previous zoological spectacles in London, and Sanger also toured a show to mainland Europe each year.[73] The elephants additionally formed part of a bridal procession sequence that included camels and horses.

By 1876, there were 13 elephants in *Gulliver on his travels or, Harlequin Robinson Crusoe, his man Friday, and the wonderful spirit of romance*, 700 performers, nine camels, 52 horses and numerous menagerie animals and birds including two lions in a collar and chain in the centre of this animal tableau.[74] In what seemed to be a response to public concern, the Lord Chamberlain wrote to Sanger with concerns about the weight-carrying capacity of the stage.

Elephants were being moved on command by the 1870s and John Cooper, who had first started working with lions when he was 11 in 1844, was credited with training the first elephant troupe in England by 1876, presenting six and later eight moving together at a time so that they seemed to dance a waltz and a hornpipe.[75] A team of four elephants was worth a thousand guineas in 1882. The elephant act was enhanced by music, and this framed the act's intention of pleasing

---

72 Speaight 1980, 86.
73 Sanger 1927 [1910], 217.
74 Sanger 1927 [1910], 235. Sanger specifies 300 women, 200 men, 200 children, and – in presumably far fewer numbers – ostriches, emus, pelicans, kangaroos, reindeer and other deer, bulls and buffaloes. Disher 1937, 259–60.
75 Coxe 1980a, 141.

spectators with an imitation of human-like actions by the largest animal – an implicit confirmation of human dominance. Cooper went on to train elephants to walk on barrels, ride a tricycle and lift him up, and these were rivalled only by the tricks of the elephants that were later presented by the Lockhart family in the 1880s and 1890s.[76] From the 1870s to 1880s, elephants were considered sufficiently manageable to be included in the ring show of the larger circuses that could afford to buy them.

During the parades to advertise Sanger's shows, elephants walked in between the carriages that carried tableaux. These included the King's Tableaux, a horse-drawn carriage with a four-high tier structure, on which three tiers of male performers were wearing 'bejeweled turbans and Oriental costumes'; the top tier consisted of one performer on a swing.[77] The other menagerie animals were paraded in 20 cages on wagons followed by horse riders costumed either as military figures or as cowboys and Indians. The scale of this spectacle was intended to impress even a queen.

As indicated, the royal family rewarded performers who worked with exotic animals with attention and often with gifts. In 1887 Queen Victoria was said to have been pleased that 'among other marks of the spread of enlightenment' was an increase in 'humane feelings towards the lower animals'.[78] A presumption of humaneness in the British treatment of these menagerie animals may have been idealistic, since elephant care was highly variable. Elephants did not breed in captivity, making the mortality rate an ongoing concern, and Sanger had 13 elephants die during his working life.[79]

Several months after having watched a parade with the elephants from her carriage on 17 July 1899, Queen Victoria inquired into an incident that brought about the death of an elephant that she would have seen in the Sanger parade. The letter, on behalf of the Queen, is reproduced in Sanger's biography and reveals a kindly interest in the fate of the elephants. Its existence implies that royal responsibility extended to elephants. In February 1900, a menagerie carpenter and

---

76 Speaight 1980, 85–86; Lockhart & Boswell 1938.
77 Lukens 1956, 51.
78 Cited in MacKenzie 1988, 26.
79 Sanger 1927 [1910], 254–55, also 251, 253–54 on Queen Victoria.

friend invited some acquaintances from a hotel back to the elephant stalls where the elephants were prodded by the group with theatrical spears that were used in a war spectacle. When the elephants duly reacted, the carpenter was crushed to death by an elephant named Charlie who had broken out of his chains. Other elephants broke loose and one, Edgar, was not caught for two days. The mishandled and physically provoked Charlie, who had been with Sanger for 20 years, had to be shot for killing the drunk carpenter. The hierarchical order of the species prevailed in practice, regardless of expressions of kind concern, even from the Queen.

Attacks in art

The painted panoramas and tableaux of conflict used in theatre and circus popularised longstanding themes of predator attack and war in more socially esteemed arts such as painting and sculpture, and these spread to the colonies. The various arts contained an abundance of depictions of animals, including those themed with emotive images of war, conflict and attacks between species. As live entertainments began to reveal comparable capacities to painted depictions during the 19th century, accordingly exhibited animals influenced themes in painting. In turn, artistic depictions of animals impinged on social expectations about exhibited animals. In considering how the arts were indicative of emotional responses within the wider society – and possibly influenced by Aristotle – Bain recognises that humans derive some pleasure from the simulation of fear in art and performance. More significantly, however, he acknowledges that there is also pleasure in viewing the infliction of pain and enjoyment derived from watching fights with animals. He argues that the bodily excitement that arises from actual danger heightened its appeal, such as with the hunting of tigers or the spectacle of bullfights or other contests. Bain considers that animal species are separated on a slim pretext into those that humans make pets of and those that are chased or put into collections for public viewing or hunting; Hume finds the passions of hunting similar to those experienced when studying philosophy.[80] Bain is clear that animal entertainments are a major social activity expressly because they stimulate the emotions.

There were notable differences, however, between depictions in performance and those in visual art and literature. The emotional significance was often generalised in live performance and more ambiguous and open to interpretation, although animals were framed within human narratives of conflict and war. An animal appearance did not by itself present a set of hostile emotions. The menagerie lion act relied on the striking visual effect of placing humans and animals in close proximity to elicit fear and excitement, drawing on pre-existing expectations and associations to colour public perceptions.

By comparison, visual art could embellish and particularise facial emotions with an example of either aggression and conflict or a harmonious compatibility between species. The violence of an attack could be graphic and studied at length. The emotional impact could be specific, its detail available for repeated viewing. In particular, George Stubbs, known for his paintings of animals, undertook a series of 17 paintings in 30 years from the 1760s that depicted a lion attacking a horse; there is a suggestion he may have witnessed such an attack. Although each painting in the series offered a slightly different perspective on the same attack, they showed the aggression of the lion on top of the horse, clawing the horse's back. Diana Donald explains that the paintings by Stubbs show four steps in the attack and were intended to reveal ferocity in nature. Stubbs followed a tradition of painting lions and tigers that went back to Rubens' painting of about 1616–18, which had been influenced by the legacy of Greco-Roman art. Donald analyses how wild animal species were used to depict and embody human qualities and ultimately to represent nature with individual animals symbolising larger patterns. 'Stubbs shows such an elemental battle for life in heroic terms . . . in a drama of raw nature itself.'[81]

The paintings reflected human emotional attitudes. In *A lion attacking a horse*, painted c. 1765, Stubbs shows a brown lion on top of a white horse whose agonised open mouth, exposed teeth, turned head, and twisted body position depict terrified surprise (Plate 2). The viewer is being positioned to feel sympathy for the horse,[82] whose innocent terror contrasts with the demonic power of nature embodied by the

---

80 Bain 1875, 253, also 170; Hume 1896, 451.
81 Donald 2007, 71, also 68–70, 74 about reviewer sympathy.
82 Donald 2007, 74.

lion; his eyes stare out towards the viewer with an ambiguous expression. A romantic natural European landscape surrounds them with the hazy mist of dark green hills and trees and botanical details in the foreground. The side of the horse, including the tail and back leg, is outlined in taut muscular profile and blocks some of the lion's body from view. The painting conveys a sense of physical fear, even terror, in the unfolding attack and leap that has propelled the lion up onto the horse's back. It further shows the lion's muscular effort to hold his position, his claws digging into the horse's flesh. This concept of a ferocious attack was part of 18th-century art well before the advent of tamer acts. A lion riding a horse and later an elephant would become the epitome of the achievement of the trained animal act after the 1890s.[83]

Elsewhere Stubbs imagines the same animal species in repose, which may be closer to Thomas' contestable assertion that Stubbs' paintings were 'controlled, detached and utterly unanthropomorphic'.[84] Donald explains: 'Stubbs' ideas on the relationship between men and fierce animals were not embodied in scenes of hunting and predation alone.'[85] He had an interest in anatomical comparisons and towards the end of his life compared human, tiger and fowl bodies and showed curiosity about how animal bodies motivate artists. In comparison, Samuel Daniell's peacefully idyllic paintings *African scenery and animals*, 1804–05, were the result of his travels in 1801 to see animals in their habitats and attracted less public attention. In Daniell's work, elephants wander freely through tranquil landscapes. But the dynamism of painting that depicted the ferocity of lions and tigers and captive animals, including staged acts from menageries, overshadowed such tranquil scenes.

Paintings of exotic animals preceded staged cage acts and exotic animals on circus and theatre stages and delivered pervasive concepts of violence. John MacKenzie writes that the gothic sentiments of 19th-century art influenced orientalist art and reflected the belief that:

> Nature, like genius and the individual human psyche, was wild and potentially uncontrollable ... Animal violence helps to illustrate this

---

83 Tait 2012, 17, 30–33.
84 Thomas 1984, 69.
85 Donald 2007, 74, also 173–76 on Daniell.

point. The destructive power and ferocity of the lion was a source of great fascination ... Nineteenth century art is full of such violence; the posed animal conflicts mirror and justify human violence.[86]

Animal attackers were surrogates for an unpredictable nature that was implicitly inclusive of humanity.

Accordingly, in comparison the live entertainment might have been somewhat disappointing. Edwin Landseer was recognised as the leading painter of animals in the first half of the 19th century, and in one portrait study of Van Amburgh and his animal act (Plate 1), Van Amburgh is positioned in the centre of the painting, standing astride, his arm extended, pointing to what appears to be a lion cringing to the side as several other big cats pull back. The emotional confrontation is implied rather than dramatised. Landseer preferred to paint dogs, stags and to a lesser extent lions, and he became best known for his emotive images of dogs and for reproductions of his paintings and engravings, which together generated half of his income.[87] His prominence was assured after commissions from the royal family. In an early set of engravings based on his drawings, he created a fighting scene with lions, tigers and leopards. Notably, however, he depicts Van Amburgh in a quiet stance of dominance, looking but not touching the animals. Less skilful illustrations of Van Amburgh's act by other artists contradict this impression by depicting handling and exaggerated physical confrontation, whereas Landseer replicated its mystique.

To achieve accuracy, Landseer studied live animals in Cross' Exeter Change menagerie and dissected dead ones. Later he would keep his own collection of live and dead animals. But MacKenzie suggests that Landseer was overwhelmed by the 'violence' in his imagination;[88] arguably, he might also have witnessed fights between species. Landseer's art was well known during the first half of the 19th century and preceded a slightly more self-reflective relationship with hunting that emerged from the practice of keeping safari hunting diaries (see Chapter 3). As MacKenzie points out, Victorian artists and

---

86 MacKenzie 1995, 54–5.
87 Donald 2007, 86, 127–58.
88 MacKenzie 1988, 34, also 31–32, 33.

travel writers transformed animals and environmental domains into nature itself.

The artistic effort to depict the emotions of an animal attack culminated in the striking effect of taxidermy. Rachel Poliquin recounts how Jules Verreaux's extremely graphic diorama *Arab courier attacked by lions*, in which two lions attacked a human on a camel, won a gold medal in 1867. Poliquin suggests that the camel was 'bellowing in fear and pain'.[89] She explains that such a composition was at once geographically informative, dramatically exciting, lurid and frightening.

The extremes of animal behaviour in painted poses and taxidermy could not be easily re-created in live exhibitions and acts. Nor could these deliver the nuances and intricacies of the painted detail of an attack – leaving aside accidents. Even literature and theatrical dialogue and song lyrics were more specific in their messages about confrontation, patriotism and conflict with animal symbols than the regular menagerie action, and there was a corresponding expansion in theatrical variety shows that presented war themes without animals. In the second half of the 19th century, a subgenre of theatrical melodramas depicting patriotism became more numerous in music hall venues. War was a perennial topic. MacKenzie lists at least 13 political events and military campaigns after 1867 that 'identify outbursts of public interest in foreign and imperial matters' and stimulate 'popular excitement'.[90] John Springhall observes that 'little wars' happened in the colonies every year of Queen Victoria's reign after 1870, and these became the substance of 'romantic adventure and heroism' in newspapers.[91]

The emotional impact of art could vary considerably, even about attack and war, and while painting fixed an image of violence, theatre remained cheerfully rousing. Penny Summerfield outlines how some historians consider that the 19th-century theatre, and especially the music hall, educated the public about political events. They also manipulated audience responses and therefore influenced public opinion more broadly to benefit imperialist rule and to advance acceptance of the propaganda about wars in an expanding British Empire. The reactions of spectators probably had some parallels across live

---

89   Poliquin 2012, 91, 92, photograph.
90   MacKenzie 1986b, 2–3.
91   Springhall 1986, 49.

entertainments. Melodramas about liberating other places were popular in working-class theatres of the 1870s in England, espousing how the dutiful sailor or soldier freed colonial populations, and these had evolved from earlier nautical tropes of liberating slaves. One interesting feature of theatre and music hall songs about war was the symbolic centrality of animals. A famous example from 1877 was the song 'By Jingo', with lyrics about how the Russians threatened Constantinople: 'we don't want to fight', claimed the lyrics, but 'the dogs of war' had been let loose because the brute of a Russian bear threatened to attack the poor lion (Britain), who was trying to avoid war by staying in his den.[92] State authority over citizens' lives was reinforced by such patriotic refrains using ideas of animals. Yet Summerfield argues that jingoistic attitudes were more likely to be found among middle-class spectators and in later narratives about a triumphant military in the colonies. She suggests that working-class audiences may have been comparatively indifferent, despite years when large numbers went into the army.

Nonetheless the inclusion of live animals made war narratives credible and heroic, and battle spectacles with animals were staged throughout the 19th century in Britain. The military were appreciative of popular entertainment involving animals, and there were reverse tributes to the circus from the military. For example, in 1872 the 'ninth (Queen's Own) Lancers' of the 'Royal Marine Barracks' put up a tent and staged their own circus, presenting well-trained 'trick' horses by non-commissioned officers and gymnastic feats for the entertainment of the garrison.[93] The horseriding skills of military men meant that they could easily re-create a 19th-century equestrian circus. In the same year there was also a touring show with a troupe of horses and 'War Arabs' in the south of England.[94]

Popular entertainment involving military iconography and endearing animals can be claimed to have distorted public understandings of war, especially in narratives staged repeatedly over time. The perpetuation of imperial ambition required force and therefore public

---

92   Lyrics cited in Summerfield 1986, 25, also 17, 25. For a discussion of animals in jingoistic attitudes, see Baker 2001.
93   *New York Clipper* 1872, Circuses, 7 September: 179.
94   *New York Clipper* 1872, Circuses, 9 November: 251.

support for soldiers sent to remote places. A music hall production of *Britannia* (without a lion) presented in 1885 in London personified the British Empire with a female performer who, confronted by the greedy aggression of other nations, was defended by the noble and loyal sons of England and brave sons from the colonies.[95] This type of show demanded pride in the English military and the lyrics unmistakably reinforced nationalist sentiments; the need to protect womanhood converged with the imperative to protect the nation, represented by a female figure or an animal. Such entertainments blatantly reinforced how colonial hierarchies of identity and status achieved control of land and of all its inhabitants, including animals, and how this was maintained through militarised regimes.

Empire-building during the 19th century has been described as 'a very masculine enterprise', and colonised peoples were accordingly viewed as 'weak and unmasculine'.[96] Animals, too, were colonised within associated emotional hierarchies. Melodramas with war themes and animals contained narrative similarities to other types of theatricalised performance, in that these were human stories about conflict and aggression in which the visual significance was enlarged by realistic animal presence. Colonial rule was also implicitly sanctioned by encounters with animals from the colonies and animals were framed in instructive ways. At the same time individual animal sensations and tales of largesse diverted attention from large-scale human predicaments in remote settlements. The ambiguity of animal presence in performance also facilitated a wide spectrum of signification and meaning that masked the underlying fundamental human–animal conflict. Imputations of violence surrounded 19th-century battle re-enactment and the staging of international conflicts and skirmishes, but the enjoyment – even pleasure – that was derived from these public entertainments with live animals may have offset understanding of the deadly consequences of war and of attack.

---

95   Summerfield 1986, 28.
96   Levine 2004b, 1, 6.

3
Imperial hunting show legends

By the mid-19th century the character of a safari hunter was appearing in menagerie cage acts in England. The hunter, holding a gun, chased lions, emulating hunters in colonial lands. The identity was associated with the military as the expansion of territorial control came to be represented by exotic animals shipped in increasing numbers to the zoos and menageries of imperial centres. This chapter outlines developments between the 1850s and the 1880s in cage acts, in travelling shows competitively claiming the greatest number of species on display, and in rapidly escalating menagerie spectacles that included pseudo state ceremonial occasions in the USA. The spectacle belied the violent methods of capture and of hunting as a type of war perpetuated on other species.

Biblical stories were supplanted as menagerie animals became trophies of adventures in foreign lands, and became popularised through biographical accounts of exotic wild nature. From 1870 the numbers of American menagerie businesses increased and, as competition intensified, enterprising showmen such as PT Barnum enhanced and embellished their menagerie exhibits with sanitised versions of safari sagas. During the 1880s hunting acts in menageries reinforced the genre of adventure fiction, particularly narratives about hunting sports that circulated in newspapers and books.

Menagerie hunters

The sport of hunting had long been a part of English country life and had featured in paintings and other representational art.[1] Similarly hunting trophies emblematic of social privilege were an accepted part of the interior design of stately mansions, and such displays in private homes were expanded with exotic wild animals, following opportunities to hunt in India and later in Africa. Public displays of hunting booty developed from the mid-19th century. Roualeyn Gordon Cumming was among the first British hunters to return from Africa and publish an account of his activities. In addition, he presented a public show of his trophies.[2] His 1850 book was subtitled 'anecdotes of the chase of the lion, elephant, hippopotamus, giraffe, rhinoceros', and Cumming admitted developing 'a love of natural history and of sport' early in his life.[3] As a young man he joined the Fourth Madras Light Cavalry in India, where he 'procured a great number of specimens of natural history' for a large collection.[4] He subsequently joined the Cape Riflemen in Africa before setting off to meet David Livingstone and become the first 'civilized man' to venture into parts of the African interior, collecting 'hunting trophies and objects of interest in science' that eventually weighed 30 tonnes.[5] These were exhibited in the 1851 Great Exhibition at the Crystal Palace and attracted considerable public attention. In a twist on menagerie hunting acts, Cumming exhibited himself as the 'lion-slayer at home' for an entry fee of one, two or three shillings.[6] The authentic hunter was on show.

A menagerie act called 'The Lion Hunt' appeared in England by 1857, in which Martini Maccomo (Macomo) fired three pistols as he chased some fairly young animals around the cage, and his act was copied by others.[7] The pistols fired blanks of wadding or paper. Maccomo was Arthur Williams, an ex-sailor from the West Indies.[8]

---

1 See Donald 2007.
2 Ritvo 1987, 249–250; MacKenzie 1988, 29. Sporting hunters took care to preserve trophies, see MacKenzie 1987a, 185; Ritvo 2002, 34.
3 Cumming 1850a, A2 (vii).
4 Cumming 1850a, A2 (vii).
5 Cumming 1850a, ix, 207; 1850b, 303.
6 Ritvo 1987 251, poster.
7 *Birmingham Daily Post* 1860, 31 July: 2.

Apparently he approached William Manders at the Greenwich Fair and began working with the successful Manders' menagerie, billed as the first 'African Lion King'.[9] He featured in a painting amid a group of big cats, dressed in a costume trimmed with leopard skin. Male and female performers might have commonly worn a piece of wild animal skin as part of the costume, but Maccomo later rejected his fake African identity with its costume of skins and feathers and, instead, wore a suit with a gold watch. Known for his sensible demeanour, Maccomo was proclaimed 'the most daring man among lions and tigers I ever saw' by another lion king.[10] Once, Maccomo was wounded while trying to separate two fighting tigers using a whip. Despite a widespread assumption that he would be torn to pieces, Maccomo survived and died some time later from an illness, probably pneumonia.

The hunting act conveyed the impression of a chase and was considered more dangerous than the longstanding style of tamer-handling performance because of the element of provocation that was almost certainly necessary to make the lions move around the cage. Maccomo's hunting act was supposed to be done with younger lions, whereas regular taming acts were done with older lions who were habituated to the interaction. A hunting act involved the tamer brandishing a weapon while making a lion run around the cage:

> It consists in chasing the lions about the cage, the performer being armed with a sword and pistols, and throwing into the mimic sport as much reality as possible. It will be obvious that this is a dangerous exhibition and it should never be attempted with any but young animals. For ordinary performances, most lion tamers prefer full-grown animals ... [but a lion] will not suffer himself to be so driven and bustled about; and so it is the animals that are put through this performance are often changed.[11]

The tone of the hunting act emphasised aggressive human dominance.

---

8   Turner 1995, 86. Mention is made of an African, Henry Porter, with Wombwell's. Also, *Manchester Times* 1884, Lion taming, 23 August: 5.
9   Speaight 1980, 82.
10 Cited in Frost 1875, 134.
11 *New York Clipper* 1872, Lions and lion tamers, 13 April: 12.

Manders' menagerie was among the 12 public menageries listed by Edward Bostock as operating in England, Scotland and Ireland during the 1860s, including his family's Bostock and Wombwell's from 1867.[12] He also briefly mentions that Wombwell's animals came from William Cross in Liverpool, and from William and Charles Jamrach in London, although Wombwell's later bought animals from Hagenbeck's in Hamburg, Germany.[13] Other menageries probably had a similar process of buying from those dealers who acquired exotic animals from safari expeditions. At the same time hunting acts with horses and hounds, modelled on English hunts, and even chasing a stag prey also became common in the circus ring from the 1850s.

At Manders' menagerie, Massarti (or Maccarte) replaced Maccomo, and by 1872 was working there under the management of Manders' wife, Sarah.[14] Sarah was reportedly also a 'lion queen', most likely some time before Maccomo was 'hired' in 1857, and after Wombwell's lion queens became famous about 1848. When William Manders died in 1871, it was Sarah who became the manager of the menagerie for four years, before their son assumed control. The business later failed.

Massarti was an Irishman, Thomas McCarthy, born in 1838, and he became the lion king with Bells and Myer circus in 1862 after working as a cage attendant, and joined Manders' menagerie in 1871. Ten years before, while working as an attendant before becoming a tamer, McCarthy's arm was so badly mauled that it needed to be amputated.[15]

There was a fatal attack involving McCarthy on 3 January 1872.[16] A feature article about lion tamers claimed that, against advice, he turned his back on some lions during the more dangerous hunting act, which caused the accident leading to his death.[17] An earlier report of the

---

12 Bostock 1972 [1927], 10. The menageries in England c. 1860 were operated by Thomas Stevens, John Day, John Simons, Whittington, William Sedgewick, Anderton and Rowland, Barnham, Chipperfield, Sargano Alicamousa, and Sidney Braham. Edward started his first menagerie in 1883, opened a second when he took over the family menagerie in 1889, and a third from Barnham in 1892.
13 Bostock 1972 [1927], 11. Bostock also lists JD Hamlyn in London up to World War I and then was taken over by GB Chapman. For more detail on earlier traders, see Simons 2012.
14 Turner 1995, 86, 87–88. McCarthy may have also been spelt 'Macarte'.
15 *New York Clipper* 1872, Lions and lion tamers, 13 April: 12.
16 Turner 1995, 86.

accident, however, said that he was undertaking the act at about 10.30 am with five lions, when one lion struck him with his paw. McCarthy struck back with a sword but fell down; another lion held him down with a paw on McCarthy's leg, tearing off his leopard skin costume while other lions attacked.[18] He used a sword that he was holding to defend himself, and extracted himself from the cage after 10 minutes. The feature article claimed that he was chasing one lion from one end of the cage to the other when he was accidentally knocked down and, while he jumped up again and drove the lions into a corner, one crept forward and sprang at him, seizing him by the right hip.[19] Initially the 500 spectators thought that this was part of the act until the other lions attacked him. Screams and confusion ensued, despite attempts by attendants to beat the lions off McCarthy from outside the cage. They sought to partition the cage and separate the lions into one section but the door was at the far end of the cage, making it difficult to reach him. The attack continued for a quarter of an hour. Finally irons were heated in a hurry and applied to the lions from outside the cage, allowing McCarthy to escape (or to be pulled out of the cage). Regardless of which version of the attack was more accurate, McCarthy had been fatally wounded.

In the same act, McCarthy also wore the older style costume of a Roman gladiator, and carried a sword with a short Greco-Roman-style blade; the costumes may have been varied to revitalise the act. John Turner's description of the attack included the additional information that McCarthy had exhibited a gorilla and a serpent before entering the lions' cage. McCarthy, distracted by one restless lion, slipped before another lion bit and held his armless shoulder. Turner's summary of the sequence of events suggests that McCarthy might have carried the scent of other animals into the lions' cage with him. Because it was a special performance, 'it had not been deemed necessary to prepare hot irons', which had saved McCarthy in the attack 10 years earlier when he lost his arm.[20] In the reports of this fatal attack, it becomes evident that iron rods were in common use for this type of act, and were regularly used as a defensive strategy, and therefore in the management of lions in 19th-century menageries.

---

17 *New York Clipper* 1872, Lions and lion tamers, 13 April: 12.
18 *New York Clipper* 1872, Circuses, 27 January: 339.
19 *New York Clipper* 1872, Lions and lion tamers, 13 April: 12.
20 *New York Clipper* 1872, Circuses, 27 January: 339.

The description of McCarthy's funeral highlighted the sensationalist appeal of the lion tamer and his act. His funeral apparently attracted a large crowd of several thousand who crowded into the chapel; the Catholic priest, Reverend Canon Carter, who was conducting the service, had to ask for silence, and for people to take off their hats. The Reverend expressed a hope during the service that 'in future persons would not be allowed to expose themselves to such danger'.[21] An inquest ruled that it was death due to misadventure, but expressed disapproval of the 'reckless custom of so-called tamers performing in the dens'.[22] Certainly a fatal attack reinforced ideas of the strength and aggression of the lion, and the risks to the tamer continued to be intermittently covered in newspapers.[23]

The hunting act was thus a distinct and more dangerous offshoot of the tamer act. The hunt, however, could not simply be enacted by the human presenter: it had to be embodied by live animals enacting a chase sequence. Meanwhile, the details of the actual hunt were obscured and the violence and loss of animal life were camouflaged within the context of entertainment.

Unnatural violent capture

John MacKenzie defines hunting as 'the pursuit, driving, ambushing and trapping of wild animals of all species with the intention of killing them for meat, other animal products, or purely for sport'.[24] This definition focuses on hunting to obtain food or trophies, rather than for live capture and sale to zoos and menageries. But the methods of hunting for live capture were often indistinguishable, and animals were incidentally killed in the process. In all cases, hunting may appeal because of what Harriet Ritvo reiterates is the 'thrill of the chase'.[25]

---

21 *New York Clipper* 1872, Circuses, 3 February: 347.
22 *New York Clipper* 1872, Circuses, 27 January: 339. There is a further report about an attack on a cage attendant at Manders.
23 *New York Clipper* 1872, Circuses, 10 February: 355; *New York Clipper* 1872, Circuses, 24 February: 371.
24 MacKenzie 1988, 2.
25 Ritvo 1987.

3 Imperial hunting show legends

The showman William Coup writes in the 19th century that

> [t]here is something thrilling in the thought of the lives that had been lost, the sufferings and hardships endured, the perils encountered, and the vast sums of money expended in the capture and transportation of wild animals for the menageries, museums and zoological gardens.[26]

He meant that the hunter's risk of dying, rather than the animals' deaths, added to the excitement of the adventure.

One hypothesis, now somewhat discredited, suggests that hunting was central to human evolution. Matt Cartmill summarises various versions of this hypothesis, including one that viewed humans as predators with weapons. He explains that hunting also involved 'estrangement from nature', and that the hunted animal needed to be free-living.[27] Cartmill defines hunting as a type of war game involving 'the deliberate, direct, violent killing of unrestrained wild animals', who are additionally defined as 'those that shun or attack human beings'.[28] He explains how hunting could be like a military campaign with strategies and subterfuge, and that both hunting and war use similar weapons. The hunting of animals was an extension of human war, a war against other species.

Live animals, like dead trophy specimens, were acquired using strategies of capture that were warlike. Ritvo explains that animal hunting provided a form of military training in most societies and that it became 'a prized requisite of colonial service in Africa and Asia', and imperialism was inherently aggressive.[29] The British Empire was forged over time from the endeavours of explorers and adventurers and organised traders, to the rule of officialdom and charter companies supported by the military in the colonies. There were corresponding stages in the acquisition of menagerie animals, with a shift from speculative captures by individual adventurers to business investment in animal acquisition.

---

26 Coup 1901, 20.
27 Cartmill 1993, 12, 13, 29.
28 Cartmill 1993, 30.
29 Ritvo 2002, 34. Hunting provided 'recreation, status symbol and para-military training', 33.

The interpretation of the ways in which European imperial powers took over human-occupied lands that were also traditional hunting grounds can be enlarged to encompass the ongoing exploitation of animals in their homelands and beyond.[30] In Australia, pastoralists went on a kangaroo hunt called 'coursing' that copied the fox hunt in England, down to horsemen wearing red jackets.[31]

David Lambert and Alan Lester explain that colonial networks were both implicit and explicit,[32] as formal networks were ghosted by an unofficial opportunism that continued and proliferated after the 1850s. Opportunistic ventures included animal acquisition and, in the example of colonial trade, some of the traded commodities that passed through network hubs were alive. Animal trading developed from informal arrangements and ad hoc sales during the 1850s and 1860s, to formally hired personnel from the 1870s. The capture of live animals in particular involved both indigenous locals and Europeans in an extended hunting process, and the capture of a larger animal, such as an elephant, required financial resources and incentives.

Foundational myths of heroic encounters with large exotic animals in remote jungles were disseminated during the 1850s and 1860s, and adventure narratives were encapsulated by the activities of individual explorers who hunted for food and for bounty.[33] Some of the exotic animals in the shows during the 1850s might have been acquired from the Reiche business created by brothers Henry and Charles Reiche. Charles was a professional hunter and he made his first expedition through Panama in 1851. The German-based animal trade made the brothers wealthy and their New York office later supplied animals to most of the menageries in the USA, including that of PT Barnum. After the Reiche brothers died the Hagenbeck family business became the leading trader internationally.[34] European explorers and hunters went

---

30 MacKenzie 1990b, 2–3, see a summary of approaches.
31 'Spirited, Australia's Horse Story', National Museum of Australia, Canberra, retrieved on 28 August 2015 from http://www.nma.gov.au/exhibitions/spirited.
32 Lambert & Lester 2006b, 7, 26–29.
33 For example, see Cumming 1850a, 89 '[w]e galloped about the plains, loading and firing for about six hours' chasing springbok and wildebeest'; 215, 'Cumming was chased by a rhinoceros'; 265, '[t]he appearance of the wild elephant is inconceivably majestic and imposing' in elephant homelands.
34 Rothfels 2002a.

3 Imperial hunting show legends

southwards from Europe into Africa, travelling the Nubian Desert on camels. Coup recounts that Paul Tuhe (probably Ruhe, who worked for the Reiches) described how mother animals fought hard to stop the capture of their young. But it was easier to capture lions, shooting them with rifles, even with the mothers defending their young, than it was to capture baby elephants. Tuhe (Ruhe) explains:

> the old ones seem to know instinctively when we are after their young, and their rage is something terrible. The trumpeting of the parents can be heard a long distance and quickly alarms the whole herd. The rifle is comparatively useless.[35]

The method used required distracting an elephant mother so that an African hunter could crawl up behind her and sever her hind leg tendons with a large knife. She would fall to the ground, at which time a hunter went close in to kill her and to collect her ivory and her baby.

Allowing for some embellishment in the retelling, Samuel Baker gives a comparable account of hunting elephants and other animals on horseback.[36] Baker confirms the presence of Johann Schmidt who brought back and traded Jumbo, and that a hunt first killed a mother by distracting her attention to allow hunters to immobilise her from behind. Paul Chambers notes that hunters of the Victorian era, such as Baker, considered that the ultimate achievement was shooting an elephant. Mid-19th-century descriptions of hunting expeditions give details of the capture of young animals and the killing of others. The promotion of animals in touring menageries, however, mostly avoided mention of the violence of capture.

Further, Coup quotes Tuhe (Ruhe) explaining, 'Of course we sometimes have a native or two killed in this kind of hunt; but they don't cost much – only five to six dollars apiece.'[37] Hunters and animals were expendable in the violence of the hunt. Human life was nearly always lost in the capture of baby hippopotamuses, because the mothers fought back strongly against boats in the water and against hunters on the land, and they proved difficult to kill. But the acquisition of

---

35 Coup 1901, 27, citing Paul Tuhe (Ruhe), see Davis 2002, 196, 284 note 14.
36 Chambers 2008, 12; Baker 1868, 369–70, Johann Schmidt joins Baker.
37 Coup 1901, 27, citing Paul Tuhe (Ruhe).

one hippopotamus could earn the same as six lions, and therefore the hunting fight was worth the greater risk and the loss of life.

Traditional hunting techniques were replaced with European methods and guns, and other hierarchies of value associated with hunted animals developed accordingly.[38] Although indigenous locals remained a vital part of hunting practices and for live capture, a distinction emerged in England and the British Empire between commercial hunters who supplied animal businesses, and sportsmen who were recognised as great hunters and could achieve social mobility.[39] The former usually brought back sufficient specimens to generate an income, albeit at the cost of human and other animal lives.

Hunting overlapped with geographical exploration and extensive newspaper coverage about the exploits of David Livingstone heightened public interest in explorers in England. The celebrity missionary worked in East Africa and became internationally known for his reports from there during the 1850s and 1860s. When his communications ceased during a search for the source of the Nile, public interest meant that an expedition by the Royal Geographical Society was mounted to find him in 1871. It was newspaper reporter Henry Morton Stanley who located him – in the now-famous encounter.[40] The dependency of European explorers like Livingstone and Stanley on indigenous locals revealed the ways in which such exploration narratives intersect with gender, race and class identities.[41]

Animal trophies added an extra dimension to exploration in new places. As MacKenzie points out, British and American notions of the frontier were interchangeable, and although 'the exploitation of animals is everywhere in the imperial record', and 'the colonial frontier was also a hunting frontier', hunting practices have been somewhat marginalised

---

38   MacKenzie 1987b, 172–73. Hunting as sport should be distinguished from other activities by indigenous Africans that might be called 'sports', see Blacking 1987, 3–22.
39   MacKenzie 1988, 38, names FC Selous, CH Stigand, Denis Lyell and Richard Meinertzhagen as gaining social mobility, and others, such as Sir Frederick Lugard, Sir Alfred Sharpe, Sir Robert Coryndon, Sir Frederick Jackson and Sir Geoffrey Archer, and Sir Harry Johnston, gaining political prestige.
40   MacKenzie 1988; Woollacott 2006, 66.
41   Woollacott 2006, 65, cites Mary Louise Pratt; 4, cites Frederick Cooper and Ann Laura Stoler.

3 Imperial hunting show legends

in historical studies of colonial empires until recently.[42] But Daniel Herman argues that because of an absence of an associated class status in the USA, hunters were initially viewed as backwater rogues before hunting acquired heroic connotations and gradually evolved into a sport, aided by biographies of Daniel Boone.[43] The acquisition of animals also subsidised colonial expansion, and they symbolised the outer reach of the empire's frontier through embodied displays in zoos and menageries in imperial centres. MacKenzie notes that in 1858 the British Association for the Advancement of Science was made aware that the British Empire provided the most diverse collection of animal and plant specimens.[44] Colonial hunters, including military men, were encouraged to keep journals and game books in which they recorded numbers and body size. But as MacKenzie indicates about Cumming, the study of natural history could not be separated from colonial hunting as it, too, propounded an ethos of 'civilization and gentlemanly conduct'. Thus 'violence and cruelty had to be appropriated in order to control and tame' raw nature.[45] MacKenzie continues that paradoxes abounded: an ideal manly identity emerged from a conjunction of investigations of animal life through science and hunting that would 'preserve to be killed, kill to conserve'.

The wider scientific and philosophical investigation of nature included curiosity about animals, but by the 1860s this supported interpretations of what it meant to be human. Nancy Leys Stepan writes that by the mid-19th century '[t]he "human" (or humaine) became transformed through scientific investigation into "the human species" and its zoological variations'.[46] She explains that the objectivity of the natural sciences disguised power relations and this unfolded through the changing paradigm of '*nature* and *naturalization*'. The process of studying nature seemed neutral while producing an 'indifference to human concerns'.[47] It might be added, indifference to animal lives.

---

42 MacKenzie 1988, 50, 7; and important work on the ivory trade and wildlife conservation, 2.
43 Herman 2007, 47–71.
44 MacKenzie 1988, 37.
45 MacKenzie 1988, 26, also, 27–28, 43.
46 Stepan 2000, 66.
47 Stepan 2000, 69, citing Gyorgy Markus and Lorraine Daston.

In his philosophical effort to re-position the human in a Dionysian wild nature, Friedrich Nietzsche also outlines a progression to superhuman capacity that seems to endorse an additional species order, especially as he finds strength in militarism. Jennifer Ham points out, however, that Nietzsche animates various animals to speak ideas and actually resists a 19th-century tendency to separation with his recognition of animality in humans.[48] The separation of non-human species for scientific study meant that they became part of a supposedly neutral process of naturalisation. Whatever the justification for hunting, its violent impact was hidden in the ensuing cultural practices of trading, exhibiting and museum collecting and, above all, within scientific approaches to studying animals.

Trading nature

Adventurers brought animals back to Europe and the USA and readily sold them to zoos and menagerie businesses, so the origins of the animals were diffused through a growing trade. Nigel Rothfels' history of the Hagenbeck family trading business details the transition to organised expeditions that brought increasing numbers of exotic animals to Europe.[49] Hamburg was a major European port and, in the first half of the 19th century, animals were brought there by sailors, bought by intermediary dealers and traded on. Gustav Hagenbeck Senior was able to purchase seals in Hamburg in 1848. There were a number of levels in the animal trade even then. Hagenbeck's bought its first African animals from a European adventurer in the mid-1850s, and these included five lions, panthers, cheetahs, hyena, antelopes and monkeys, acquired mostly from the region of the Sudan.[50] After buying a larger shipment in 1864 than in the 1850s, Carl Hagenbeck

---

48 Ham 1997, 145–63.
49 For detailed accounts of the hundreds of animals traded in businesses in 19th-century Europe, see Rothfels 2002a; Simons 2012.
50 Rothfels 2002a, 49–50; Hagenbeck 1909, 7–8, 12; Hagenbeck 1956, intermediary traders included Gutschmidt, Breitweiser and Rath, and the painter of the animals of Hagenbeck Zoo was Heinrich Leutemann whose drawings were published from the 1860s in the magazine *Daheim*.

contracted the adventurer Lorenzo Casanova in 1865 to supply the family business. In 1870, in Suez, Carl supervised loading Casanova's 60 cages of animals. As well as rhinoceroses, lions and panthers, there were tethered elephants, giraffes, antelopes, buffaloes, and free-roaming ostriches. In the latter part of the 19th century, Hagenbeck's gained pre-eminence in animal trading in Europe and supplied animals for other menageries and circuses and operated their own. The family business also presented an extensive zoo collection for public viewing. Hagenbeck's developed from a business buying from adventurous explorers into one that commissioned from designated agents, and eventually came to dominate the worldwide trade in exotic wild animals for entertainment.

In addition, Hagenbeck's supplied numerous private menageries and European royalty with animals. Carl was given the title of 'Court Supplier to the Emperor of Germany', and the business also supplied the emperor of Austria-Hungary, the Russian tsar, the sultan of Morocco and the mikado of Japan.[51] Carl became known as 'The King of Menagerie Owners', especially after his profile was enhanced by the English and American press. Although this suggested some curiosity on the part of the royals, exotic animals had become a necessary component in the display of state imperial authority.

Animal trading was found in diverse regions of the world, and animals could be acquired from a wide variety of sources including from indigenous traders. Lorenz Hagenbeck gave a detailed account of how Hagenbeck's was supplied by agents attending long-established animal trading fairs towards the closing decades of the 19th century. Hagenbeck's sent Breitweiser to purchase animals at an important animal fair held annually in Gorki (Lower Novgorod), trading animals found in the Russian empire including Russian marals or stags.[52] Lorenz went to India c. 1902 to meet up with the Hagenbeck representative there, Jürgen Johannsen, and attended a big elephant fair with hundreds of elephants for sale in business deals held in conjunction with a religious festival at Sonpur. Some of those elephants were sold with several levels of ownership and purchase, and the sale involved debt. Up to the mid-20th century, Hagenbeck's had 48 men and one

---

51 Hagenbeck 1956, 16.
52 Hagenbeck 1956, 26–27, 39–40.

woman under contract to obtain animals on their behalf.[53] Senorita Erika Cook, from Mexico, was not a stereotypical hunter – she held a pilot's licence, carried a gun, and supplied flamingos and rattlesnakes. Lorenz claims she looked like a 'fashion model'.

Demand expanded with an increase in the size of major public menageries in Britain and the USA by the early 1870s. A tally of the species numbers that survived capture and transportation was difficult to establish. The species that eventually reached the British menagerie might be estimated from advertising, which was indicative of the scale of these businesses. When Wombwell's Royal Menagerie was put up for sale in 1872 by George Wombwell's nephew, Fairgrieve, the advertisement listed some of the animals, starting with a 'stud of black maned lions and lionesses',[54] indicating the lion's continuing pre-eminence. The sale took place in Edinburgh, from whence the animals could be easily shipped to anywhere in Europe. Animals that were part of special cage acts were highlighted in the advertisement as 'performing'; they included Bengal tigers, leopards, hyenas, wolves and two elephants, one of whom, Maharajah, was only eight years old (and therefore more manageable than older elephants) and proclaimed the cleverest elephant ever exhibited, able to be instructed by anyone, even a child. The measurements of the two elephants were given, a common practice throughout the 19th century. Most were bought by traders.

The capture of wild animals for the menagerie trade was done for profit, in keeping with values that sanctioned the conquest of nature and blurred distinctions between hunting and exhibiting. Public promotional strategies meant that wild animals became inseparably associated with the expansion of opportunities for safari hunting in Africa and Asia. Menagerie exhibition continued to enact dominance over animals, diverting attention from the financial imperatives that led to their slaughter or violent capture.

---

53 Hagenbeck 1956, 212–13.
54 *New York Clipper* 1872, 23 March: 408. There were also zebras, wolves, camels, dromedaries, polar bears, brown bears, Indian bears and spotted hyenas.

3 Imperial hunting show legends

Showmen adventurers

In turn, showmen recognised that exotic animal shows sparked public interest in adventurous journeys to remote regions and some showmen undertook their own travels. Animal exhibition was fused with ideas of geography and foreign travel. It was touring menagerie promotion that inspired G Van Hare to undertake trips abroad, including to Africa to obtain animals. As a young man Van Hare had gone to every visiting menagerie, including Wombwell's, and his working life included being a performer, showman, adventurer, hunter and lion tamer. After a journey to Africa, Van Hare performed in an act with lions in Cuba, billed as 'Professor Van Hare, the African Traveller'.[55] During the 1850s and 1860s Van Hare presented shows in London and Europe that included affordable domesticated species and monkeys. After travelling and working in Spain, Van Hare seems to have been encouraged by financial problems to venture southwards and undertake an African expedition for several months to obtain animals. It was then that he acquired several gorillas.

Van Hare observed the catching of elephants without guns by indigenous Africans. The men scared the elephant into a tactically placed barrier of vines by crawling around on the ground. The elephant's frantic efforts to struggle free caused the vines to become more entangled, and the trapped elephant was eventually killed with spears. Van Hare noted the capture of seven elephants in one day.

Although he joined these hunting expeditions, Van Hare called himself a traveller rather than a hunter. It was possible that the hunter figure was not yet well established as a theatrical identity, even in the 1860s. Van Hare took over a lion act with five lions in Havana, Cuba, after the death of the English tamer, William Braithwaite, who had performed under the name Herr Jounglar. Van Hare recalled that the lion act received the greatest applause that he had witnessed, not to mention a sizable fee of four shillings and two pence from each spectator. He describes rushing into the cage, upon which 'the animals were at once struck with awe, and crouched into their usual corner'; he coaxed them to jump through a hoop by use

---

55   Van Hare 1893, also 154–69, 170–83, 218, about hunting in Africa.

of a whip.⁵⁶ He put them through this sequence each day for several weeks. Van Hare's act was in the older tamer style; it was unusual for the showman to be the adventurer, and so he could rely on the novelty of having visited Africa. But Van Hare, like a number of others, only presented his lion-taming act for a short time. When he left, he wished that they would have 'a kind master' since 'animals appreciate kindness more than human beings'.⁵⁷

In the USA, Barnum had, by 1851, used the circumstances of the safari hunt to promote his show with 10 elephants. Janet Davis points out that a poster bill for Barnum's Great Asiatic Caravan, Museum and Menagerie proclaimed how 'a drove of elephants was captured in the jungles of Central Ceylon, by Messrs Stebbins, June and George Nutter, accompanied by 160 natives'.⁵⁸ On this poster the explorers doubled as safari hunters and were billed like stars of the show, even though they were not present in it. Advertising the large numbers of indigenous people involved in the expedition promoted its importance. It was the elephants on show, however, who embodied the fantasy of a safari adventure for the public.

Barnum had first promoted displays of hunting with buffalo hunters using lassos in 1843, and he later promoted New York's first Wild West Show with Native Americans, which developed into a distinct genre.⁵⁹ During the 1840s, however, when Barnum was establishing his reputation as America's pre-eminent showman through his strategies for promotion, the main attractions at his New York American Museum were the chimerical half-monkey, half-fish Feejee Mermaid (a hoax) and the composite woolly horse, and these were being concurrently managed with the famous little person, General Tom Thumb (Charles Stratton). The museum's publicity was supported by constant promotion, placed in newspapers on Barnum's daily visits to editors and printing offices. The natural history component of Barnum's exhibition was less sensational than a large component of 'wonders', and AH Saxon writes that these might conceivably be termed

---

56   Van Hare 1893, 242, 243, the menagerie included two tigers, a bear and two jackals.
57   Van Hare 1893, 246.
58   Davis 2002, 196.
59   Werner 1923, 68–69, 71, 72.

'ethnographic', consisting of humans exhibited for their physical difference.[60] Nearly every well-known performer of this type worked for Barnum, and Saxon points out that the menageries were more socially acceptable entertainment in the USA than the 'wonders' and humbugs that made Barnum's reputation, although it was by managing the European singer Jenny Lind that he first became wealthy. While Barnum relied on other adventurers for animal acquisition, he also travelled to Europe to develop and to promote his acts, and he toured his shows to Britain.[61]

Travelling menageries were directly connected to permanent zoos and travelling circuses through the exchange of animals and the way all three were attributed the capacity to provide an education on foreign geography. Biblical associations, however, helped to provide an imprimatur for American menageries to make them acceptable and therefore viable. In the 1850s in the USA, exotic animals were still mainly acquired from ship captains and crew, and individual animal exhibits could be profitable. Barnum's expansion of his menagerie reflected increased diversification in sources. In 1861 'two living whales' in a large tank had top billing at Barnum's American Museum, above the 'man monkey, Madagascar albinos, pure white negroes, or moors, seal lion, and the mammoth bear, Sampson'.[62] When the whales died, Barnum found another use for the tank and advertised the 'first and only real hippopotamus', 'the Great Behemoth of the Scriptures', from the Book of Job, 'the marvel of the animal kingdom' as 'frightful antagonists', capable of overcoming attack.[63] The description explained how the hippopotamus lived in and out of water and floated invisibly under the surface.

Barnum had been buying animals from the Hagenbeck business for several years by the time he visited Germany in 1873 and met Carl Hagenbeck.[64] At that time Hagenbeck's was supplying animals to menageries accompanying German circuses including, in one example, two giraffes for a Queen of Sheba pageant at Renz's circus.[65] In 1873 Barnum was planning a grand New York hippodrome and Carl gave

---

61 Speaight 1980; Assael 2012, American circus in Britain.
62 Werner 1923, 246–47, bill reproduced (original in capitals).
63 Werner 1923, 248–49, bill reproduced (original in capitals), Job XI, 15–24.
64 Saxon 1989, 246.

Barnum advice about the animals Barnum was buying from Hagenbeck's for US$15,000. Barnum made notes about elephant races in India, and Carl's suggestion that an ostrich might make a feasible riding steed for races. Barnum's later shows would have elephant races and his semi-fictional adventure stories included ostrich riding. It was the prominence of elephants in increasing numbers, however, that made them the animal show travellers of distinction in the USA, and supported Barnum's expanding entertainment empire.

Elephant travelogues

Small travelling menageries date from 1813 in North America and sometimes there were several animals in cages on wagons travelling with circuses. American menagerie showmen formed a Zoological Institute as early as 1835 to integrate all existing menageries, but it was abolished by 1837.[66] In the mid-19th century in North America, big cats were usually viewed in their cages, but circus ring parades did periodically include camels, bears and one rhinoceros by 1857, and by 1859 also included lions and a leopard. However it was individual elephants from Asia that took centre place in these walking displays.

The popularity of elephants in the USA can be traced back to Old Bet, although it was the legendary Jumbo that Barnum promoted in the 1880s who later became inseparable from public perceptions of the elephant (see Chapter 4). An elephant arrived in 1796, but it was Old Bet, acquired in London, who became a profitable exhibition from about 1805 in the eastern states of the USA.[67] She was shot to death in controversial circumstances that were publicised as a dispute about ownership, and her skeleton was exhibited from 1816. An elephant appeared in an American circus from 1833 and was without

---

65 Hagenbeck 1956, 18. Rothfels 2002a, 47, Carl had initially purchased animals from the Christian Renz travelling menagerie in 1862 and resold the lion, wolf, jaguar and panther for a profit.
66 Thayer 2005, 130–32. This was in contrast to permanent menageries, such as New York's menagerie in the Bowery. Also, see Flint 1996, 98.
67 See Flint 1996, 98; Durant & Durant 1957, 25; Culhane 1990, 14–16; Kreger 2008, 185–203; Nance 2013, 15–38; Nance 2012, 233–49.

3 Imperial hunting show legends

competition until 1848 when others began to appear including Romeo, Abdullah and Lallah Rookh.[68] Elephants were known to keepers by name and they were walked along roads beside the menagerie wagons or in advance of them in the early hours. They continued to be walked between performance sites in 19th-century shows without train transportation.

Lallah Rookh was very cooperative and was trained to walk a thick rope in 1856, probably by Charles Noyes.[69] The name Lallah Rookh was derived from an 1817 poem by Thomas Moore about an Indian princess, Lalla-Rookh, destined for marriage to a foreign prince. The poem was adapted as a pantomime that had a lion tamer character who was an Englishman, Lionall; with the help of the lions he saved Lallah's romantic interest, Pinion, from the Tartars.[70]

Elephants could be considered uncooperative, although at that time their scarcity meant they could not be easily replaced. Romeo stood 11 feet 2½ inches (more than 3.4 m) in height and had lost an eye. He was acquired in about 1847 from a brickyard in Calcutta, where he had been used to grind clay, and was reportedly bought for US$10,000.[71] But he attacked his keepers, possibly fatally: Long John in 1852, and Frenchy in 1855. Romeo was soon known as a 'bad elephant', as was Chief.[72] In 1860 Stuart (also Stewart) Craven was called in to manage Romeo. Craven secured ropes around the animal and subdued him with shotgun pellets.[73] Forepaugh's circus acquired Romeo in 1863 for US$25,000 and Romeo was still there when he died a decade later, worth at least twice that amount.[74]

---

68 Thayer 2005, 130–31. Allen & Kelley 1941, 69. Later elephant arrivals were also called Hannibal, Bolivar, Columbus, Virginius, Mogul, Siam and Pizarro.
69 Thayer 2005, 131; Slout 1998, 222–23. Slout also has a brief entry on John Carter as an elephant performer and trainer of Lallah Rookh.
70 *New York Clipper* 1872, To Lalla Rookh, 30 March: 414. The identification of a menagerie elephant as the poem's heroine predated the staging of the full drama in 1872 in the USA.
71 *New York Clipper* 1872, Circuses, 15 June: 87.
72 Allen & Kelley 1941, 71.
73 Conklin 1921, 114.
74 *New York Clipper* 1872, Circuses, 15 June: 87. Forepaugh bought Romeo from Mable's menagerie.

A circus that could afford an elephant for the menagerie might also walk him or her around the circus ring, but those elephants did not initially perform tricks. Craven, the first elephant tamer in the USA, first presented a group of elephants for the Van Amburgh menagerie in 1853, and worked with a number of touring shows until the 1880s. Craven developed a troupe for Forepaugh's, although there was a dispute over payment that Craven resolved by bringing along a lawyer and witnesses.[75] Craven, a tall, slim man, learnt to ride standing up on an elephant, and even standing on one leg. These were unique feats in the mid-19th-century American circus. The elephants were being used in the same way that horses were used as steeds for the display of human acrobatic skills and were not yet trained to do physical tricks. Craven also stood on the elephant Tippo Saib, juggling and doing a backflip from the animal's tusk.[76] Later Craven taught a group of 12 elephants to form a pyramid and move in unison. As the numbers of elephants increased, their value depended on their cooperative passivity and what they could do. The transition to small groups of trained elephants executing clever feats regularly in the circus ring happened from the 1870s and 1880s.

While George or Adam Forepaugh presented some of the elephants in the circus ring, they had been trained by Craven, and his pupil, the legendary Ephraim Thompson.[77] Thompson, a tall and muscular African-American performer, was in demand internationally during the 1880s and 1890s. He rode an elephant like a horse, impressive in his evening dress with diamond shirt studs. His act included four elephants playing skittles, walking a rope and playing instruments; one was ejected from a chair, and together they enacted a pantomime depicting a rescue from a house fire. Despite their size, elephants can be dexterous and fast-moving and there was a group of elephants trained by Thompson in a 'Musical Prodigy Elephants' act; it went on tour in the USA for a number of years with a presenter called Rossi. Using their trunks, the elephants played the chimes and moved the bellows of an organ with their feet. Thompson was working

---

75   Conklin 1921, 112, 114.
76   Slout 1998, 65.
77   Slout 1998, 301; Kober 1931, 46–47; Allen & Kelley 1941, 50, citing Sturtevant about notable trainers.

for Hagenbeck's as they established a circus in Hamburg after 1887, and his major competitors were the Lockhart family act and Miss M'hamedin's act with two elephants.[78]

In the USA from the mid-19th century, a single elephant or small groups of them might appear in the circus parade through the main street of a town and then in the ring parade; they were also lined up in human acrobatic vaulting or leaping acts in which the acrobat leapt over assembled animals.[79] By the late 19th century some elephants had been taught physical feats to present in performance, while behind the scenes they were deployed to do loading and lifting offstage as the menagerie travelled between locations. Their versatility made them very important to the travelling menagerie and to the circus. Charles Fox and Tom Parkinson write:

> Then elephants made the march – the grand free street parade at noon. Next it was time for the afternoon performance in which elephants were dressed in spangled blankets for the spec [spectacle] and later walked back for the featured elephant display.[80]

Elephant travellers of distinction became the stars of American animal entertainment.

American circus menageries

During the 1870s in the USA, a travelling menagerie with a circus and/or a museum or sideshow, each operating out of a separate tent, became commonly known as a 'combined travelling show', and it was promoted by the number of menagerie cages.[81] This was a far larger enterprise than the menagerie or regular tenting circus of previous decades that had a single tent presenting equestrian acts, acrobats and

---

78 Hagenbeck 1956, 18; Kober 1931, 47.
79 For example, see the Barnum and Bailey Program 1891, 37: Display No. 1. Leaping, vaulting somersaulting over elephants (Billy Rose Collection, Performing Arts Library, New York Public Library).
80 Fox & Parkinson 1969, republished posters, 275.
81 *New York Clipper* 1872, The tenting season, 13 April: 12.

clowns. Smaller circuses continued to visit small towns and co-existed with the increasingly larger combined enterprises that required a more populated centre to be profitable. A larger show might also travel by rail between larger centres.

As Stuart Thayer explains about American circuses, however, even side by side the menagerie and the circus were usually separate shows, and this was not always made clear to the public. He writes, 'A circus and menagerie title did not guarantee a ring appearance by the animals', and there was ambiguity when menageries claimed also to be circuses.[82] He found that the archival sources about these wild animals, which are mainly advertisements, did not make clear whether a caged animal was only displayed in a menagerie sideshow or whether a menagerie cage was also wheeled into the ring. It was a minority of menagerie animals that were paraded, with the rest viewed in cages or in the confinement of stalls and other areas. It can be presumed that most menageries remained separate tent shows with a distinctive history for much of the 19th century. One entry fee for everything was only instituted towards the end of that century. But a menagerie travelling with a circus could become the dominant business.

There was growing competition among menagerie owners as those businesses generated more opportunities and expanded from 1870. Barnum entered into business partnership with William Coup and Dan Castello in 1871, to open 'P.T. Barnum's Museum, Menagerie and Circus', exhibiting exotic animals and humans with Barnum-hyped wonders.[83] When their mammoth show opened on 10 April 1871 in Brooklyn, New York, the lead attractions were the so-named Fijian cannibal family and a giraffe, since the high mortality rate of giraffes meant that other showmen had stopped importing them.[84] But it was Coup's advance publicity that became important for the 1872 tour. Barnum's tendency to buy expensive animals and to make other business gambles caused his more cautious partners considerable anxiety about how the box office takings would cover costs. The partnership had developed a railroad show by 1872 with their Great Traveling

---

82 Thayer 2005, 132; Thayer 2006, 10–16.
83 Saxon 1989, 238. The name of a show did vary in the advertising.
84 Werner 1923, 309–10; Saxon 1989, 240. See Dennett 1997.

3 Imperial hunting show legends

World's Fair, which included animal stock cars among the rail cars, with partitions and troughs for feeding the animals.[85]

In 1872 there were at least 20 big shows in the USA that had both menagerie and circus, and some additionally had museums. The number of menagerie cages was nominated as the distinguishing feature of those combined shows. For example, as well as the number of employees, menageries were listed as having: PT Barnum's, 20 menagerie cages; Sells Brothers, 13 cages; WW Cole's, 20 cages; Adam Forepaugh's, 32 cages, with three new cages; John O'Brien's, 30 cages; and Kleckner and Conklin Brothers, eight cages.[86] 'Howe's Grand London Circus and Sanger's English Menagerie of Trained Animals' did not specify the number of cages, and there were also four larger circuses touring that were circus-only ventures. The 'Van Amburgh & Co., Great Golden Menagerie', however, remained a menagerie with 26 cages and promoted a large number of new arrivals in 1872 as competition escalated.[87]

There was clearly a commercial benefit to the menagerie business in promoting its size through the number of animal cages, even though other animals were kept in stalls. Competition for audiences drove this strategy. The number of tents also became significant, with one show advertising 12 tents and 41 'dens' and a two-mile-long (3.2 km) parade

---

85 Davis 2002, 20.
86 *New York Clipper* 1872, The tenting season, 13 April: 12. The full titles of these shows were: 'P.T. Barnum's Great Traveling Museum, Menagerie, Caravan and Hippodrome Combined with Dan Castello's Circus', 'Sells Brothers Mammoth Quadruple Alliance Museum, Menagerie, Caravan and Circus', 'W.W. Cole's Colossal Museum, Hippodrome and Menagerie', 'Adam Forepaugh's Grand Menagerie, Museum, Caravan and Equestrian Aggregation', 'John O'Brien's Consolidated Shows' and 'Kleckner and Conklin Brothers Monster Menagerie and Circus'.
87 *New York Clipper* 1872, The tenting season, 13 April: 12. *New York Clipper* 1872, 18 May: 55. A report on OJ Ferguson, who was buying animals for Van Amburgh's in Europe, listed: 'one two-horned rhinoceros, a giraffe, black tigers, one adday [sic], one dano and one Sardinian mouflin [sheep] antelope, the three latter being new to America, a pair of black African ostriches, Royal Bengal tigers, king vultures, a maribou stork, a young anodad [aoudad], an adjutant [stork], ibex, crossoptillon [pheasant] gold, silver and Bohemian pheasants, hyenas, wombots [wombats], ocelots, a nylghau, porcupines and many rare birds and monkeys'.

in 1873.[88] The financial investment to mount a 20- to 25-cage show after 1872 also necessitated significant returns. While noting that the circus was competing with political events and a presidential election for public attention, a newspaper commentary explained that investment in shows had gone up that year.[89] Shows usually paid a separate licence fee for the menagerie and the circus at each location. For example, in a small town in 1872, those fees might be US$50 for the circus, US$25 for the menagerie and US$5 per sideshow; the total annual revenue from licences in one state could reach US$75,000.[90] When one show reduced the admission fee to 25 cents for adults and 15 cents for children, the other show managers argued that this entry fee could not cover costs of licences, advertising, accommodation and 'hay, oats, and raw meat for the animals' to 'yield anything like a remunerative profit to the management for the labour and capital invested'.[91]

It should be pointed out that the practical competency and loyalty of the animal keepers became an important part of animal survival in the larger shows, and therefore was critical to menagerie profitability.[92] Knowledgeable menagerie managers became a crucial component of viable shows from the 1870s, but there still did not seem to be much concern about the animals' living conditions while held in cages for years, although CG Sturtevant notes that some animals suffered from a condition called 'cage paralysis'. This condition was seemingly more evident in animals living in zoos, because animals in travelling menageries that were transported in cages had to use their muscles to maintain balance, and would leap up at sudden noises and jolts. This may have been one incidental benefit of travelling in a menagerie.

---

88 *New York Clipper* 1873, 8 March: 392, The Great Eastern Menagerie, Museum and Aviary Circus.
89 *New York Clipper* 1872, The tenting season, 13 April: 12.
90 *New York Clipper* 1872, Circuses, 29 June: 103. This was the licence fees at Poughkeepsie. *New York Clipper* 1873, Circuses, 1 February: 351.
91 *New York Clipper* 1872, Circuses, 13 April: 15.
92 Sturtevant 1925, 76. Circus historian Sturtevant lists 23 'outstanding' menagerie superintendents in the USA working in the 50 years before 1925 and 17 elephant superintendents.

3 Imperial hunting show legends

Species contests

A pre-show parade through the streets of an American town, featuring wagons (known as 'cars') containing major attractions, advertised the arrival of the circus and menagerie. The wagon cages were increasingly elaborately decorated as the parade evolved into a distinctive spectacle in its own right.[93] Some decorated wagons had themes, or even presented a free glimpse of the performers, including the lion tamers, who would later perform in the menagerie tent. The menagerie itself was rapidly increasing in size. In 1872 Barnum's menagerie included a baby elephant, a giraffe, camels, dromedaries, zebras, lions, tigers, hyenas, rhinoceroses, leopards, eland, a large white bear, grizzly bears, a panther, sea lions, a kangaroo, a tapir, crocodiles and other reptiles.[94] The range of animals seemed typical of an American menagerie collection by the early 1870s, although a large show, such as Forepaugh's, advertised some additional species.

While the menageries tried to outdo each other on size and on the variety of species, elephants and lion cage acts were common elements. Elephants were given names inspired by legendary identities, the lion tamer act accorded a high profile. For example, Sells Brothers had an elephant called Julius Caesar, and the lion tamer, Robert Elwood, appeared in the parade before the show, although Mademoiselle Amelia was also billed entering the lion cage, but most probably only appeared once in the menagerie tent show. Adam Forepaugh's had George Forepaugh as a performer with the elephants, Herr Alexander Darious as a performer with other animals, and H[J] Childers as a lecturer.[95] Forepaugh's show had four tents that would become crowded. The first contained automaton curiosities, including mechanical bellringers, and the second and third tents were the menagerie, and the fourth was the circus.[96] Only WW Cole's promoted

---

93 Fox & Parkinson 1969, 174–87, 143, 150, 207 (posters).
94 *New York Clipper* 1872, The tenting season, 13 April: 12. For example: Sells billed monkeys, anteaters and Australian birds; WW Cole's billed sacred cattle, llamas, ibex, jaguars and emus; and Adam Forepaugh's billed two rhinoceroses, four sea lions, a white caribou, sulphur-crested cockatoos, and an orangutan. *New York Clipper* 1872, 6 July: 111, John Robinson's Combination Circus featured sea lions.
95 *New York Clipper* 1872, 13 April: 12.

a different lead attraction, in 1872 billing the 16 musicians in the band as wearing Prussian uniforms. The JE Warner & Co.'s 'Great Pacific Museum, Menagerie and Circus' had AJ Forepaugh as the lion tamer and, for the parade, the aerialist, Leona Dare, was positioned in a tableau on a wagon roof with a Bengal tiger,[97] presumably below her inside the cage. Van Amburgh's promoted Professor C White as the lion tamer, but the car with an Egyptian theme had a live lion on the rooftop. White had survived an attack in 1872,[98] but there had been a fatal accident at O'Brien's that year during a rehearsal by the new lion tamer, Joseph (Joe) Whittle (see Chapter 5).

The threat of fire remained a major business risk in menageries with restrained or caged animals. On 24 December 1872 a fire started by a furnace at Barnum's circus, museum and menagerie spread and killed the animals in cages because the keepers did not have keys, and only the three elephants could be rescued.[99] The loss due to the menagerie fire, and Coup's sale of his share of the menagerie and the Madison Square Gardens enterprise to Barnum, provided him with an opportunity to increase the scale of the spectacle. He would outdo his competitors once again.

In 1873, as well as purchasing new animals, Barnum asked that George Sanger provide him with duplicates of the costumes worn in the Sanger's Congress of Nations in London (see Chapter 2), which he had seen, and he paid US$165,000 for the costumes, armour and chariots.[100] Saxon writes that these made up a substantial portion of 1000 historically accurate costumes to represent the 'Kings, Queens, Emperors and other potentates of the civilized world'.[101] While the replacement building in New York at Madison Square Gardens could seat 8000 for the

---

96   *New York Clipper* 1872, 13 April: 15.
97   *New York Clipper* 1872, 13 April: 12.
98   *New York Clipper* 1872, Circuses, 1 June: 71.
99   *New York Clipper* 1873, Burning of Barnum's circus, museum and menagerie, 4 January: 316. The animals in the menagerie were reported as: '[t]wo lions, two Bengal Tigers, a leopard, Rocky mountain sheep, an albino deer, an African wart hog [sic], a llama, a yak, an élan, two ostriches, five snakes, four giraffes (which were probably the most valuable part of the collection, being the only ones in America)'. There were also monkeys, a porcupine, a badger, two sea lions, two polar bears, a horned horse, four deer, two seals and 10 camels.
100 Werner 1923, 315; Saxon 1989, 248.

3 Imperial hunting show legends

hippodrome show in August 1874, Barnum described having a large tent made for touring – approximately 880 feet long and 400 wide – to create a hippodrome that would seat 11,000 spectators twice a day.[102] There were 1200 people involved with the show, 750 horses, and the show cost US$50,000 to transport from New York to Boston. Although the touring hippodrome show did not include the full menagerie, it did include the larger exotic animals such as elephants, camels, ostriches and giraffes, who were presented in processions. Some were put in races – possibly influenced by Barnum's discussion with Carl Hagenbeck. Barnum and his team greatly enlarged the scale of indoor menagerie spectacles in combination with imitation state ceremonies (Plate 5).

The 1875 hippodrome program was even more extensive, with Chinese warriors and Tartar soldiers in supporting roles to the performers playing their respective royal rulers in an overwhelmingly large orientalist spectacle.[103] Armies of soldiers enhanced the spectacle of royals, and exotic animals were amalgamated into a military parade through time and across geographies. There were Roman chariot races

---

101   Cited in Saxon 1989, 248. Saxon lists how they represented: Britain, France, ancient Rome, Germany, Turkey, Italy, Egypt, Russia, Ireland, Spain, China, India and the USA.
102   Saxon 1983, 189 (162) to Samuel L Clemens.
103   'P.T. Barnum's Great Roman Hippodrome Bill of the Performance for the week ending Jan. 2nd, 1875' (John and Mable Ringling Museum, Archive). The opening spectacle was: 'Fete at Pekin. Holiday of the Celestials. Grand Reception of the Emperor Haamti, A.D. 1690 seated in a Royal Palaquin, borne by Mandarins of the first class, followed by a grand procession of the Tartar Cavalry, Mongol, Manichou and Kathaian Soldiery … Warriors of the Yantse, with the emblems of the Celestial Empire, The Winged Dragon.' 'Feats of the Agility and Ledgerdemain by Mons. Aymar, Le Petit Eugene, Ling Leek, Yamadiva, Satsuma and Little All Right. Victoria on the High Wire. Gorgeous Chinese Ballet.' Subsequent acts were as follows: 2. Flat Race by five Ladies on their English Thoroughbreds. 3. Monkey carriage. 4. Roman standing race – 2 horses abreast. 5. Liberty horses. 6. Two horse chariot race. 7. Mad. D'Atalie, the female Sampson. 8. Indian Life a chase for a wife. 9. Race by Monkeys on ponies. 10. Race between English and American Jockeys. 11. Boy race. 12. Hurdle race by ladies. 13. Chariot race 4 horse D'Atalie and Mons Arnaud. 14. Satsuma and Little All Right – Most Wonderful Japanese Equilibrists in their Ladder Balancing and other Acts. 15. 'Pantomime equestrian spectacular $53,000'; 'first grand Dramatic Equestrian Pantomime'; 'Elephants, Camels, Dromedaries, Giraffes, Reindeer, Horses, Ponies'. Also, there was a Moorish village and Bluebeard's Castle.

and Colosseum acts, and 'a scene called "Indian Life on the Plains" wherein scores of Indians of various tribes appear with their squaws, pappooses, ponies, and wigwams', and 'engage in buffalo hunts with real buffaloes'.[104] The buffalo hunting was enacted alongside cowboy and Native American war re-enactments on horseback.

Saxon reported that Barnum joked that Queen Victoria and her company could not match the grandeur of the royal processions of his hippodrome.[105] His ambitious intention to outdo state pomp was unmistakable. Barnum continued that he would pay the cost of the Ashanti (or Ashantee) War (probably the 1873 to 1874 period of conflict) in Africa if he could have the British royals to show in the USA for a couple of months. In this proposal, the realities of fighting a war were displaced into a triumphant parade with processional figureheads and symbolic soldiers emulating an official occasion, and military action was reduced to a costume contest. The entertainment spectacle and state ceremony became interchangeable.

After the 1870s, advertisements and posters that depicted one or more elephants at the centre of elaborate costume parades were increasingly associated with circus and its pageantry. Although horses dominated Barnum's hippodrome spectacle, the entourage in the geographically themed displays with elephants were clearly in the grand pageant, and a separate act by 1877.[106] A spectacle with the impression of an Indian raj became a regular feature of American circus and at Forepaugh's by 1881, with 'Lallah Rookh's Welcome'. Charles Fox and Tom Parkinson note: 'Defying geographical and historical accuracy, elephants effortlessly appeared in any setting, whether it be Roman or medieval French or Oriental.'[107]

Sturtevant describes the last decades of the 19th century as the heyday of menageries accompanying the travelling circus in the USA. Sells' had 51 menagerie cages in 1884, O'Brien's had 50, and the 'superior' Adam Forepaugh's circus – the largest in North America – had 50 cages

---

104   Saxon 1983, 190.
105   Saxon 1989, 248.
106   PT Barnum Daily Show program 1877 (Billy Rose Collection, Performing Arts Library, New York Public Library).
107   Fox & Parkinson 1969, 219 (poster).

3 Imperial hunting show legends

and 25 elephants. But Sturtevant recalls a visit to a menagerie about 1890 that had:

> very large displays, but many of the dens in fact, the majority of them, were small two-horse cross cages, there were many duplications in the collections, and a relatively large number of small and unimportant animals and birds such as wolves, foxes, porcupines, badgers, various parrots, etc, was carried [sic]. Of course there also were big dens of large and rare animals.[108]

Interestingly, the well-established Barnum and Bailey Circus 'The Greatest Show on Earth' menagerie (BB) probably had 25 cages at the most, about the average number. According to the 1886 BB route book, among the animals exhibited were Asian elephants, three Bengal tigers, four African lions, four African leopards, four panthers, monkeys, rhinoceroses, a polar bear, two sea lions, a hippopotamus and a yak.[109] An African elephant remained a rarity.

Menagerie exhibition grew in conjunction with opportunistic economic exploitation and business competition and provided the basis for the presentation of increasingly elaborate indoor and outdoor spectacles from the 1870s and 1880s (also see Chapter 6). Large-scale exotic animal acquisition only became systematic once entertainments such as menageries with circuses generated the public demand to ensure sufficient financial return. Henceforth the scale escalated to encompass thousands of animals.

---

108 Sturtevant 1925, 76. The information about Forepaugh's comes from WC Boyd.
109 Sturtevant 1925, 76. There were also a nyighau, a wolf, two Russian bears, a lioness and cubs, one striped and three spotted hyenas, three kangaroos, an Australian emu, a warthog, a pelican, a leopard and cubs, a tapir, azis deer, a sacred bull, a black buck, a mandrill monkey, a dog-faced baboon, a porcupine, a gnu (horned horse), a llama, a sacred goat, a double-horned rhinoceros, four white camels, 12 dromedaries, and one Nubian buffalo.

Advertising sporting chases

Show posters underwent changes as the numbers of menagerie animals increased and as shows expanded on ideas of safari hunting.[110] Illustrations on lithograph posters initially depicted a single animal body, often set against a backdrop of flora. As the public became more familiar with the appearance of species and their numbers increased, advertisements promoted animal groups against a natural setting. Depicting nature in the background might have downplayed the presence of confining cages in the menagerie tent. Poster bills also advertised menagerie animals in stylised formations. For example, 'A Scene in Africa' was the headline on a lithograph used for generic promotional purposes in the USA during the 1870s; it showed a male lion in the centre, standing on a rock with an ordered line of leaping tigers and leopards below him and moving camels behind him.[111] The grouping might also be interpreted as a hierarchical ordering of the animals.

The advertising of animal exhibits increased in complexity, especially after 1871, when Barnum expanded his travelling menagerie and sideshow to include circus.[112] As images of elephants and lions began to be routinely included in circus and menagerie advertising, a circus required at least one elephant and, if possible, some lions, suggesting Africa, to remain competitive. The Great Eastern Circus Menagerie in 1872 proclaimed 'Zoological Triumph' on a poster with an illustration of a hunter firing a gun from each hand at two pouncing mid-air lions (Plate 6).[113] While the image may well have promoted a hunting act in the menagerie, it also drew spectator attention to an idea of the safari hunt. The action of the hunter carried a direct association with colonial lands, and the fear and excitement of a lion attack. Sometime later, poster images would deliver those ideas, using only the

---

110   Bills viewed at Billy Rose Collection (encompassing the Townsend Walsh Collection), New York Public Library of Performing Arts, and Joe E Ward Collection, Harry Ransom Library Special Collections, University of Texas at Austin.
111   Pfening 2004, 13.
112   Davis 2002, 42, citing Fred Dahlinger and Thayer.
113   Slout 2006, 28.

3 Imperial hunting show legends

enlarged head of a lion or a tiger menacing, their fangs bared ready to pounce, in condensed images of aggression.[114]

Print publicity took advantage of the ways in which the connections between hunting and collecting were expanding, as social practices converged within a scientific paradigm. In 1880 in London, taxidermist Rowland Ward published a best-selling book, *The Sportsman's handbook to practical collecting, preserving and artistic setting-up of trophies and specimens: to which is added a synoptical guide to the hunting grounds of the world.*[115] As MacKenzie notes, '[t]he striking thing about nineteenth-century science was indeed that it was ubiquitous ... [e]very hunter was a zoologist and reader of natural signs'.[116] He outlines how the material exploitation of colonial regions had always been a combination of science and economics. The pursuit of natural sciences and collecting became integral to the spread of colonial power, and individuals were quick to identify the opportunities in new places.

Even before Rowland Ward's book on sporting hunts for trophies became a bestseller, Barnum, the master of advertising, directly exploited the link between the hunting safari and the menagerie collection in semi-fictionalised accounts derived from the diaries of hunters. In the later years of Barnum's working life, adventure stories made the menagerie interchangeable with the safari hunt as a sporting pastime. This was a perceptual shift from killing for financial gain (or food) to hunting for enjoyment and leisure.[117] Barnum worked as a journalist in his early years and his publications included two controversial autobiographies and a collection of jungle adventure stories published in serial form in 1876 and in book form as *Lion Jack*, in both the USA and in England.[118] The latter featured Jack, a 16-year-old adventurer; the Jack identity seemed to have its origins in the travel adventures of the sailor character Jack Tar in the late 18th century. A subtitle for *Lion Jack* included the explanation 'a story of perilous

---

114 Fox & Parkinson 1969, 27, 201 (posters).
115 MacKenzie 1988, 35.
116 MacKenzie 1990b, 5, 7.
117 See Baker & Mangan 1987; MacKenzie 1988, 3, a shift from the 'practical to pleasurable'. Joys 1983, 15, citing Coup.
118 Saxon 1989, 290.

adventures among wild men and the capturing of wild beasts: showing how menageries are made' and Barnum admitted to publicising his show with his book.[119] The sequel was *Jack in the jungle*, which developed into a genre of collected stories that Saxon suggests also drew on 'two thick notebooks [that] Barnum filled during his meetings with the animal dealer', Hagenbeck.[120]

A growing field of juvenile literature with hunting in the title fuelled the aspirations of young men in the 19th century.[121] JS Bratton found precedents for childhood adventure stories in nautical serials of the early 1870s, which were subsequently expanded.[122] In the first of the boy stories set in colonial frontiers, Canadian writer RM Ballantyne published *The young fur traders* in 1856, and Rider Haggard's classic *King Solomon's mine* was published in 1885.[123] The most well known of the British authors writing for adolescent boys was GA Henty, with his first book, *Jack Archer: a tale of the Crimea*, published in 1884; in this and his subsequent stories, he offered a portrait of masculinity based on battle bravery and honour. Henty's stories were mainly war stories using his experiences as a soldier, and later as a war journalist during the major campaigns of the 1860s and 1870s. Henty's Jack had a naval career that also took him to India.

It is likely that Barnum's influential stories contributed to the development of the genre, and his original 'Jack' hunting stories were illustrated in the 1880s, possibly with further additions to the text. An illustrated volume narrated in the first person – supposedly by Barnum – called *Animal stories*, features Jack Harvey, a Texan cowboy in Africa, with a titlepage carrying the descriptor, 'Natural history from a new standpoint'. Stories about the hunting of animals for their live capture were assumed to contribute to the study of natural history. In his set of adventure stories, Barnum hires a group of hunters to enter 'the wilds of

---

119   Werner 1923, 373, 347, a publisher suggested Barnum employ a writer but use his name. The bibliographic record of the books published in the 1880s lists the press agent as a co-writer, but does not name him, although Morris H Warner was the press agent c. 1886. See 356–60, also 371.
120   Cited in Saxon 1989, 290.
121   MacKenzie 1987a, 190–91, lists examples of hunting adventure stories; MacKenzie 1988, 45–46.
122   Bratton 1986, 84.
123   Woollacott 2006, 64, also 61.

3 Imperial hunting show legends

Africa in quest of curiosities' and 'valuable prizes for The Greatest Show On Earth'.[124] The leader of Barnum's semi-fictional hunting group is an American, Carl Godkin, who had worked for him in India, and Godkin is described as having 'knowledge of natural history and was one of the most successful sportsmen that ever lived'.[125] The members of the sporting group are named as Diedrick, Pongo, Abdallah from Senaar, 'Govozy, Wart, Adz, Bormo, Divak, Valmur, Orak and Goobo' and a Hottentot and a bushman. But Godkin's main assistants are presented as three Americans, Harvey and 17-year-old cousins Bob Marshall and Dick Brownell. They set out from the east coast of Africa, from Port Natal, and move northwards to the Transvaal near the Kalahari Desert. Pongo reports that he knew Cumming and Livingstone; the *Animal stories* book was based on the biographies of hunters.

A visual impression of the safari is highlighted at the beginning of the stories through descriptions of clothing and weapons that might have been familiar to readers as the costumes and props of circus equestrian spectacles. Harvey is a good horseman and rifleman who could 'throw the lasso with the skill of a Comanche chieftain'; he always wears 'flowing hair, [a] thick flannel shirt' and a 'broad sombrero', and introduces the cowboy costume to southern Africa.[126] Marshall and Brownell wear hunting coats, helmet hats and trousers tucked into cavalry boots. The costumes conflate hunting and Native American wars of resistance and colonial military conquest. The so-named natives are armed only with spears and knives and walk beside the wagon and horses, although Pongo does carry an African throwing weapon that is described as being comparable to the boomerang used in Australia.

In Barnum's adventure narrative of hunting sports, the African characters are crucial to the venture and work at considerable risk. For example, the group first encounters a lion who attacked Orak during the night; the lion is shot and wounded by Harvey, who follows the lion out of the camp and eventually kills him and rescues Orak.[127] Meanwhile a lioness attacks Divak, who fights back with a javelin and causes

---

124 Barnum 1926, 19, 109.
125 Barnum 1926, 14, also 13, 15, 19, 20–21, Barnum based this narrative on accounts by the hunters.
126 Barnum 1926, 15, 123, also 17.
127 Barnum 1926, 26–32, 34.

her skull to shatter. Pongo, who is adept at locating lions' dens, retrieves a lion cub. The next hunt sequence is in a chapter called 'The champion of stupidity'. The hunters are on horseback in a valley in pursuit of a flock of ostriches for their saleable feathers when the frightened birds appear to flee in the direction of the hunters, making themselves easier targets for the hunters' lassos.[128] But the ostriches are not stupid and fight back; despite being shot, one kicks Marshall and knocks him unconscious. As the birds escape at speed, Brownell jumps onto the back of one until Pongo's throwing weapon clips the ostrich's head and the bird falls down. Harvey's attempts to lasso an ostrich only end with him being dragged off his horse and along the ground; the ostrich is only stopped by a bullet to the head.

Brownell and Marshall set off to hunt giraffes, and Marshall climbs a tree and comes face-to-face with a male giraffe that dislodges him from the tree branch. While lassoing a giraffe, Harvey says that he found it hard kill the giraffe because 'Those eyes are too human' and therefore if she behaved well, he would not harm her.[129] (Readers may not have accepted the death of a giraffe.) This episode is followed by the pursuit of an African buffalo being hunted by lions at the same time, and Godkin recounts his experience in India of riding on the back of an elephant who was attacked by a buffalo and lost. The group hunts a fast-moving oryx also stalked by a hyena, who is gored by the oryx. They lasso a zebra, shoot a snake, encounter monkeys, baboons and hippopotamuses, and a long-horned white rhinoceros charges at them. 'Nothing inspires a sportsman with courage so much as the sight of his fleeing game.'[130] They do not hunt elephants because Barnum had a large number in his show.

In these stories, animals exist to be either captured or shot. Equally unnerving is the way the safari sportsmen in the stories were oblivious to how the African men were constantly at risk of their lives, while the American hunters remained more protected with their rifle power. As the human characters were competitively pitted against a range of fleeing species in different episodes, and the Europeans and Americans came away the victors, animals were positioned as if they were warring

---

128   Barnum 1926, 43–56, 65, 60, 66.
129   Barnum 1926, 86, also 103.
130   Barnum 1926, 186, also 236.

3 Imperial hunting show legends

enemies to be defeated. Such stories depicted hunted wild animals who fought back; that is, hunting for sport was a process of fighting nature. It seemed like waging war on other species.

The entrepreneurial showman Farini (William Hunt), who was Barnum's contemporary and, after 1880, his business colleague, undertook an African safari to the Kalahari (Botswana) in 1885. He later published a widely read account of his safari adventure, with extensive appendices on Kalahari flora and fauna.[131] Farini had previously relied on agents to acquire human performers from Africa.[132] He recounted being told of adventure in southern Africa by an indigenous hunter he met in London, digging up diamonds in Kimberley, South Africa, and travelling in a 'hunter's paradise'. Farini travelled with his adopted son, Sam Hunt, who since 1870 had been performing as Lulu Farini, the very lovely, secretly cross-dressed, adolescent trapeze performer; although Lulu was exposed as a man in 1874, she continued to perform to a curious public.[133] Importantly, Lulu took camera equipment so that the expedition was promoted on their return by Farini's book and Lulu's photographs (Plate 6).[134] Farini's biographer, Shane Peacock, gives an extended description of the expedition (which included hunting lions) and the specimens it collected, and evaluates the validity of Farini's claim to have found the ruins of a city. They travelled with horses, mules and ox-drawn wagons, depending on bushmen who often went their own way. The trip involved numerous mishaps, betrayals and miscalculations – early in the expedition, Farini nearly died. Farini's observations about hunting constituted only some of the experiences, and there were what seem to be comparatively honest accounts of clumsy accidents while trying to shoot, missing out on spotting lions, a lion grabbing one of the party at night, and firing in mistake at one of their own party. For example, when Farini did succeed in what he thought was the shooting of a lion, he crept forward only to find the lion dead,

---

131   Farini 1886, 450–68. There are appendices on flora, reptiles, insects, birds, mammalia and geology, and a table of distances.
132   Peacock 1996, 311, 306. One was WA Healey.
133   See Tait 2005, 66–67.
134   Farini 1886, vi, 36, 358–459, Farini 1886 nearly dies 140–41, misadventures 161–65, 191–202. Lulu's photographs were exhibited separated and with Farini's papers presented at Berlin Geographical Society, 7 November 1885, and Royal Geographical Society of England, 8 March 1886. Peacock 1996, 305–57, 344.

impaled on the horn of his bok prey. Farini is atypical in revealing his inept effort.

Intentionally or not, Farini exposed some of the terrible consequences of colonial rule alongside hunting misadventures. He gives an account of slaughtered indigenous prisoners, and Hottentot children offered for sale. In addition, he writes in empathetic acknowledgement of how a wounded giraffe looked back at Farini with 'despair in his drooping eye', to ask, 'what harm have I ever done you?' (Plate 6)[135] Farini's well-known account differed from most perhaps because he was not trying to make his reputation through hunting achievements. To some extent the numerous difficulties of the adventure in this widely read book countered, if not dispelled, illusions that safari hunting was an enjoyable sporting challenge.

It was the circulation of unrealistic, embellished adventure stories of hunting in Africa and Asia, including those associated with menagerie entertainment, that fuelled the proliferating ambition to undertake a safari. As newspaper graphics were supplemented by photographs of safari hunts, hunters increasingly aspired to travel to Asia and Africa (see Chapter 7). With its lion chases, gunfire and overtly aggressive gestures, the menagerie act seemed to involve hunting; it unmistakably added to the spectrum of entertainments that presented fighting behaviour and war re-enactments. Menagerie entertainment helped to foster 19th-century illusions about hunting escapades, much like adventure stories for boys. While it is arguable whether military campaigns in the colonies continued to receive popular support throughout the 1880s and 1890s, an imperialist hegemony of individualistic hunts for animals remained entrenched in popular culture through its manifestation in the safari adventure story genre.

---

135   Farini 1886, 370, 384, 292.

4
Mobs and hooligans, crowds and fans

Menagerie spectators took liberties. The inclination to touch or even taunt meant that menagerie staff had to remain vigilant to forestall harm arising from contact between animals and curious spectators. Yet many menagerie visitors developed and expressed strong allegiances with exhibited animals and, when Barnum was planning to transfer the elephant Jumbo from London to the USA, he encountered considerable public resistance.

Audiences could be fickle. This chapter is about the extreme responses of 19th-century audiences to menagerie animals – placid or otherwise – and to workers. It outlines instances of spectator misbehaviour and fighting that occurred in menageries and in towns visited by a menagerie. The travelling menagerie could become a catalyst for individual hooliganism, but it sometimes brought with it law-breaking activity, not to mention questionable dealing, scams and hoaxes. A menagerie's capacity to attract large crowds proved an incentive for crooks and criminals.

Unruly spectators

The behaviour – and misbehaviour – of the public seemed unpredictable to workers in menageries.[1] Instances of hostile behaviour that had been evident in the smaller-scale 18th-century animal show continued in

19th-century animal exhibitions. William Cameron Coup outlines how care had to be taken by workers to avoid being caught up in situations of threat towards animals, and he describes fights among workers and with members of the public. Admittedly some of the antagonism from locals may have been due to the deceptive show practices and unpaid bills widely associated with touring shows, but this did not explain spectator misbehaviour towards the animals. Whether it was a spur-of-the-moment response or a calculated one, some spectators could be dangerous.

Coup's account of touring with a mid-19th-century American menagerie depicts conflicts between individuals and groups in and around the exhibition tents. In 1852 the 16-year-old Coup joined PT Barnum's touring caravan, which included a menagerie and a so-named 'freak museum'; Coup remained associated with menagerie businesses until he died in 1895.[2] Coup was inspired by the show created after Barnum and Seth Howes brought 10 elephants from Ceylon (Sri Lanka) to the USA in 1850 to add to the 11 camels that had arrived the year before.[3] The menagerie also included 100 horses and an elaborately carved, painted wagon.

In one small town on tour in the 1850s, the elephant, Old Romeo, was tormented by a group of locals led by a young woman. Old Romeo ignored her annoying provocation for some time. Coup explains what happened:

> The ringleader in this reckless sport was a veritable young Amazon. For a time the patriarch of the drove, who had more good common sense than all his tormentors, stood the annoyance with dignified forbearance. But at last the big country girl succeeded in arousing his ire, and the huge elephant raised his trunk and gave her as dainty a slap, by way of warning . . . Her pride was wounded before her companions. With her face flaming with anger, she leaped over the guard chain and made a vicious lunge at the shoulder of the elephant with the point of her gaudy parasol.[4]

---

1 For a summary of studies of visitor behaviour in zoos, see Davey 2006, 143–57.
2 Slout 1998, 63.
3 Saxon 1989; Coup 1901, 3, 143–44.
4 Coup 1901, 11.

Apparently, an elephant keeper rushed forward and rescued the female spectator before the situation escalated further. Despite Old Romeo's reputation, Coup defends Old Romeo as placid in his own early experiences with him. Once Coup had been sleeping on hay and Old Romeo used his trunk to gently lift Coup off the hay that he wanted to eat. Coup's explanation for Old Romeo's encounter with the female spectator is that the girl was showing off to her friends and was angered and/or embarrassed by the animal's resistance. Regardless, Coup claims that this type of tormenting behaviour was typical. Menagerie animals were victimised by unruly spectators.

There were spectators who inadvertently provoked responses from animals because they did not perceive a risk from venturing too close. For example, some would hold children up to a cage with a chimpanzee or baboon or orangutang in order to shake hands.[5] George Conklin, who started out as a lion tamer and later became an animal trainer, confirms that the menagerie workers had to ensure the animals were not poked with umbrellas or fed the wrong food or patted to see how they would react. He explains: 'The more you warned people about an animal and said it was dangerous, the more most of them seemed to want to get up to it and pet it.'[6] In another example given by Conklin, someone who fed peanuts to an elephant, after being told not to, let the elephant take them from his pocket, and complained vehemently when his coat was badly ripped.

While contributing to an ideal of rational recreation for the populace, a visit to the zoo (or travelling menagerie) was enjoyed in part because opportunities for leisure excursions were limited, especially for children.[7] There was a positive benefit to a two-way interaction, and potentially even feeding animals, albeit with careful management. Arthur Munby visited London's Zoological Gardens in 1864 and describes how:

> the animals were mostly resting after food or sleeping: which was all the pleasanter for me. Elephants & camels, giraffes & hippopotami [sic] – such as these simply bring back the awe of one's childhood,

---

5 Hagenbeck 1956, 86.
6 Conklin 1921, 12, 153.
7 Akerberg 2001, 108.

one's boyish love of the marvellous East: but why are the Carnivori so horribly human – why does the lioness lie on her back & stretch her great arms & yawn; why does the lion clap his broad hand to the side of his mouth & tear down his horse-bone, just as Hodge does that of his mutton chop?[8]

A perception of similarity through what Munby deemed human-like qualities and behaviour had the potential to change social attitudes towards other species and towards processes of captivity. At the same time perceptions of either difference or sameness may explain misbehaviour.

Spectators were not necessarily well behaved, thoughtful onlookers like Munby – that is, looking passively; protected by the anonymity of the crowd, a number indulged in the freedom to ignore instructions and menagerie protocol. Some even became belligerent. The comments of showmen revealed that caged and restrained animals were targets of human hostility. Anecdotes of spectator misbehaviour confirmed that the animal keeper's job was to prevent direct contact by which a member of the public could abuse an animal, and maintain order among the crowd. In hindsight, descriptions may actually have been circumspect about the extent of the problem in order not to detract from a show's reputation. While explaining that misbehaviour is atypical of most visitors to zoos today, Gareth Davey writes:

> Unruly visitor behavior presents problems for every zoo. Teasing, feeding, shouting, throwing stones, vandalism, and even animal poisoning, cause distress, or death to captive animals.[9]

Davey continues that recent research reveals how the position of spectators and crowd size can physiologically stress animals.

Some misbehaviour may have been due to the dynamic in spectator groups, including showing off or starting fights, and some of this activity was clearly preceded by alcohol consumption. The public had to be constantly watched for everyone's protection. Major disruptive behaviour ranged from ignoring the warning not to pat the

---

8   Munby 1972, 185.
9   Davey 2006, 149, citing Hediger and Thompson.

animals to poking them and abusive provocation, as the prodding of Old Romeo illustrated.

Some of the behaviour around menagerie entertainment seemed at odds with what JM Golby and AW Purdue outline as a progressive 'civilization of the crowd' during the 19th century when working-class entertainments converged with those of the middle class and bourgeois respectability, and they argue that the crowd became less unruly and less violent.[10] The pursuits nominated as tending to lead to riotous responses – such as cock fighting and dog fighting – involved animals, which Golby and Purdue admit had gone underground, and various sports games had become more rule bound. The menagerie crowd may have resisted civilising restraint evident elsewhere. While there probably were a large number of working-class spectators in the crowd, violence surrounded the animals on display and this tacitly encouraged fighting behaviour in an atmosphere with comparatively few familiar social restraints.

The travelling menagerie was a place of organised leisure, but its transient character may have made it appear less regulated than comparable entertainments. It was a popular, seemingly classless entertainment and menagerie audiences in the mid-19th century wandered through in groups at their own pace. There were few inbuilt restrictions imposed, such as the organised seating in a circus show, which additionally had a small barrier around the ring. In the USA, the seating in the largest circuses from the 1870s reflected social hierarchies of race and class, but even the circus was viewed as having some potential for violence because of the diversity of spectators.[11] In the absence of formal viewing arrangements that positioned spectators at a distance, the menagerie became a space in which protocol could be more easily ignored.

Taunting actions played out in the menagerie reflected the values of the wider social sphere. Anecdotes about individual spectator provocation and bullying provide a glimpse of how humans who might have had limited social power – such as the woman tormenting Old Romeo – potentially took out personal and/or social frustrations on animals. A captive animal might have been viewed as passive – an objectified

---

10   Golby & Purdue 1984.
11   Davis 2002, 32.

Other – and comparatively powerless to retaliate. Individual spectators might have been considered adventurous and admirable for confrontation and physically aggressive behaviour, rebelling against the restrictions and confinement imposed in everyday life. Animals were considered outside of human society, so the menagerie presented a contained world for individuals looking for excitement.

Showmen were also confronted by groups that ranged from those who refused to pay, to mobs intent on dispensing what they felt was rough justice, often on the slimmest pretext. Coup outlined how groups of people posed a regular threat to the American travelling show and menagerie, often with guns. The 'tough' elements of some towns were a constant problem and could comprise 'several hundred hoodlums' and the show rarely escaped 'a pitched battle with these desperados'.[12] The refusal to pay could reduce income for a show from $5000 to $800. Menagerie workers were defensively on guard and responded to perceived threats by fighting back.

Problems with unruly spectators did occur in all entertainments, and could escalate regardless of whether behaviour was fuelled by alcohol consumption, and these did sometimes develop into situations of confrontation with weapons. In the USA there were newspaper reports of an ejected spectator returning to a permanent entertainment venue to fire a gun, narrowly missing performers, and on one occasion, ironically, shooting at a female performer costumed as the Goddess of Liberty.[13] In another report, 'a man intruding upon the show was beaten by some of its employees and died of his injuries'; one of the employees, despite professing innocence, was arrested for murder.[14] Public gatherings, in general, held the risk of violence.

Conklin did not believe that he needed a gun for protection in most of the incidents that he experienced in a travelling circus and menagerie. There were misunderstandings among local townspeople and on one occasion an uninvited group of drunken criminal cowboys had attached themselves to the show.[15] One of the drunk cowboys

---

12 Coup 1901, 196–97, also 211–12.
13 *New York Clipper* 1872, Miscellaneous, 1 June: 71. Mrs E Howorth in a 'Hibernian Tableau' in Philadelphia.
14 *New York Clipper* 1872, Circuses, 22 June: 95.
15 Conklin 1921, 212–13.

4 Mobs and hooligans, crowds and fans

shot a Native American person, and this crime made the performers anxious about their safety. Because the menagerie workers were also considered outsiders by the townspeople, they were therefore guilty by association.

The size of the crowds increased progressively as menageries grew in popularity, as mentioned in reports about touring routes. For example, in Chicago in 1872, Forepaugh's 'mammoth tents have been filled to their utmost capacity'.[16] Occasionally the crowd was too large to be controlled. The tents became very crowded, sometimes to the point where a performance in a circus tent could not take place, even with an elephant brought forward to clear a space to allow passage.[17]

In England, similar trouble with unruly spectators was noted. George Sanger describes 'mob brutality' from the 1850s onwards and recounts several major mob attacks that included some particularly violent behaviour. He writes about Lancashire:

> Rows were frequent, and now and again terrible scenes were enacted, men and women being literally kicked to fragments by the formidable iron-tipped clogs which formed the general foot-wear. Lancashire men in those days gave very little attention to the use of their fists. The clog was their weapon, and they considered there was nothing unmanly in kicking and biting to death.[18]

Crowd gatherings were rough, and could be dangerous. There was a description of a fairground stallholder who was stomped to death by local rioting spectators wearing clogs. Sanger also explains that animals like elephants who were upset by the public became dangerous to keepers.

A young boy who had teased an African elephant called Lizzie was crushed to death at Wombwell's in April 1872. But '[m]any local witnesses came forward to testify that the unfortunate boy had given the elephant great provocation'.[19] Apparently Lizzie was usually compliant, even expressing 'joy' at seeing a chemist again who had cured her of colic

---

16 *New York Clipper* 1872, Circuses, 15 June: 87.
17 *New York Clipper* 1872, Circuses, 25 May: 63, Great Eastern Menagerie.
18 Sanger 1927 [1910], 169.
19 Bostock 1972 [1927], 31, also 40.

with a potion four years previously. Lizzie's routine involved walking around the menagerie tent and standing on a raised area. In a separate incident, she accidentally knocked the lighting rope and the skin on her back caught fire, but she healed and recovered. Extreme responses by spectators were only some of the risks facing travelling animals.

Ongoing problems with unruly spectators, however, got to such a point in one city that Edward Bostock applied for police protection for his menagerie. He recounts that 'we had been in a few rough quarters in England, Ireland, and Wales', but in Glasgow the company experienced the worst of what he termed 'hooliganism'.[20] The Glasgow authorities provided an older policeman as a watchman, but he proved ineffectual.

The continuing problem of human-to-human fights with locals and with other circus workers has been downplayed in circus history. Peter Verney, however, explicitly writes that 'the arrival of the circus was the signal for every tough in the district to start limbering up for action, for a good fight against worthy opponents'.[21] The word 'clem' described 'a fight on the lot' and 'Hey Rube' meant that a visitor was looking for trouble and to be prepared. 'Hey Rube' was called a 'battle cry', and used at the end of each stanza in a poem by William Devere about such conflicts that Verney reproduces, claiming that there could be a serious fight at least every two weeks. He continues that even though the law often viewed showmen as 'undesirable vagrants', the police ignored conflicts and were often pleased to see aggressive locals challenged. Workers at smaller circuses struggled to defend themselves – George Sanger's father sat up at night with a shotgun.

Recognition of what was called 'ruffianism' in London theatres was outweighed by reports of orderly audience behaviour in most venues and even in the 'cheap theatres', despite the poverty in the surrounding area.[22] In their major study of audiences in London theatres, Jim Davis and Victor Emeljanow present only a few examples of uproar, although disorder was not a focus of their study, dispelling ideas of 19th-century theatre attendance divided and localised by class.[23] As indicated, a distinction could be made between entertainments with more regulated

---

20   Bostock 1972 [1927], 36.
21   Verney 1978, 260–62.
22   *New York Clipper* 1872, 6 July: 108.
23   Davis & Emeljanow 2001, 26, 228.

4 Mobs and hooligans, crowds and fans

entry and seating and a focused stage area for spectators who attended the venue regularly, often more than once a week year-round. The arrangement of the menagerie facilitated unwarranted responses because of its transience.

The practices in tamer cage acts may have indirectly incited spectator misbehaviour. An implicit idea that aggressive animals in small, confined cage spaces should fear and obey humans was conveyed by these acts. Combined with harsh animal management, confrontation and submission could be said to permeate travelling menagerie exhibition. As 19th-century circus historian Hugues Le Roux explains, the 'tamer's performance' provided 'the most valuable evidence of the superiority of man over animals'.[24] The tamer appeared to make the lion obey with only a whip for protection. The tamer must 'astonish the beast and overawe him' and make him 'execute from fear of the whip those leaps which he would naturally take in his wild state'.[25] Animals should fear the human.

Tamer hunting acts in particular attracted larger crowds and the tamer could earn a big fee. The perception of them, however, could be decidedly critical. Englishman Frank Fillis repeats an oral account about tamer Tom 'Baddy' (Batty), who replaced a drunken handler and entered the menagerie lion cage.[26] It was probably Thomas Batty, who Carl Hagenbeck describes as an example of a trainer with an unacceptable hunting act in which he fired pistols and antagonised the animals.[27] Fillis claims that the popularity of the act caused a rival to offer Batty his weekly £50 fee not to appear, but a replacement handler was fatally attacked, and Batty made one more appearance for £250 to a crowd of thousands. Batty was probably an experienced tamer: the Batty family was involved in the English circus, and the generation after Thomas also presented animal acts. This anecdote reveals that the hunting act, with some chasing action and weapon display, was perceived as an overt

---

24   Le Roux & Garnier 1890, 133.
25   Le Roux & Garnier 1890, 150.
26   van der Merwe 2007, 42–43. Batty was not at the Copenhagen Winter Gardens as claimed where there were no Winter Gardens, but Batty may have been appearing at the Berlin Winter Gardens. (Email inquiry, Circus Museum, Copenhagen, 15 April 2008.)
27   Hagenbeck 1909, 12.

display of aggression towards animals. Spectators may not have appreciated that this hunting act was repeatedly staged – Batty's act did seem ad hoc. As well as attracting large, excitable crowds, tamer acts tacitly encouraged provocative and threatening behaviour towards all caged and restrained animals.

In France, Paul Hervieu was an eyewitness to an accident in which a lion attacked a tamer. Hervieu cynically summarises the behaviour of the spectators. He explains that, firstly, "'[a] female spectator never faints until there is nothing more to see"; secondly, those at the back rushed forward and clambered over barriers at the first opportunity; thirdly, women even pushed men aside "to get a better view".[28] Although he implies that women were more aggressive in their effort to see what was happening, this could mean that he noticed them because, unusually, there was minimal distinction between the behaviour of male and female spectators attending the incident. Certainly such an occurrence could cause a disturbance if not also inadvertently provoke some to discard conventional gender roles.

While circuses with menageries toured widely in their respective countries, they also toured internationally and the impact of national events at a local level may not always have been fully appreciated by such companies (see Chapter 5). In one graphic example that took place shortly after the Prussian siege of Paris (1870), Prussian-like uniforms were worn by the band in an American circus for a parade through the streets of Amiens, France, playing the *Marseillaise*, so that the 'utter bad taste of this proceeding raised the just indignation of an excited crowd', and the circus was forced to leave quickly.[29] The military uniforms increasingly used as costumes by circus bands and performers conveyed not only connotations of aggression but specific identities in conflicts.[30] Unquestionably some American circuses touring to Europe were more successful than others and it was becoming apparent that the

---

28 Cited in Le Roux & Garnier 1890, 155. This was Sultan's attack on Bidel (see Chapter 5).
29 *New York Clipper* 1872, Circuses, 7 September: 179.
30 In the early 1870s, as happened during the American Civil War, menagerie and circus proprietor John Robinson was said to have paid for US army uniforms worn by soldiers, including his son. *New York Clipper* 1872, Circuses, 21 September: 199.

4 Mobs and hooligans, crowds and fans

knowledge of the lion or elephant keeper was an increasingly important element of success.[31]

While there may have been numerous reasons for individual spectator resistance and aggression towards animals in a menagerie and for crowd attacks, they also took place in a socio-political context. The social world of the 19th century could be harsh, with physical impositions within the workplace and also in the domestic sphere for women and children. A hidden problem of domestic violence among entertainers seemed to come to public attention only in extreme cases resulting in death. In one example, a manager, James C Davis, shot his partner, the trapeze performer Mademoiselle La Rosa; he claimed it was an accident, saying the gun had gone off when he moved a cocked pistol at her request.[32] There appeared to have been a domestic dispute – two other guns were found in his possession, and apparently the couple were not married as initially claimed.

Outbursts of mob violence that seemed spontaneous during visits to menageries could also expose aspects of class dissension and political frustration that erupted periodically out of ordered social life.[33] It might be argued that a latent violence in society more broadly was exposed by the fighting behaviour of individuals and groups. Caged and restrained animals were considered to have come from remote regions perpetually at war and the military forces sent to these colonial regions came from the home country populations, which may have contributed greater complexity to local tensions. There may have been an insidious contagion of violence. Billie Melman points out that the 19th-century crowds in Britain attending these spectacles of violence as entertainment could also attend the public hangings of criminal prisoners until 1868.[34] The connections between government systems and violent punishments in public and private spheres might have become more oblique in European and American 19th-century social

---

31   *New York Clipper* 1872, Circuses, 21 December: 298. On 16 November 1872 Myers circus opened in Hamburg in a building seating 5000, with John Cooper as lion tamer and elephant keeper.
32   *New York Clipper* 1872, Mlle La Rosa accidentally shot and killed, 30 March: 415.
33   Melman 2006, see Part I.
34   Melman 2006, 100.

worlds, but they remained unmistakable in the treatment of indigenous inhabitants in the colonies.[35] Confrontational responses by locals were the manifestation of societal conflict already imbued with the violence perpetuated by the official imperatives of nation-states.

Crooks

Misbehaviour motivated by curiosity or hostility happened in a crowded environment, additionally encompassing the less acceptable practices of showmen and the drunken behaviour of workers. Questionable business practices in the USA ranged from organised games to entice spectators to part with as much money as possible and short-changing them on their admission fees, to more blatant activities such as pickpocketing; these may have been less evident in shows in Europe. Janet Davis identifies a carnivalesque element to performer identity and behaviour in American circus and recognises that there were problems with thefts that invariably happened on the town's seasonal Circus Day.[36] In addition, American workers known to be associated with a menagerie did not always pay their bills to hotels and other local businesses. This led to accusations and problems, even if that town was not part of the touring route the following year. Some of those associated with, or who simply attached themselves to, a show engaged in outright criminal activities, such as pickpocketing and stealing.

Performers would often become involved in fights. Amid his mid-19th-century accounts of threatening behaviour from people outside the touring show, such as horse thieves and conmen making false accusations about harbouring escaped slaves, Coup recounts witnessing his first fight among the menagerie workers that caused him to try to leave the show.[37] A larger worker was physically bullying a smaller man who seemed to put up with it, but one day he suddenly retaliated, took out a pistol and fatally shot the bully. Coup explains that he and

---

35 For example, see McCulloch 2004, 223, 226–27. McCulloch argues that flogging and caning were standard treatments in British Africa, so assaults on workers in the colonies could be located within a 'political economy' of violence.
36 Davis 2002, 174, 29–30.
37 Coup 1901, 9–10.

other workers had to be constantly alert to trouble. Workers were also vulnerable to false accusations.

There were numerous confrontations in hotel bars. In one incident several drivers working with Forepaugh's went for an early evening drink in a saloon in Jerseyville, Illinois, and were joined by others later. At the suggestion of a driver, Jones, they started singing. A town officer, Neece, entered the saloon and ordered the men to stop singing because they were disturbing the peace. The drivers ignored him and when the marshal, James McKinney, arrived, he seized Jones by the collar and shot him with a revolver. McKinney hurriedly left town; Jones later died. The dead worker was described as a quiet, inoffensive person and 400 of the show's workers, or attachés as they were called, threatened to take 'dire vengeance upon the whole community'.[38] Adam Forepaugh had to intervene to calm down the crowd. In a similar incident, circus men refused to leave a local drinking house when the African-American owner wanted to close, culminating in an altercation in which the owner was shot by one of the show workers, who then disappeared.[39]

An incident in a hotel may have detracted from a performer's reputation. For example, in a letter sent to the trade paper where performers advertised for work, one performer gave a disclaimer about his alleged involvement in a fight in which a gun was fired.[40] Singer-actor Charles Cochran, who tried unsuccessfully to join Barnum and Bailey Circus The Greatest Show on Earth (BB) in the USA during the early 1890s and later became a manager and show entrepreneur, provided a detailed account of his own bad behaviour as a young man attending the theatre in 1897. He arrived after he had been drinking and was refused entry, but he forced his way inside past the attendants. He claimed that he did not realise he was 'tight' and out of control. When a manager tried to physically persuade him to leave, a fight ensued, and the attendants joined in. The five-minute fight was reported in the next day's newspaper in the language of a boxing match, 'blow for blow, move for move, in the

---

38 *New York Clipper* 1872, Circuses, 12 October: 223.
39 *New York Clipper* 1872, Circuses, 16 November: 263.
40 *New York Clipper* 1872, Circuses, 17 August: 161.

parlance of the prize ring'.[41] By then spectators could also easily attend more formalised displays of fighting in boxing and wrestling shows.

In addition to this type of violent incident, the practices associated with travelling shows could be manipulative, if not outright criminal. The menagerie that accompanied a circus from the 1870s in the USA also contained performers who were not an obvious part of the main show or even an accompanying sideshow, and were specifically attached to the menagerie. George Conklin writes about an African-American man, Jeremiah Backstitch, who rode a 'meek, innocent-looking' mule; spectators were invited to ride the mule for $5.[42] The mule was trained to move to the signal of a whip, and throw off everyone until Backstitch volunteered from the audience as if he were one of the spectators, and rode the mule successfully. Such practices were designed to maximise revenue. Enterprising workers conceived of all manner of ruses. For example, balloon sellers for the menagerie parade would pop spectators' balloons with tacks so that they could sell more later.

Conklin explains that the workmen and keepers were constantly looking for ways of making extra money, such as selling fake magic stones with healing properties or miracle oil or even miracle soap. In further examples, one man took the quills out of the porcupines to sell, while another was selling goose eggs as ostrich eggs to farmers.[43] Small performances happened wherever crowds gathered and, for example, a sleight-of-hand performer would use cards to entertain and trick spectators. One, Spaf Heiman, would call for a knife from the audience and make it disappear; if it was of good quality, he appeared to swallow it so he could keep it.

There were numerous games and devices that accompanied large live shows, and these were often used to fool the crowd. The 'fixer' accompanied games of chance, paying off the police or working in the crowd to calm down a 'victim' with sympathetic words or, if that failed, providing payment.[44] As well, 'cappers' were planted among a crowd to appear to win in order to induce people to take part. In a variation, one crook played a well-dressed doctor who was called if a spectator fainted

---

41 Cochran 1929, 60.
42 Conklin 1921, 148–49, 150–51.
43 Conklin 1921, 153–54, 174–75, also 156.
44 Conklin 1921, 166–68, also 172–73.

4 Mobs and hooligans, crowds and fans

after losing a large amount of money in a game. This apparently happened regularly, and the doctor was able to get the person carried out of the crowd before there was a disturbance.

Drawing on sociological studies of the 1960s and 1970s, Joseph Rogers defines terms such as 'grifting', to denote the more common crooked games played by 'grifters', duping members of the public aided by dishonest public officials.[45] The bad feeling that a show left behind was called a 'burn up' and the discovery of grifting often led to violence and fights.

While these types of behaviours were duplicitous, some practices associated with travelling shows in the USA were unmistakably criminal and unquestionably gave travelling shows a bad reputation. Thus the shows that upheld honest practices became individually known. In the USA, travelling shows were almost expected to be the epicentre of illegal activities. Some managers accepted dishonest practices as inevitable, while others tried to stop them. Conklin writes that during the 1860s and 1870s, '[t]he gambler, the pickpocket, the short-change artist, and the faker travelled with the show and in return for goodly sums of money, paid to its owner, were left undisturbed to prey on the crowd which the circus brought together'.[46] Conklin writes of two performers with O'Brien and then Cole's circuses; Pat Ford got into more fights than anyone else, and Jack Rogers was 'an all-round crook', who would sneak through town while the show was happening and steal clothes from washing lines.

Cochran describes attending the World's Fair in Chicago in 1893 where 'crooks had gathered from all over the world'.[47] Some awareness that con artists would be present in the crowd did not deter spectators, and it may have added to the thrill for some, and encouraged others to take licence. There was great excitement among the public but the crowd made the fair seem wild. Cochran considered the spectacle and electric lighting displays extraordinary. Even though they were show workers themselves, Cochran and a companion spent their last US$100 during their first visit, so he found a job at the fair selling fountain pens.

---

45 Rogers 2007, 116–18.
46 Conklin 1921, 165, also 151.
47 Cochran 1929, 23, also 25.

At travelling shows and fairs, the games were commonly rigged to allow spectators to appear to win at first and then to lose. Lorenz Hagenbeck recounts trying to sell the Hagenbeck elephants to the American showman, Benjamin Wallace, well known for show grifting. Wallace replied, in colourful language, that he did not want the elephants because they cost too much to feed and because, '[i]f ever I want to earn some dollars, I think up a new game.'[48] Lorenz claims that the games he saw in the USA were unknown in Germany. He explains:

> Crowds would flock in their thousands round a stage, on which was a man selling lottery tickets, and all would be astonished to see that people were actually winning – here five, there ten, even twenty dollars. Indeed, at first there was hardly anyone round who did not win something. Of course, the winners were almost all stooges of the man on the platform.[49]

Spectators were duped by the ease with which the planted fixers initially appeared to win and they continued to buy tickets or to play the game, often with all the money they had. Lorenz was dissatisfied that the Hagenbeck name became associated with the business practices of Wallace when he bought the Hagenbeck circus in 1906. Certainly illegal business practices may have been less tolerated at the local level in Europe, but the menagerie show was theatrical entertainment and prone to duplicitous exaggeration.

---

48   Hagenbeck 1956, 76, also 58–60; Hagenbeck's Giant Circus and Wild Animal Show toured three riding rings and two stages in the circus tent and a menagerie tent in 1905. The circus show ran for one hour and 45 minutes, twice a day. The parade presented lions and tigers in menagerie wagons and, to satisfy spectator expectations, included a 'veiled "Indian Princess"' in a howdah on an elephant. But a range of factors impacted on attendance, such as the day of the week, the weather, other recent entertainments, and how far the performance day was from payday. It was eventually sold and amalgamated into the Hagenbeck–Wallace circus after 1906. The Hagenbeck–Wallace included an act featuring Bombayo, 'The Man from India', leaping over elephants. Lorenz believed that the three-ring circus may have been very ambitious, as he would subsequently successfully tour the world with a one-ring circus for 10 years. Slout 1998, 313–14 on Wallace.
49   Hagenbeck 1956, 76.

A 1910 newspaper article suggests that teams of 'fakers' associated with some circus and menageries might number 30 out of 80 workers.[50] There was clearly a theatrical element in that highly experienced fakers might dress poorly and appear inept at the trick to dupe suspicious members of the public who came expecting trickery. By that time, however, such tricksters were only really effective in smaller towns since the public in the cities were now familiar with crooked games. The heyday of such scams coincided with the peak in the popularity of the travelling menagerie.

Educational animal fights

Wild animal exhibiting in the second half of the 19th century was often justified with rhetorical statements about educational value, with performers even adopting the title of 'professor', no doubt intended to offset a poor reputation. Some claims about the merit of the study of natural or 'animated' history in zoological displays for young people seemed to be sincere, although the elevation of menagerie practice to schools for the 'cause of science' with declarations that 'education has triumphed over ignorance and the great door of knowledge' revealed hyperbole that was more about business marketing than pedagogy.[51] Ferguson stipulates that: '[T]he moral effect ... improves the mind, instructs and enlarges the common fund of human knowledge, and may be looked upon, as the only pure and correct school'.[52] The idea that observing animals could be beneficial for children did become entrenched and was proclaimed extensively by menageries and circuses through succeeding decades.

Animal exhibitions in menageries were sometimes accompanied by talks and lectures, and the delivery of these was more theatrical than scientific. A crowd gathered around the menagerie cages listening to the lecturer, who greatly embellished the commentary. Lecturers appealed to the predictable sentiments of the viewing public, and baby animals were particularly popular with crowds. While a menagerie

---

50 Kelly 2012, 30–33, reprinted.
51 Ferguson 1861, vi, vii.
52 Ferguson 1861, 14.

lecture might have provided the public with some basic information about an animal species, it was often framed by a human melodrama of struggle and loss.

Conklin recounts how the display of menagerie camels had a roster drawn from camel attendants who were mostly Irish, but who dressed each day as Arabs. The lecturer (John) Childers elaborated on the life of the costumed Arabs with the camels in the desert, adding more details with each successive lecture. One day he recounted how they spent their days huddled together in sandstorms, 'saved from dying of thirst by killing one of the faithful animals and drinking the water stored in its stomach'.[53] The attendants quit the show together to avoid what they perceived as further humiliation from make-believe stories.

A commitment to delivering menagerie shows with some educational value was undermined by the exploitative attitudes held by showmen, since the more sensationalist aspects of animal life could attract a crowd. The organisation of animal fights and 'animal-baiting' had been legislated against in Britain by the mid-19th century.[54] There were still covert animal acts that promised fighting when incompatible animals were placed together, as when, for example, a lamb or small dog was placed in a lion's cage. Additionally, fights between animals arose because of the conditions under which they were kept; the keeper's lack of knowledge about animal behaviour meant the keepers were often taken by surprise. Two leopards with Van Amburgh's had been in an act with Lester for four years, and lived in the same cage.[55] All concerned were left stunned when the leopards had a serious fight that left them both badly injured.

In another example, when a group of ostriches showed a capacity to fight one another, Coup regretted that this fighting capacity had not been predicted and presented to a paying audience. He suggested that ostrich fights might rival the appeal of a bullfight. Two males among 40 ostriches were identified by the keeper, Delaney, as "'spoiling for a fight'" and Coup describes how 'their mouths were wide open, their eyes red and hideous, and their magnificent plumage ruffled, until the spectators, while deploring the fight, could not help admiring the

---

53   Conklin 1921, 147–48.
54   Thomas 1984, 160–61; Ritvo 1987, 151–52.
55   *New York Clipper* 1873, Circuses, 8 March: 391.

4 Mobs and hooligans, crowds and fans

splendid appearance of the birds in their rage'.[56] Coup describes how the fighting birds circled each other with loud screams, delivering body blows. Delaney risked injury when he tried to stop the fight to save the animals, and eventually delivered two heavy blows that forced one ostrich to the ground, while the other assumed the position of victor and walked away followed by the female birds. Yet it was human vandals who broke into the menagerie and destroyed these birds. Within 12 hours of the fight, the male ostriches had been completely plucked, their feathers stolen for profit. Thus menagerie animals were also at risk of unscrupulous opportunistic attacks from outside.

Coup's aquarium business with Charles Reiche was completely unprepared for a fight between alligators crowded into a tank. He writes that the attendants were 'paralyzed [sic] with fear', because the alligators 'would snap at each other so violently as to break each other's jaws', with a noise like a gunshot.[57] Once the fight subsided, to prevent a recurrence or escape, the adult alligators were shot in the eyes and buried.

A report about fights between animals in 19th-century newspaper coverage under an entertainment subheading made clear the assumption that fighting displays were of public interest. A report about tiger fighting in Java, Indonesia implied that it was a common practice to stage a tiger against a buffalo in a bamboo cage; although the buffalo was usually the winner of the 20- to 30-minute fight, few survived the fight more than a few days. The fight was stimulated by throwing boiling water over the buffalo and poking the buffalo with nettles tied to the end of a stick. The animals had to be harmed to make them fight. In Java, the tiger tried to avoid the fight until 'goaded by sticks, and roused by the constant application of burning straw', after which the tiger was gored by the buffalo.[58] In this instance, animal fights manifest ideas of colonial struggle. 'The Javans are accustomed to compare the buffalo to the Javan, and the tiger to the European'.[59] While this report describes a staged animal fight during the colonial era, the tradition of a buffalo fighting a tiger or

---

56 Cited in Coup 1901, 146–47, also 149.
57 Coup 1901, 150–51.
58 *New York Clipper* 1872, Tiger fighting in Java, 25 May: 60.
59 *New York Clipper* 1872, Tiger fighting in Java, 25 May: 60.

humans attacking a tiger with sticks was a ritual developed under Javanese kingship and allowed rulers to confirm their power.[60]

There was a contradiction between the proposition that simply viewing animals in menageries was educational and the existence of less acceptable, surreptitious animal displays on which promoters sought to capitalise. While animal fights, accidental or not, might have held the promise of quick box-office gains to a showman, it was animals that offered a capacity for spectator–animal interaction that gained affectionate popularity and often acquired the largest following of fans. Even so, supposedly placid animals could become the centre of considerable controversy and conflict.

Fans of Jumbo nationalism

In 1882 the African elephant Jumbo became famous in Britain through newspaper publicity about Barnum's purchase and proposed removal of him to the USA.[61] Barnum's agent approached the secretary of London's Royal Zoological Society, who accepted an offer of US$10,000 (£2000) for Jumbo. The events surrounding what became a popular movement to keep Jumbo in England, and which became known as the 'Jumbo Craze', were underpinned by a newspaper campaign to stir up controversy (and sell newspapers). The campaign made Jumbo into a national figure. Why did an elephant imported from eastern Sudan via France become central to an emotionally charged public campaign that made him into a figure of national pride in Britain? As events unfolded, it became clear that the animal management concerns that motivated the sale were not widely known. Instead, Jumbo appeared stoic in public, popular with children and therefore imaginatively endearing.

Paul Chambers provides a detailed biography of Jumbo's life, and explains the importance of the keeper, Matthew Scott, to his wellbeing.

---

60   Sramek 2006, 660, citing Peter Boomgaard.
61   Jumbo features in most circus histories and is discussed in zoo histories: for example, see Culhane 1990, 125–43; Hancocks 2001, 1–5, photograph. The purchase price would be the equivalent of over £200,000 today, although Jumbo cost Barnum considerably more in total costs.

4 Mobs and hooligans, crowds and fans

Jumbo's increasing popularity during his decades in the London Zoological Society Gardens came from his capacity to provide rides for children on a specially built howdah, belying the ongoing concerns of zoo staff regarding Jumbo's behavioural problems. Direct contact with Jumbo galvanised public opinion: adults who had taken rides on Jumbo's back as children wanted their own children to have the same opportunity, preferably on the same elephant. When the Royal Zoological Society's secretary, Mr Sclater, tried to publicly explain that when elephants reached adulthood they were subject to what was termed 'bad' or 'uncertain' temper, this was rejected because Jumbo had benignly given rides to children for years.[62]

The Jumbo controversy provided a further example of the undeniable connection between exhibited animals and newspaper publicity; this was initially escalated by the *Daily Telegraph* and sustained by its editor, who was known to be critical of the London zoo.[63] Disagreement among the Fellows of the Zoological Society about the sale of Jumbo unfolded in letters to the editor of *The Times*, escalating the controversy. The news that Jumbo's sale had been completed led one of the Fellows to write an anonymous letter to *The Times* under the pseudonym 'Penitent Fellow'.

> An attempt was made on Saturday to remove a distinguished and, by children, a much-loved resident from London, but, happily, without success. I allude to Jumbo, the great and docile elephant who has for very many years been one of the chief attractions of the Zoological Gardens, but who, for reasons difficult to understand, has lately been sold to an American showman. In common with many other Fellows of the Society, I have found my disgust at this sale intensified by the pathetic and almost human distress of the poor animal at the attempted separation of him from his home and his family. Our hearts are not harder than those of his keepers . . . is it too late to annul the bargain?[64]

---

62 *Times* (London) 1882, Jumbo, to the editor of *Times*, 24 February: 10.
63 Chambers 2008, 125.
64 *Times* (London) 1882, 21 February: 10.

The Penitent Fellow ends his letter with the claim that a subscription would raise the funds to save Jumbo. This polarisation in the Zoological Society offered Jumbo's supporters a stronger case, based on the sentiment that Jumbo was loved by all. They deemed Jumbo's sale akin to selling a family member to the USA. An attempt to encourage Jumbo into a large box on wheels for transport to the Millwall Docks was unsuccessful due to his resistance. Jumbo's following increased once it became widely known that he was the largest elephant in the Zoological Gardens, and seemingly the first African elephant to survive there. The elephant should therefore not be sold and shipped to the USA.

Leaving aside the legacy of elephants in sentimental theatrical pantomimes, the patriotic dimensions to the possession of this particular elephant stirred up public opinion by intersecting with a collective nostalgia for childhood experience. There were numerous letters from the public sent to newspapers to protest the removal of Jumbo from the zoo, 'as if Barnum had purchased an English institution'; in poetic jest it was suggested Barnum exchange Jumbo for William Gladstone, the British Prime Minister.[65] Even Queen Victoria and the Prince of Wales had taken rides on Jumbo and they, too, contributed to the protest about the sale. The saga played out in newspapers throughout Britain.[66] For *The Times*, Martin Skeffington wrote an eight-point rebuttal of Sclater's explanation of the sale, arguing that it was clearly motivated by the 'excessive price' and asking why, if Jumbo were so dangerous, a sale had not been initiated earlier? Additionally, why had children been allowed to continue to ride on him.[67] Conversely, William Agnew writes that based on his 34 years of experience as a magistrate in Goalpara, India, where he had 'owned' an elephant that became dangerous and 'did great mischief while loose', elephants should not be kept in zoological gardens.[68] He argued that the passengers on the ship transporting Jumbo needed protection.

---

65 Werner 1923, 334.
66 For example, see *Bristol Mercury and Daily Post* (Bristol) 1882, 6 March: 8; *Belfast Newsletter* (Belfast) 1882, The sale of Jumbo [by telegraph], 6 March: 5. Also see Hancocks 2001, 3, citing Brightwell.
67 *Times* (London) 1882, Jumbo, to the editor of *Times*, 24 February: 10.
68 *Times* (London) 1882, Elephants, to the editor of *Times*, 18 March: 5.

4 Mobs and hooligans, crowds and fans

Certainly the public did become protective of individual animals. Jumbo, as well as Zafara, a giraffe in France facing a similar fate,[69] became national emblems because they were inadvertently caught up in a legacy of political events and national rivalries. But Jumbo's biography also illustrates the manner of the trade between institutions; he had arrived in London in 1865 in poor condition from the Jardin des Plantes in Paris, in exchange for a rhinoceros from India and having been originally traded to Paris from Africa by Johann Schmidt in 1861.[70] Zoo superintendent AD Bartlett describes Jumbo arriving in London in a 'filthy and miserable condition'. He continues:

> none of the keepers except Scott dare go near him; but, strange to say, he was perfectly quiet as soon as he was allowed to be free in the Gardens. I was perfectly well aware that this restless and frantic condition could be subdued by reducing the quantity of his food, fastening his limbs by chains, and an occasional flogging; but this treatment would have called forth a multitude of protests from kind-hearted and sensitive people, and, in all probability, would have led to those concerned appearing before the magistrates at the police court charged with cruelty.[71]

The keeper Scott and Jumbo became inseparable companions, with Jumbo seemingly depending on the loner Scott, and possibly vice versa; Bartlett resented Scott's proprietary control over Jumbo.[72] Jumbo's behaviour depended on one person and this was unacceptable. There were struggles at a personal and a national level enacted about this particular elephant.

By 1881, Jumbo was causing ongoing concern with attendants because he was unpredictable, regularly trying at night to break out of the elephant house – that is, out of confinement. Selling him on was a pragmatic decision that reflected the common practice with difficult large animals – a better option for an elephant, given how others were killed (see Chapter 6). Meanwhile Barnum understood the special

---

69   Allin 1998.
70   Werner 1923, 333, about Schmidt; Chambers 2008, 10–19; Baker 1868.
71   Bartlett 1898, 45–46.
72   Chambers 2008.

appeal of elephants in the USA, especially since Old Bet had produced notable financial gains. It has been argued that Jumbo gained more attention internationally with this controversy than had any of Barnum's previous business ventures, including those that had toured to Europe since the 1840s.[73]

There was mounting public indignation at the prospect of depriving English children of a chance to ride an elephant considered a pet by many. The Jumbo craze illustrated how an idealised animal figure that was placid in contact with the public could attract affection. A committee was formed to prevent the Zoological Society's sale of Jumbo, proclaiming his value to science and zoological study, and this led to a highly publicised court case. The Zoological Society disputed the scientific worth of Jumbo on account of the increasing availability of African elephants in the preceding four decades, as well as the commercial worth of the animal against the cost of keeping him. Justice Chitty ultimately upheld the Zoological Society's right to sell him, noting the hypocrisy of those who traded their horses without qualms.[74]

The delay in the departure of Jumbo meant that in the intervening time he attracted more than 10 times the usual number of visitors per day, so that there were thousands, instead of hundreds, visiting Jumbo.[75] When Jumbo was finally transferred to the ship on 25 March 1882 he was saluted and celebrated as if he were royalty, and most of his chains were removed so that his 'head, body, and trunk were thus entirely freed' to assist his stance during the voyage.[76] There was also a plan to send back messages about his health in bottles dropped at sea. The party who came to farewell him at the docks included Bartlett, members of the aristocracy, and Mr Tallett from the Society for the Prevention of Cruelty to Animals. A description of the process of settling him on deck took up most of a column in *The Times*.

The publicity surrounding Jumbo was invaluable to Barnum's efforts to make him a distinctive attraction. Les Harding writes that Jumbo was not a performer, even though he appeared in the circus

---

73 Werner 1923, 333, see 345 for a poster bill showing Jumbo's trunk reaching the third storey of a building.
74 *Daily News* (London) 1882, The Zoological Society and Jumbo, 17 March: 6.
75 Chambers 2008, 130.
76 *Times* (London) 1882, 27 March: 10.

4 Mobs and hooligans, crowds and fans

ring: 'Jumbo did not do anything.'[77] As a celebrity in the USA, he made Barnum a fortune, becoming a household name and featuring in advertisements for household goods.[78] Unfortunately there was a tragic accident just a few years after his arrival in the USA. Jumbo was being moved across a rail line when he was hit and killed by a freight train on 15 September 1885. Another smaller elephant called Tom Thumb survived with only a broken leg.[79] Barnum, however, kept a noted taxidermist and businessman Henry Ward, on call; Barnum regularly donated specimens to museums and had already been involved in discussions about Jumbo with the Smithsonian National Museum for two years. Thus was Jumbo's fate decided. Ward was assisted by the young Carl Akeley, who pioneered the realistic mounting of taxidermied animals in natural settings. They took six months to create two Jumbos, one of skin and one of the skeleton.[80] Both Jumbos toured for two years with a live female elephant, Alice, billed as Jumbo's widow. The popularity of his skeleton, which was later displayed at the American Museum of Natural History, confirmed that elephants continued to be good business even in death.

Jumbo's reputation was established before the Jumbo craze and Barnum's decision to obtain him was no doubt indicative of this pre-existing prominence. In England, Jumbo's prominence galvanised sentiments derived from memories of pleasurable leisure activities, underscored by beliefs about differences in national attitudes towards animals. The Jumbo craze only evoked public sentiment about the fate of an individual animal, since that popular movement was not contesting the fate of all elephants in captivity.

The co-option of Jumbo's name followed. Edward Bostock recounts how Wombwell's acquired a young elephant, also called Jumbo, in 1880 from William Cross in Liverpool. This elephant proved so energetic and noisy that the menagerie could not contain him. Bostock recounts: 'One moment he was on his hind legs, the next on his fore, and anon

---

77 Harding 2000, 6.
78 See advertisement reproduced on the back cover, *Bandwagon* 2005, July–August: 47; also see advertisements in Harris 1973.
79 See Harding 2000; Chambers 2008; and most American circus histories.
80 Harding 2000, 9, 100–1. Ward initially thought that it would only take him two months.

he seemed to be clear of the ground altogether.'[81] Once, untied, Jumbo took off, but stopped when he spied Wombwell's older elephant, Lizzie. He headed to her side and was quickly tied to her neck. Soon after, Wombwell's decided to return this young, unmanageable Jumbo to Cross. He was sent by rail in a wooden box, breaking a tusk on the journey. He, too, was eventually sent to the USA.

Interest in elephants also extended to scientific attention to their emotional attributes. Elephants had acquired a reputation as 'models of domestic virtue' with the capacity to fall in love.[82] Charles Darwin was told that the Indian elephant had been observed to weep in times of grief and upon separation from other elephants. But he found conflicting accounts and he asked Bartlett to arrange an experiment with elephants trumpeting to see if the contraction of the muscles around elephants' eyes produced tears as it did in humans.[83] The results were inconclusive, as were investigations into other physiological similarities in displaying emotions. Regardless, life in captivity may have distorted the elephant's emotional reactions. Nonetheless the elephant's reputation for human-like emotional qualities persisted, serving both entertainment and scientific inquiry. The capacity of individual animals to arouse strongly felt human sentiments was irrefutable.

Whitewashed elephant wars

Competition between American menageries to maximise entry fees after the 1870s encouraged a relentless search for novel exhibits. Elephant attractions were especially favoured and, accordingly, new acts were quickly copied. In an interesting twist, however, it was a copy of Barnum's 1884 elephant exhibit that attracted the most spectators. As so-named white elephants reveal, fake animal attractions also proved profitable.

In 1883, before Jumbo was accidentally killed, Barnum acquired the elephant Toung Taloung, after prolonged negotiations. Taloung was one of a scarce number of 'white elephants', inhabiting the region of Burma

---

81   Bostock 1972 [1927], 66, 65–67.
82   Hagenbeck 1909, 148.
83   Darwin 1999 [1872], 169–70.

4 Mobs and hooligans, crowds and fans

(Myanmar) and Siam (Thailand), where they were revered in religious traditions. Taloung, eight feet (2.4 metres) in height, turned out to be a pinkish, pale grey with blotches, rather than a distinctly white colour by European standards. It is probable that Barnum's elephant displayed albanism, indicative of sacred elephants, but publicity suggesting that the elephant's skin would be white raised unrealistic expectations in audiences. Such a misleading advertising campaign may have contributed to this unsuccessful venture. Barnum's competitors, however, sought to present unmistakably white elephants.

In Britain, in a characteristic display of entrepreneurial opportunism, Sanger's National Amphitheatre, Hippodrome, Menagerie and Great Pantomime advertised that a perfect specimen of a 'prodigious sacred white elephant' would be on view in the Christmas pantomime before 'its departure to America, to join Adam Forepaugh's gigantic show', and before Barnum's Taloung arrived in London.[84] According to Sanger, the Prince of Wales came to see his white elephant, whereupon Sanger confided in the prince that the animal was whitewashed, and was rewarded for his honesty with Indian jewellery.[85] In the USA, Forepaugh presented an elephant as the 'Sacred White Elephant', possibly the one imported from Sanger's.[86] Ringling Brothers Circus also acquired an albino, Kheddah, seemingly named after the system of bamboo enclosures that entrapped wild elephants in India.[87] Yet it was Barnum's Taloung who was branded as a fake because the elephant was not expressly white, even though Taloung may have at least been an appropriate religious icon.

Taloung's journey between Siam and New York was broken by a brief stopover at the London Zoological Society Zoo between January and March 1884. Perhaps Barnum was attempting to continue the newspaper furore over Jumbo when he placed an advertisement in *The Times* promoting 'the first and only genuine white elephant ever imported'. In her analysis of Taloung's presence in London, Sarah Amato finds a wider set of discourses that were current in the culture at the time, and a correlation with racist ideas of whiteness. Amato notes

---

84 *Times* (London) 1883, 22 December: 8.
85 Sanger 1927 [1910], 241.
86 Hoh & Rough 1990, 219.
87 Lockhart 1938, 94, 23.

that stories of white elephants had already been brought to Britain by travellers and circuses. She argues that the ensuing disappointment in Taloung's apparent lack of whiteness had parallels with 'anxiety about the maintenance of racial purity and white privilege'.[88] This alignment was made explicit when white elephants appeared in advertising for Pear's Soap – advertising that also presented racially marked human bodies to denote that whiteness was equated with 'cleanliness'. When two monks were introduced to perform Buddhist rituals near the elephant, the ensuing debate prefigured relations between Britain and the South-East Asian colonies.[89]

National rivalry once again manifested itself in relation to different religious beliefs. The controversy about the elephant's pink-grey appearance was compounded by questions in newspaper stories about the monks' authenticity. The slippage around the word 'white' may also have indicated the difficulty of conceiving of an elephant (or any animal, for that matter) as god-like within a Christian framework with notions of purity. Rituals of reverence towards animals may further have been unacceptable to those holding traditional ideas of religious practices.

Opportunistically, Barnum and his press agents ran a poetry contest with a $500 prize about the arrival of Taloung in the USA – as he had when the celebrity soprano Jenny Lind had arrived 30 years earlier. The poem 'The sacred white elephant – Toung Taloung', by Joaquin Miller, was one of three to win the prize, encapsulating narratives about Taloung that assumed that the West had conquered the East. Miller explains that spectators perceived the elephant as embodying the East and foreign ways, and that they identified the material achievements of the West as better than the tyranny and mysticism evident in elephant homelands.

> They see the storied East in thee
> See vast processions, kneeling priests . . .
> A land of tyranny and tears.

---

88 Amato 2009, 251.
89 Kober 1931, 45. While difficulties in the management of elephants arose with the increased numbers, in Europe the employment of keepers from the Indian subcontinent assisted the process of working with Asian elephants.

4 Mobs and hooligans, crowds and fans

And this is a lesson, royal beast,
God recks not pagod; beast or priest...
From land of dreams to land of deed. [90]

The poem depicted the arrival of the white elephant as signifying cultural conquest and confirmation that the West was superior to foreign countries, characterised by tyrannical repression. Public reactions to the Taloung competition poems included a number of witty satirical send-ups.[91]

Despite this competition and other masterful pre-publicity stunts by Barnum, his animal exhibit did not lead to expected box office returns. Barnum obtained testimonials to confirm that Taloung was a sacred elephant, including by one knowledgeable Captain Richelieu who wrote that the Siamese divided elephants into categories.[92] Barnum admitted that American audiences might find Taloung disappointing, as if part of a dream or myth, although this recognition was potentially also part of a publicity ploy. Despite the publicity, Taloung did not become an exhibit to rival Jumbo, and once crowd numbers dwindled, Taloung was retired to a barn in Bridgeport, Connecticut.

Instead it was Adam Forepaugh's fake white elephant, called the 'Light of Asia', who proved highly effective in drawing large crowds. The year 1884 became known as the 'White Elephant Year' because of the rivalry between the two elephant attractions. Forepaugh advertised that the Prince of Siam had visited Forepaugh's 'white elephant', although the prince and his entourage left quickly, possibly shocked by the sight of the whiteness.[93] It was known to some behind the scenes that Forepaugh's white elephant was created with white paint. In the circus ring tent, the elephant appeared on a stage and a performer in a black suit, called a 'professor', proclaimed that this was a genuine sacred elephant. Apparently the painted elephant would recognise the performer (possibly the keeper), forcing the professor to evade the friendly overtures to avoid getting paint on his dark suit.

---

90 Werner 1923, 350–51. The word 'recks' is probably wrecks and the 'pagod' spelling may be a version of the French word 'pagode' for pagoda.
91 Saxon 1989, 306.
92 Saxon 1989, 305.
93 Werner 1923, 354.

Coup gives an account of Forepaugh's white elephant that suggests a more harmful and permanent substance may have been applied to the elephant's skin to achieve undeniable whiteness. The elephant was covered with a black velvet cloth and, as Coup writes, 'the trunk had been manipulated in such a way that visitors could touch it, and as no colouring matter came off on their hands I presume that part of body had in some way been "sized" or enameled [sic]'.[94] Such faked whiteness would have almost certainly been injurious to the animal.

The 'show warfare' between Barnum and Forepaugh had supposedly ended by mutual agreement in 1882.[95] But as the Taloung competition indicates, Barnum may have been vindicated in his continuing distrust of Forepaugh's agreement. Accordingly, Barnum created a third exhibition with an elephant called Tip who had whitened skin and marched in a street parade with Barnum and a banner proclaiming 'The White Fraud'. Barnum also wrote to the newspapers that Forepaugh's white elephant was an ordinary elephant who had been painted in Liverpool and shipped to the USA.[96]

Eventually, in 1890, the combined Forepaugh and Barnum elephant troupe would contain 60 elephants, and, in 1903, they became part of circuses under Ringling Brothers management, who claimed to be exhibiting half the trained elephants in the USA.[97] Barnum's Taloung tragically died in a fire in Bridgeport in 1887. Forepaugh's hoax white elephant, however, probably survived into old age performing as a boxing elephant.[98] Show hype for white elephants persisted well into the 20th century.[99]

---

94   Coup 1901, 41.
95   Saxon 1989, 288.
96   Saxon 1989, 307.
97   Allen & Kelley 1941, 26, about Forepaugh. *Ellis County Mirror* (Texas) 1902, 9 October: no page. An advertisement for Ringling Brothers Circus, 'The Last Giraffe Known to Exist'. 'More than half of all the elephants in America trained in an act' (Harry Ransom Library, University of Texas, Austin, Joe E Ward Collection, Box 18). Ringlings had to retract the boast about the giraffe.
98   Allen & Kelley 1941, 26, an obituary by Edwin C Hill appeared in the *New York Sun*, 1932. Forepaugh's elephant was possibly named John.
99   Lockhart 1938, 95. George Lockhart Junior claims that an albino elephant appeared at the London Zoo in 1926, described as having '"an unwholesome pink hue, with china-blue eyes, and a wealth of flaxen hair upon its pate"'. Also, see Allen & Kelley 1941, 17–18. In 1927 BB imported Powah, a white elephant, into

Manipulative show practices did not improve the reputation of menageries, and competitive businesses generated an environment of risk in which questionable dealings were commonplace. Public responses to menagerie animals ranged from affection to abuse, both responses ignoring the plight of countless animals kept in captivity for entertainment. The elevation of a few individual animals to celebrity status could not compensate for the plight of many. While public victimisation of animals belongs within a continuum of human bad behaviour towards other humans in and around menageries, the exposure of an aggressive impulse to animals in vulnerable circumstances also sets it apart. There is no doubt that a few spectators went hunting for opportunities to taunt helpless animals in the menagerie.

---

the USA, and he toured to England, although the deaths of two Burmese keepers, who were apparently murdered, also raised doubt about the sacred identity and how he was obtained.

Plates

Plate 1 This well-known painting of tamer Van Amburgh shows him wearing a Roman costume and standing in the centre of a cage of cowering lions and tigers. Edwin Landseer, English, 1802–73. *Portrait of Mr Van Amburgh as he appeared with his animals in London theatres*, 1846–47, Paul Mellon Collection, Yale Centre for British Art.

Plate 2 A graphic image of a brown lion on the back of a terrified white horse. The lion is digging his teeth and claws into the flesh of the horse. George Stubbs, English, 1724–1806. *A lion attacking a horse*, circa 1765, oil on canvas 69 x 100.1 cm, National Gallery of Victoria, Australia, Felton Bequest, 1949.

Plate 3 Cartoon drawing of politicians in top hats and suits attempting to climb up onto a seated elephant with a crown howdah. Several of the politicians have already failed to climb the elephant. John Doyle, *A lesson in elephant riding*, 1844, author's collection.

Plate 4 The black and white advertisement for the Great Eastern Circus Menagerie illustrates a menagerie hunting act showing a hunter firing pistols surrounded by attacking lions. *Advertisement for Great Eastern Circus 1872*, courtesy of Pfening Archive.

Plate 5 The back cover of a 1883 Barnum and London Circus program contains seven black and white drawings depicting: P.T. Barnum's vast hippodrome venue, three circus rings, two menagerie tents, a stage with acrobatic performances, the elephant Jumbo, a baby elephant and mother and the museum of human curiosities. *Program back cover for Barnum and London Circus 1883*, courtesy of Pfening Archive.

Plate 6 Hunters with rifles in the African grasslands hunting giraffes. Lulu Farini (Sam Hunt), *Photograph Hunting Giraffe, Kalahari*, 1885, The National Archive, UK, copy 1/373/439.

Plate 7 Photograph of horses playing dead in Frank Fillis' Anglo-Boer war re-enactment. It appears to be a battlefield except for a visible section of raked seating to one side and the top of a Ferris wheel in the far background. Photograh *St Louis Exposition 1904*, courtesy of Floris van der Merwe.

Plate 8 Five lions on raked pedestals sit behind Madame Pianka. The uppermost maned lion reaches out a paw, probably to touch the bow in her hair. Photograph of Mme. Pianka, *The lady of lions and her class*, circa 1902.

Plate 1

Plate 2

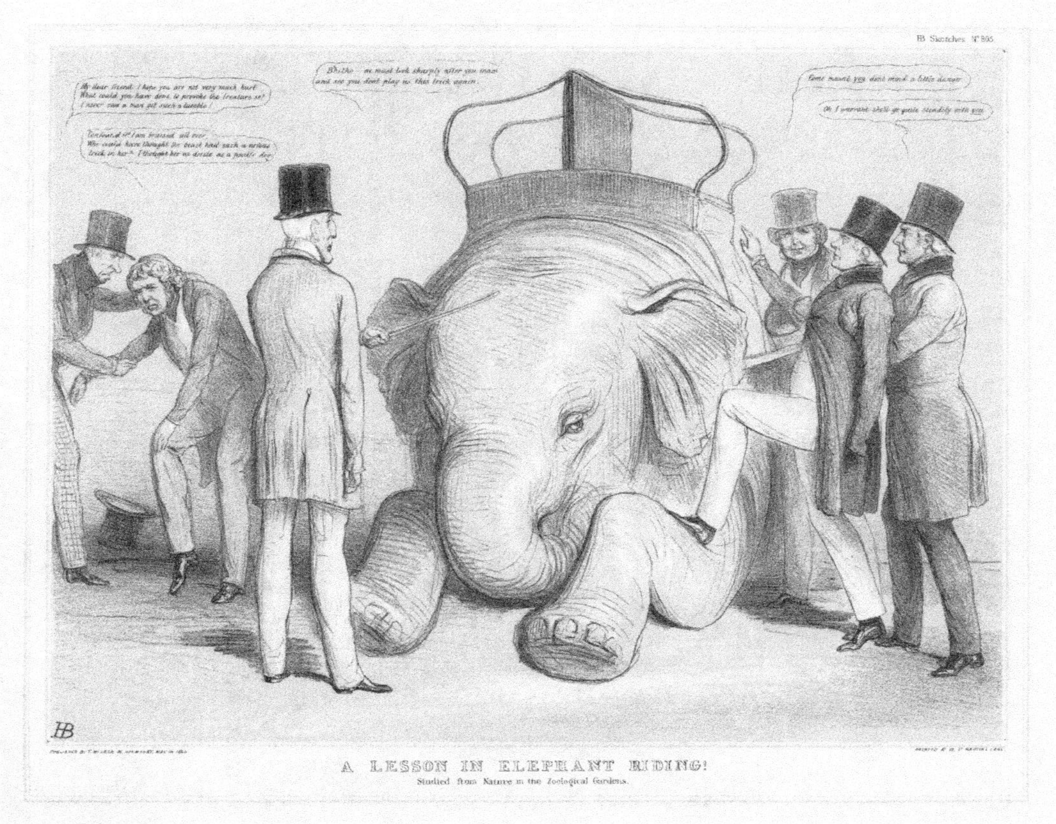

Plate 3

Plate 5

Plate 6

Plate 7

Plate 8

5
Head in the colonial lion's mouth

An animal tamer act with lions and tigers in a small cage remained the major menagerie attraction in the second half of the 19th century, and it now routinely involved the handler putting his or her head in a lion's mouth. But some spectators were not convinced that this feat, or the display of carnivores eating raw meat, should be entertainments. One of the main criticisms was that such stunts demeaned the humans involved and reduced them to the level of brute nature.[1]

This chapter considers animal tamer acts, fighting acts and other theatrical war scenarios with animals presented in Britain, France, the USA and British colonies from the 1870s to the 1890s. Spectacles in the colonies in Australia, New Zealand and southern Africa depicted colonial hostilities and insurrections in shows that consisted of a menagerie, a circus and a theatrical enactment of war. The tamer act might have gained social acceptance in Europe and the USA by the 1870s, but it proved controversial in the colonies during the 1890s for both the head-in-the-mouth feat and for the inclusion of female tamers. In a colonial milieu in which human fights were commonplace, menagerie human–lion acts tested the limits of social respectability.

---

1 For example, *New Zealand Mail* 1894, 19 January: 21.

Feeding frenzy

In England, Bostock and Wombwell's menagerie charged extra to watch the animals being fed at set times.[2] These shows involved carnivorous animals including lions, tigers, bears, wolves and hyenas being fed quantities of raw meat in front of spectators. The attendants would also become covered in animal blood during the process of delivering the meat to the cage, so it was literally a bloody spectacle.

The practice of feeding the animals was presented to the public throughout the 19th century and was compelling, even if some members of the public found it repulsive. If social abhorrence of the 'putrid and loathsome filth accompanying animal life' arose as much from an idea of what was disgusting and repulsive as from visible activity, the reaction at least seemed justified for carnivore feeding displays.[3] Prejudices about the way in which animals lived in nature were reinforced by feeding displays in the contrived and unnatural circumstances of captivity. The spectacle of animal feeding, however, became fused with notions of human degradation because of human proximity to the animals.

Cage acts that included the feat of the tamer putting his or her head in the lion's mouth often followed or preceded displays in which the lions were fed. The juxtaposition of a tamer act and a feeding spectacle led one to be associated with the other. There was an impression that tamers who entered cages and undertook acts with wild animals were at risk of becoming animal food. It was compounded by the inclusion of smaller feeding stunts during tamer cage acts.

The opportunity to observe menagerie animals being fed was widely publicised when Queen Victoria visited Van Amburgh's act on 24 January 1839, and when the animals were reportedly deprived of food prior to the Queen's observation of feeding time.[4] Van Amburgh's subsequent publicity contained a graphic account of the feeding. The practice became widespread and the delayed feeding of hungry animals maximised the effect. There was, however, some variation among the expectations of spectators in different countries. On

---

2 Bostock 1972 [1927], 82.
3 Bain 1875, 281.
4 Rothfels 2002a, 158–59.

tour in Europe, Bostock and Wombwell's found that French spectators would not pay extra to see the animals being fed, thus reducing the menagerie's income.[5] In France horsemeat used for feeding was expensive because humans also ate it. This reflected variations in the social utility of other species.

Vivid poster images of lions eating raw meat were used to advertise feeding spectacles in the USA in the 1880s and 1890s.[6] In one image, the feeding lion is in the foreground with a menagerie hunter firing a gun in the background. Such images contrasted with the posters showing images of animals standing unrealistically close together, in ordered lines, billed as 'The Realistic Jungle Menagerie'.[7]

The feeding of lions and other carnivores also brought to the fore the visceral sensory dimensions of viewing menagerie animals, involving smelling and seeing the activity. Hugues Le Roux describes the experience of watching lions, tigers, wolves and bears being fed as part of a menagerie exhibition in France. The spectator enters a darkened booth that has a strong smell and, as a gas light was turned on, two keepers enter, covered in blood from the horsemeat in a barrow, which they wheel in. A third keeper calls out that the animals are about to be fed. Initially, the keepers pretend to put the meat forward to the lions while presenting an empty hook. Le Roux's vivid account continues:

> As they pant with rage, their breath rises in clouds of smoke, scattering the sawdust of their litter. They roar and dribble with hunger. At last the meat is within their reach, and they drag the huge pieces towards their jaws, too large to pass through the bars at first, there is a moment's struggle ... [Afterwards] the expression of satisfaction after rage.[8]

---

5   Bostock 1972 [1927], 83, includes a full article from an English newspaper, 'Consumption of horseflesh in Paris: startling statistics'.
6   Jando 2008, citing 1882 *The children's circus and menagerie picture book*, 275; and 1891 advertisement for Barnum & Bailey's Circus Greatest Show on Earth, 295.
7   Jando 2008, 1897 poster, 280–81.
8   Le Roux & Garnier 1890, 134–35, also 148–49.

Le Roux's description implies that the animals were kept hungry for the demonstration, and that feeding was the focus of intense interest. Some cages were even open to the public to enter. A sleeping lion was woken, pulled by the ears, and Le Roux was invited to step into the cage; he nervously moved forward and touched the lion's leg.

In 1879 during Bostock and Wombwell's feeding show, two lionesses leant on their cage doors, opening them. They leapt out among the spectators, who seemed to think that this was part of the show and so did not disperse.[9] The lionesses were eventually enticed back into their cages without further mishap. By 1880, the feeding was followed by a pet dog being placed in the cage of a docile tiger – they had been raised together. An elephant keeper, Thomas Bridgeman, however, mistakenly let the dog into the cage of a different tiger, leaping into the cage to rescue the dog upon realising his mistake.[10] The dog did not survive, but Bridgeman became known as a lion tamer, replacing a performer called Captain Cardona, but retaining the stage name.

As Le Roux explains, it took 'nerve' to work with lions, and it was only '[t]he boldest of individuals who put their heads two or three times a day into the lion's mouth'.[11] A spectator's perception was that a lion with frightening jaws obeyed because he or she feared the sting of the tamer's whip – but this was probably not the case. Despite the widespread use of the word 'mouth' in the advertising, the act involved placing the head somewhere near the upper and lower jaw of the lion.

By the 1880s, the most well-known French lion tamers were François Bidel and Nouma-Hava, as well as Jean-Baptiste Pezon, whose enterprise had 30 lions, and who employed his sons Adrian and Edmond in the family's acts.[12] Edward Bostock sold to Pezon, Bidel and others some of the lions who had been bred from Wombwell's original lions; their lineage traced back to Wallace, the lion who toured with George Wombwell in the 1820s. One group sold to Bidel were accompanied by the keeper, Thomas Crouch, who worked with Bidel and who became known as the tamer Captain Ricardo; this group went to the USA.[13] The American Colonel Bone toured France in the

---

9   Bostock 1972 [1927], 69–70.
10 Bostock 1972 [1927], 68; Turner 1995, 21.
11 Le Roux & Garnier 1890, 150.
12 Le Roux & Garnier 1890, 138–46.

1880s with a lioness, billed as being extremely ferocious, although Le Roux recounts an anecdote suggesting that such fierce lions were not as aggressive as their promotional material claimed.[14] There were a number of tamers touring Europe including Miss Cora performing with a lion named Senide in Germany.[15]

The finale of Bidel's act involved a lamb's head being placed in the lion's mouth. As testimony to the social acceptance and even admiration of tamers, a poem by French actress Roselia Rousseil, 'The lion's death or the tamer by love', was dedicated to Bidel, who had become quite wealthy by then. It began by praising the beauty of a performer with Apollo's grace and Hercules' strength, and how his 'soft, dark eyes, are dear to me'.[16] Bidel was described as a 'famous' tamer working in a large cage with 'lions, lionesses, bears, hyenas and a lamb' and presenting 'feats of leaping ordinarily shown in such exhibitions but the main feature was the simultaneous approach of the wild animals to the lamb, and the exchange of "the kiss of fraternity"', which involved the animals touching noses and the lamb's head being placed into a lion's mouth.[17] In a performance in Turin, Italy, on 23 December 1872, the lion closed his jaws around the lamb. Suddenly, 'streams of blood were running from his mouth' as the spectators screamed and fainted. Bidel had to strike the lion on the head to get him to release the lamb. A lioness saw this as a chance to claw and bite at Bidel, but he managed to avoid serious injury, the thick fabric of his costume protecting his skin.

Gruesome occurrences that overlapped with the feeding exhibition did give notoriety to such shows, which were, by then, relatively common. Le Roux asks whether concern about an attack prevented a spectator from attending a show.

---

13 Bostock 1972 [1927], 253.
14 Le Roux & Garnier 1890, 146–47.
15 Kober 1931, 109. Hagenbeck 1909, 123. Those working in German menagerie acts included Kreutzberg, Martin, Kallenberg, Preuscher, Schmidt, Dagersell and Kaufmann.
16 Le Roux & Garnier 1890, 148, also 151.
17 *New York Clipper* 1873, Circuses, 18 January: 335. The details of the attack are from this source.

> Can I say that fear of such an accident is ever sufficiently strong to make me pause on the threshold of the menagerie? No, I cherish, and like me, you also cherish, the hope that some day perhaps we may see a lion-tamer eaten.[18]

Paul Hervieu was an eyewitness to a mishap in July 1886 in which Bidel tripped on his fork and fell during a performance at Neuilly. Sultan, a black-maned lion, took the opportunity and attacked. Bidel's coat was completely ripped, and his torn flesh exposed; Hervieu outlined the crowd's emotional reactions to this event. There were cries from the audience, followed by complete silence, and the hissing of the gas lighting could be heard as Sultan stopped and Bidel lay motionless. Then Sultan took two steps forward and put his paws on the tamer's shoulders. There was uproar among the audience with shouting and screaming. Hervieu felt that the lion played with the tamer, almost accidentally causing flesh and head wounds, until two attendants pushed forward with iron bars, and the lion stopped and retreated. Hervieu was 'distressed, horrified' but his companion was keen to see the attack unfold, and Hervieu also quoted someone behind him saying, 'I was for the lion.'[19]

The use of irons and heated irons with lion acts may have been contentious by the 1880s in Britain, even if head-in-the-mouth stunts and female tamers were permissible. A defence of menagerie practices in England implies that there was ongoing public concern about the spectacles, and about the treatment of menagerie animals. A story in an 1884 newspaper article claims: 'Among other erroneous ideas concerning the details of lion taming is that red-hot irons are kept in readiness in case of an accident.'[20] The article claims that the story arose because Manders' menagerie had older menagerie paraffin lamps that could glow red-hot. A spectator asked if they were used for the lions, and ever the showman, Manders gave a theatrically exaggerated response that they were used to support the tamer. The article indicates an effort to redeem the reputation of menageries by rejecting practices in which irons were routinely used on the animals or kept ready for emergencies.

---

18 Le Roux & Garnier 1890, 151, 152–57, citing Paul Hervieu's notes.
19 Cited in Le Roux & Garnier 1890, 157.
20 *Manchester Times* 1884, Lion taming, 23 August: 4–5.

Certainly Frank Bostock admitted that he stopped heating irons by 1890, and instead claimed that they were only used in winter to provide warmth and to heat water.[21]

Even in Britain, protective legislation against animal cruelty did not extend to exotic animals in menageries until 1900.[22] The law stated that depriving animals of food only applied to domesticated species and there did not seem to be restrictions on the use of iron prods against lions. Edward Bostock's rebuttal of the 19th-century claim that elephants, lions, camels and other large animals attack when they are ill treated pointed out that all male animals were liable to attack at certain times, which could be gauged by unusual feeding patterns, such as refusing food.[23] Eventually it was systematic animal husbandry and knowledgeable approaches that made it possible to discard irons and older crude methods of control by force for big cats. Feeding displays were phased out with the advent of, and touring of, more complex acts with trained animals by the turn of the 20th century.

Pomp and Conklin

By the 1870s a menagerie act in a lion's cage – sometimes wheeled into the circus ring – involved a jumping display and the animal lying down in a handling trick. The jumping trick was achieved by getting a lion accustomed to jumping over a low plank, then by raising the height of the plank, and sometimes placing a hoop on top of the plank for the lion to jump through. This could progress to the lion jumping over the bending figure of the tamer. In the handling trick, a lion could be made to lie down with the flick of a whip, and with pressure applied to his back, the tamer could stand over the lion and pull the jaws open. While this handling feat proved popular in attracting crowds, their responses

---

21 Bostock 1903, 162. Also see Ballantine 1958, 8, as the story continues in the 20th century with Clyde Beatty and Bill Ballantine repeating the story presented by Frank Bostock that dismisses the use of hot irons, claiming these were used for heating drinking water in cold weather. Bostock seems to be repeating a version of the 1884 newspaper story.
22 Assael 2005, Appendix, 161.
23 Bostock 1972 [1927], 256.

were mixed and often critical. For example, one commentator stated, 'This is a fool-hardy feat, in which risk is incurred, without exhibiting any intelligence, grace or docility on the part of the lion.'[24] While simple feats could be achieved as a result of repetition, this was not yet systematic or based on a full understanding of the bodily reactions of a species to others in proximity. The menagerie cage act still deployed basic forceful handling.

George Conklin's unusual working life spanned menagerie cage acts and circus ring performances, tamer and trained acts, and lion and elephant acts. One of Conklin's brothers was an acrobat, and another was a singing clown, so perhaps it was inevitable that Conklin would join a circus. He was hired to put up posters in advance of the show, although his father had wanted him to join the circus band.[25] Conklin became a cage boy to the lion tamer Charlie Forepaugh in the John O'Brien circus from 1867, then a night watchman, and eventually a lion tamer, performing at night in a menagerie tent that was lit by hundreds of candles in wooden racks. He moved to WW Cole's circus in 1875 when O'Brien sold the cage of lions. Conklin's account of how he began working with animals suggested that he was a keen observer and had taken the initiative, but he was well connected and by 1886 his brothers operated a menagerie, the Conklin Bros Great American Circus and Menagerie. They continued to do so in various partnerships in later years, but Conklin remained outside the family business, eventually becoming a leading American animal trainer. He stayed with Cole's for a decade, during which time Cole's undertook a tour to Australia and New Zealand, and sometime after 1886 became the head animal trainer with the Barnum and Bailey Circus The Greatest Show on Earth (BB), working with BB until 1906, including on tours to Europe.

Conklin achieved increasing complexity in his acts through close observation of the animals, and his work set precedents – although probably not as many as he claimed. His act in the late 1860s involved a lion cage that was placed on top of a wagon pushed into the circus ring by an elephant, and pistol shots indicative of a hunting act. For the anticipated and best-known feat, Conklin put his head halfway into the mouth of the lion Pomp. Conklin explains how, with one hand on

---

24 *New York Clipper* 1872, Lions and lion tamers, 13 April: 12.
25 Slout 1998, 55-56; Conklin 1921, 11–12, 79.

5 Head in the colonial lion's mouth

Pomp's nose and the other on his lower jaw, he would 'open his mouth as wide as possible and put my head in it as far as it would go which was about halfway.'[26] This act was intended to make 'the crowd hold its breath.'[27] While putting his head in Pomp's mouth was a crowd-pleasing feat, Conklin explained that it was less dangerous than it looked, because his hold on the lion's nose and the body around the jaw allowed him to detect even the smallest muscle movement. The act's climax was a contest over a piece of meat, and although Conklin did not chase the animals around the cage in a hunting action, he exited the cage while firing two or three pistol shots.

Conklin had watched Charlie Forepaugh at work for a season, including observing the head-in-the-mouth feat. After noting the audience's applause and the tamer's superior earning capacity, Conklin decided to try to become a lion tamer. He began to secretly rehearse with the lions at night. Forepaugh used three cages, one with the main lions Pomp, Nellie and George plus a leopard, Belle, and two cages with another eight lions. During his clandestine night-time rehearsals, Conklin practised the same feats as Forepaugh, but with all the lions in the same cage. When Forepaugh's contract was due to expire, Conklin approached the circus owner explaining that he could do a better act with all the lions together. Conklin perceived that the behaviour in a big group was not due to the tamer's mastery, but instead reflected the lions' social hierarchy. The lions followed a leader, and would even follow a lion leader who jumped over an object. Conklin also noted that a lion's noisy roars were misleading, since they were usually not a prelude to aggression.

In 1867, Conklin's first costume at O'Brien's was a Roman-style shift with spangled tights and a belt of leopard skin that cost him US$100.[28] The tamer act, which he had embellished based on Charlie Forepaugh's, was of a standardised, theatrical style, though the costuming reflected the aesthetic forged by Van Amburgh's generation. The action was also similar to Van Amburgh's: a ringmaster began by spruiking and exaggerating the danger that sent 'shivers down the spine

---

26   Conklin 1921, 37, also, 34.
27   Conklin 1921, 37, also 44–45.
28   Conklin 1921, 39–40, also 36–37. This would be equivalent to about six months' wages for the average worker.

of everyone'. The act involved the lions jumping over Conklin's raised leg, over a leopard with her hind legs held up by Conklin, and then, to confirm submission, he would lie across all three lions. After the head-in-the-lion's-mouth feat, 'I fed them all meat with my naked hands.'[29] This was followed by a type of 'tug-of-war' around the cage between Pomp and Conklin with a specially prepared, long thin strip of meat that Conklin and Pomp each held in their mouths. Here the feeding display was integrated into the act as a feat. The act's 'grand climax' involved the lions 'snarling and growling' and Conklin firing a pistol – later, a revolver. After the act finished, an elephant pushed the cage out of the ring.

As Conklin explained, his cage act had novelty value c. 1870, and was a lead attraction because the lions were loose inside the cage. He was also credited with getting a lion to dance. Conklin had observed how one lion seemed to respond to the band's music in each performance, and Conklin made waltzing gestures to frame an interaction with the lion, who did a 'dancing' movement on all fours. It was during an enactment of the waltz feat that one of the other lions bit into Conklin's thigh, and he was unable to perform for several weeks. Conklin's position as tamer seemed assured as the only replacement who came forward was, in the end, unable to enter the cage.

During the 1870s, the combined circus and menagerie shows that Conklin worked for consisted of as many as seven menagerie tents, erected along a path that led to the main circus tent.[30] Audiences had to walk through the tents with as many as 50 cages to enter the tent, which hosted the circus performance in the ring.

Over the course of three decades, Conklin conditioned 25 cages of lions, which he believed was more cages than anyone else in the USA at that time. In confronting a rebellious tiger, Conklin recounted throwing a stool as a last defence, giving Conklin the few seconds he needed to extract himself from the situation. A big cat found it hard to quickly visualise the four legs of a stool or chair, so a trainer had the advantage of additional seconds, if needed. Conklin's claim to have discovered the usefulness of holding up chair legs as a defensive

---

29 Conklin 1921, 37, also 38.
30 Conklin 1921, 152–53.

5 Head in the colonial lion's mouth

strategy may or may not be accurate, as Coup also mentioned this practice, and it was widely adopted.[31]

In addition to big cats, Conklin worked with elephants for 40 years. For a feat in which he lay on the ground while an elephant walked over him, he kept a long nail in his hand as a defensive strategy, which could be put into an elephant's foot (also see Chapter 6). He made competitive claims about his capacity to condition the movement of a wide range of animals, including bears, lions, tigers and elephants, and claimed that he was the first person to coach spotted hyenas to jump and run, and to teach a team of zebras to pull a cart.[32]

Conklin reports that for publicity in a newspaper feature, the hair was shaved off a monkey performer, who was described in before and after photographs as a missing link in evolution, reflecting 'some of Darwin's theories regarding animal expression', not to mention showmen who copied each other's ruses.[33]

Slightly before 1870, Conklin taught George the lion to growl and then jump at him when he blew on the lion's nose. Conklin would fire a pistol twice before exiting the cage as George jumped towards the closing door.[34] While the feat worked well for Conklin, he claimed, contradicting other reports, that it caused the death of another tamer. O'Brien managed a second cage tamer act with an ex-coachman, Joseph Whittle, and sent Conklin and Whittle's acts on different engagements during the 1871–72 winter season; Conklin performed two shows a day at Colonel Wood's Museum in Philadelphia. But Whittle attempted to usurp Conklin – as Conklin had Forepaugh – eventually replacing him after Conklin was refused more money for the 1872 season. Conklin claimed that he did not consider that Whittle would be given his cage of lions, and thus did not forewarn him about the routine with George. Consequently, when Whittle unwittingly gave the cue by exiting the cage, George did his usual action of jumping for the door, grazing

---

31   For example, see Cooper 1928, 30–31. The ex-Bostock trainer, Captain Ricardo, managed big cats with kitchen chairs. The prop of a stool or a chair became integral to 20th-century trained big cat acts.
32   Kober 1931, 48; Conklin 1921, 52–53, 73.
33   Conklin 1921, 206. See Goodall 2002, on PT Barnum and others and the 'missing link'.
34   Conklin 1921, 38–42.

Whittle's leg. This minor incident was followed by a second, far more serious attack when Whittle returned to the cage to assert his authority over George. When Whittle turned to again exit the cage, George jumped a second time.

A newspaper report about this attack on 2 April 1872, however, claimed that Whittle was attacked during a rehearsal of the head-in-the-mouth feat. The paper reported that just as he put his head in the lion's open jaw, the lion closed his jaw, 'the teeth cutting his chin and neck'.[35] It sounded more dramatic if Whittle was attacked during this feat, but it was more likely that Conklin's account was accurate, even if there were only one attack from George. Conklin also had a vested interest in claiming that George did not attack during the practised head-in-the-mouth sequence, as he might not have wanted to divulge his knowledge of the body-handling technique used in this feat, because his techniques set him apart from competing presenters. The newspaper account reported that several attendants tried to get the lion to unlock his hold on Whittle but this was only achieved when the cage scraper was forced between the lion's jaws. He released Whittle, but the lion sprang again at Whittle, jumping on his chest and grabbing him by the leg. The attendants forced the lion back into the partitioned cage, and eventually reached Whittle. He had his wounds sewn up by a doctor and was taken to hospital, but died two days later. Whatever caused the accident, in both accounts Whittle eventually died of blood poisoning. Conklin was asked to return to O'Brien's and he resumed his usual act, although in his first reappearance, attendants stood ready 'with irons to beat' off a lion.[36]

The 1872 *New York Clipper* edition describing Whittle's accident has an illustration with the caption, 'The beast tamer and his beasts', and shows the tamer dressed in tights and a body-fitting acrobat's suit of the type worn by a 19th-century circus gymnast, holding a whip. One lion jumps through a hoop held mid-air by a tamer, watched by a lioness who seems ready to spring up through the hoop, while three others crouch nearby. There was a second front-page illustration published shortly afterwards with the caption 'Perils of the lion tamer', and

---

35 *New York Clipper* 1872, 13 April: 15. The details of the attack for the second account come from this source.
36 Conklin 1921, 43.

it shows the tamer in a cage wearing a loose-fitting tunic, being attacked by two lions with their teeth sunk into his body.[37] Horrified spectators watch in the background beyond the cage bars, with vivid facial expressions and open mouths as if screaming.[38] The reader would have been left in no doubt as to the potential of the tamer becoming animal food.

Although there was a gradual cessation of auxiliary feeding displays, staged confrontation remained part of some big cat acts. Cage acts that fulfilled audience expectations with confronting stunts proved a durable attraction. But an act needed to be dynamic to remain competitive, and this could be achieved through noisy feats and energetic actions, although these carried more risks for presenters in small cages. Such approaches were discarded once lions, and to a lesser extent tigers, became a regular part of the circus performance during the 1890s. Trained individual animals were reliable performers of complex tricks and enriched the showmanship inside a much larger arena cage in the ring (see Chapter 6). While lions were ideal performers for these feats, since they communicate vocally in their social worlds, it was the performed reactions and gestures of a human to a rehearsed roar that highlighted ideas of danger and risk. The hunting big cat act, and its later versions, suited circus and its promotion of danger, an effect that was enhanced by the act's props, usually a whip and a gun firing blanks.[39] The theatricality confirmed a social preconception that big cats were innately aggressive.

Local 'crack fighting' goes global

Human fighting acts were programmed into travelling shows with animal acts, notably within colonial regions in the competitive decades after American circuses and menageries had travelled around Australia and New Zealand (Australasia). There had been some animal exhibition in British colonies prior to the establishment of zoological gardens in the 1850s.[40] But colonial concerns at that time were different from

---

37 *New York Clipper* 1872, 17 August: 153.
38 *New York Clipper* 1872, 17 August: 153.
39 The hurrah act was only phased out in the 1960s in American circus.
40 Gillbank 1996, 80–81.

European concerns about acclimatising introduced exotic animals; for example, acclimatisation debates in the colonies centred on the introduction of domesticated species from Britain and the rest of Europe. Animal collections only began to tour within the colonies after the 1870s with the precedent of menageries arriving with travelling American circuses that followed the trade networks. By then, the menagerie functioned as a form that can be equated with David Lambert and Alan Lester's trans-imperial forms, recognisable across the world (see Introduction).

Animal exhibition had developed in Australia and New Zealand about the same time as the circus, presenting animals from geographical regions nearer to Australasia than to Europe and North America. Mark St Leon writes: 'The exhibition in the colonies of wild animals – animals of African or Asian origin – dates from about the same time that the circus was introduced.'[41] By the late 1840s Beaumont and Walker's menagerie was installed in the grounds of a Sydney hotel, with elephants, kangaroos and emus roaming freely. While equestrian circuses in Australia date from 1847, they did not tour with an accompanying menagerie until the mid-1870s. As entertainment forms standardised globally, it is interesting to find that human fighting in and around a circus with a menagerie was also evident across colonial domains, and seems to have been even more pronounced onstage and offstage than in the empire centres. This can be contrasted with noticeably more prudish colonial attitudes to circus tamer acts in the colonies, even during the 1890s.

From the 1870s, whole large circuses regularly travelled global trade routes, long used by performer groups and small troupes; American circuses crossed the Pacific, and European ones travelled southwards through Asia following the shipping trade routes and ports.[42]

---

41   St Leon 1983, 55, also 22, and see for a short history of circus in Australia and its family circus histories; St Leon 2011.
42   See St Leon 1983, 35–39, 41, 47, about the Ashton's, Burton's and Jones' circuses in the 1850s to 1860s, and JA Rowe and Chiarini's circuses. Downes 1975, 27, 29; the first circuses to reach New Zealand were JA Rowe from San Francisco en route to Australia in 1852 and Foley's coming from Australia and reaching Nelson by 13 September 1855 with a 'temporary menagerie'. Foley's arrived with four cases of animals, including a 'wild and ferocious Bengal leopard'. Chiarini's would tour with a larger menagerie two decades later; an early example of a

5 Head in the colonial lion's mouth

There was 'a steady stream of the largest of American circuses' touring to Australia between 1873 and 1892.[43] The Cooper and Bailey Great American Circus arrived in Australia in 1876 with a lion act in which the tamer put his head into the lion's mouth. The accompanying menagerie animals included three elephants, one of whom, Titania, was billed as trained, and there was a giraffe that might have been stuffed, rather than alive. While most of the acts in the circus ring were still equestrian and/or acrobatic, including a solo trapeze act, the two novelty acts were those by Professor GW Johnson, presenting Titania and working in the lion's den. His act was advertised as compelling:

> the lions to perform various feats in full view of the public. He will discharge pistols while in the cage, and place his head in the lion's mouth, and feed them with raw meat from the naked hand.[44]

This was a hunting act with a head-in-the-mouth stunt and a feeding stunt.

George Wirth saw his first elephant at Cooper and Bailey's in 1876 – he also mentions that the first hippopotamus arrived in Australia in 1891.[45] Three circuses arrived in Australia in 1876; Cooper and Bailey's, John Wilson's circus from San Francisco, and the Royal Tycoon Circus from Asia with Indian and Japanese acrobats. But the latter could not survive financially and was bought out by Mr Ridge and the Wirth family, and the remnants of the Royal Tycoon became part of an Australian show that toured regional Australia. John Wirth, a musician, had played with the Australian Ashton's circus band for a short time after 1870, where his sons became circus trained. Later, the John Wirth family formed Wirth's Circus in 1880, and it developed into one of the larger tenting circuses touring Australia and New Zealand, accompanied by a human fighting act. Wirth's toured to South Africa

---

touring circus with some menagerie animals was Chiarini's Royal Italian Circus and Performing Animals.
43 St Leon 1983, 73; Wittmann 2012.
44 Wirth 1925, 142, reproduction of the Cooper and Bailey Circus program, 25 January 1877.
45 Wirth 1925, 10–11, 61. The Ashtons worked with Royal Tycoon Circus. Two hippopotamuses arrived with Sells Bros Circus and Hippodrome and were paraded around a hippodrome track.

in 1893 and 1894, continued on to South America and Britain, and returned to Australia via Asia in 1900.[46] The Wirth's acts with horses were highly skilled, and in the early 1900s May Wirth became a world-leading equestrian working in the USA.

Fights seemed to be an unavoidable consequence of the travelling life in Australasia, and George Wirth recounts how his father, John, broke up a three-person fight in a hotel between Ashton's star acrobat and horse rider, the Indigenous Australian performer Combo (Combo Combo), another Indigenous Australian performer, Callaghan, and the bandmaster George Smidth. John had to bodily separate the two men, depositing Smidth outside through a window, and throwing Combo.[47] The fight may or may not have involved a racial slur, since skilful Indigenous performers were respected in the circus, if not in society. Members of Wirth's circus touring after 1880 encountered fights and comparable troubles in a range of situations, from an insulting confrontation in the street to the more generalised threat that newcomers to a town faced. The memoirs of the Wirth brothers, George and Philip, outlined staged fights, spontaneous street fights, and encounters with colonial soldiers. George also outlined the struggle of maintaining an entertainment business; Wirth's faced intense competition from rival circuses trying to reach a town before them. In Australia it was inevitably the weather that caused the most difficulty for a tenting circus touring most of the year.

The staging of a fight within a show required an accomplished fighter. Wirth's hired the American tumbler and horizontal bar performer Dick Mathews, who was more than six feet (1.9m) tall. Initially Mathews watched as several of Wirth's 'champions' were beaten by 'the best of the town fighting men'.[48] He became Wirth's fighter after he won a fight with a cheat at a game of cards. Mathews very effectively

---

46 Wirth no date, 56, 106. This book is similar to Wirth 1925, although shorter with a less continuous narrative, and Philip claims the initiative of the menagerie. The foreword describes how Wirth's travelled in the early decades of the 20th century by rail in a special train, with 10 elephants in eight rail cars and rail cars with other menagerie animals. The menagerie reached small towns without zoos and opened at 4 pm, well before the circus performance began at 8 pm.
47 Wirth 1925, 10, also 30–32. For a history of Indigenous circus performers who became world renowned, see St Leon 1993.
48 Wirth 1925, 31.

evaded wild swinging punches and those who rushed towards him. Philip Wirth explained that there was an expectation of a fight with the arrival of a touring show. He writes:

> It was a long established custom at the time, for the crack fighting man of each country town to challenge any member of a show that was showing there. There were many fine fighters in most of the places at which we stopped and one season through the Monaro [region of southern New South Wales, Australia] we could produce no boxer to cope with the local men until a young man named Dick Mathews joined up with us ... [H]is continued success made him, for a time, our greatest drawing card.[49]

Mathews had to fight several men in the Monaro, including the local champion, and henceforth undertook the contest with any local fighter who came forward. A district's recognised strongest fighter would try to outdo an opponent on behalf of the locals. But there were also separately organised travelling sideshows with boxing exhibitions that invited and thrived on the participation of the locals – possibly raising expectations that all travelling shows involved that type of fighting.[50] The practice of hand-to-hand fighting became more formalised once there was a champion.

George explains that Wirth's encountered 'plenty of opposition in those days, and many a fight to gain supremacy.'[51] It was not that fighting behaviour was simply assumed to be indicative of an innate nature. George also suggests that the fighting behaviour of young men was influenced by stories about a schoolboy character, Jack Harkaway. Clearly, influential Jack adventure stories circulated within the colonies, too.

Colonies in the Pacific region began settlement as military garrisons and transplanted fighting cultures. A Wirth's tour to Noumea, New Caledonia, in 1888 encountered French soldiers stationed there, operating an island prison for convicts. It was here that Wirth's

---

49 Wirth no date, 37. The quote in this version is more succinct than in Wirth 1925.
50 See Broome & Jackomos 1998.
51 Wirth 1925, 32.

slack-rope performer, Charlie Redman, was killed in a street fight.[52] Back in Australia, Wirth's circus men were attacked by a local football crowd and were only saved from serious injury by the intervention of the local police. Performers provoked fights offstage, at times through drunken behaviour.

The performers were presented in onstage fights and wars that seemed to offer an implicit invitation for fighting responses from the public. In 1890 in Auckland, New Zealand, Wirth's presented a Wild West Show – most probably riding Australian horses – reproducing a version of 'Barnum and Bailey's Three Ring Circus, Hippodrome and Wild West Combined Shows'.[53] Harry Wirth had travelled to San Francisco and engaged Jack Sutton, an originator of Wild West performances, to hire a group of Native Americans and several cowboys from ranches to perform in the show. Native Americans might have been legendary fighters in battle, but the loss of their land and other enforced circumstances led a number to work – often unhappily – in entertainment spectacles. While New Zealand audiences were not overly impressed by the warlike fighting and horseriding, the lassoing displays provoked a craze that led authorities to ban the practice in public places. Emulating their staged battle re-enactments, the American cowboys and the Native American performers were constantly in trouble for fighting each other or the townspeople. George Wirth claimed that on one occasion, he had to have some performers knocked unconscious and carried to the train in order to get them to the next town.

In another instance, the lack of warlike fighting promised by a show sparked the fighting responses of the townspeople. The 1890s Wirth's show usually finished with '"The Hunter's Cabin" – a scene in which Indians shoot the hunter, scalp him, and burn his cabin', but for one show in the New Zealand town of Palmerston North, the cabin did not arrive. Instead, a lassoing display finished the show, and the disappointed audience hissed and demanded their money back. The aggravation spread, and audience members began cutting ropes and destroying the tent. There was a 'tearing down and breaking of seats' until the cowboy and Native American performers lined up on their horses, 'like an army of cavalry with drawn revolvers well loaded', and

---

52 Wirth 1925, 40–43.
53 Wirth 1925, 49–50, also 52–53.

5 Head in the colonial lion's mouth

fired over the heads of the crowd.[54] An audience member climbed onto a pedestal and urged the crowd to attack, but George Wirth had mobilised the rest of the performers and, armed with pick handles and sticks, they marched against the mob and dispersed them.

The issue of crowd control remained a constant concern. In Australia, Wirth's had competition from the British Harmston's circus. It hired Wirth's cowboys but presented fake, painted Native Americans. In Sydney, thousands of local men rushed into Wirth's enclosure without paying for the show, which featured horsemen lassoing bulls. But the horsemen galloped through 'the crowd of larrikins',[55] 'and virtually mowed them down', with several casualties.[56] By 1893 Wirth's competition came from another Australian circus – that of the Fitzgerald Brothers[57] – and the circus of Frank Fillis, which included a menagerie and arrived from southern Africa via Singapore. Wirth's went directly to southern Africa.

To further complicate matters in southern Africa, staged fighting acts began to converge with the offstage conflict. Wirth's staged episodes of colonial conflict from the Matabele wars of 1893 and 1896 in what is now Zimbabwe, called 'Major Wilson's Last Stand or Fighting to Save the Queen's Colours'.[58] The performance re-enacted a battle in which a handful of soldiers from the British South Africa company were surrounded by the Impi indigenous people of Matabele.[59] The latter, however, were played by 100 Zulu warriors with spears and cowhide shields, who became enthusiastically involved in the re-creation. George Wirth describes how the fight became a serious battle as the Zulu performers 'came at me with such ferocity' with clubs, forcing him to gallop through them. He continues: 'They were all very much excited over their seemingly [sic] success over the whites, and for

---

54   Wirth 1925, 55–56.
55   Larrikin, in the Australian vernacular, can mean a social nonconformist or a rowdy or mischievous person. The older usage here has a negative connotation, meaning lout, and implying a person in search of a physical fight.
56   Wirth 1925, 59, also 62–63. One of the cowboys from the USA who had been working with Wirth's had been in trouble with the law and, deemed an outlaw for stealing cattle, he had escaped to Australia.
57   See Arrighi 2009.
58   Cited in Wirth 1925, 82.
59   Wirth 1925, 82.

a long time that night after the performance they were still yelling and making passes at the people who attended the performance.'[60]

The government feared an uprising and instructed Wirth's to stop re-enactments of the conflict. In the colonies, the requisite separation between current warfare and mock fighting in theatrical battle re-enactment was tenuous, if not non-existent, for disenfranchised indigenous peoples.

In South America, Wirth's encountered violence that ranged from local street fights to the crowd's indignation about war between nation-states. There were spectators who refused to pay; a spectator who fired a gun at moving acrobats mid-air; unscrupulous businessmen; and fights with locals in public.[61] Philip Wirth recalls that

> [i]t was also quite startling to see the youths of the city indulging in fights with daggers, in the streets, just as we see the youngsters at home sparring good naturedly, but these lads are, however, so expert with their weapons that there is rarely any damage done.[62]

But in Pernambuco, Brazil, in 1895, Wirth's circus suddenly found itself in the middle of a crowd enraged by the threat of war. During the performance, '[t]he news had got about that England had annexed the island of Trinidad [in the Caribbean] from Brazil', causing Brazilians in the crowd to seek out British spectators to attack.[63] Most of the British escaped from the Brazilians by leaving at interval by boat, rather than over land. Wirth's departed quickly from South America, and became the first Australian circus to perform in England, working there for 18 months. On 18 May 1898, the company performed for the Prince of Wales at Southport. Wirth's return trip to Australia by way of southern Africa was cut short due to the escalating Boer War, and the circus hastily departed again, travelling instead through South-East Asia to complete a world tour.

While circus productions expanded on earlier 19th-century war shows, all types of fighting and conflict seemed unavoidable for circuses

---

60   Wirth 1925, 82.
61   Wirth 1925, 89, 93, 94–95, 98–99.
62   Wirth no date, 74–75.
63   Wirth 1925, 100, also 107.

and shows with animals that travelled in Australia and New Zealand and other colonial regions. Since there does not seem to be any circus depiction of the resistance of Indigenous Australians to colonial rule or the Maori wars of resistance, it is likely that war re-enactments followed the precedents set in British and American shows (see Chapter 6). Maori war arts, however, would eventually be performed in Britain.[64] While shows in the colonies exposed a continuum of violence from street fights to war re-enactments, geographically specific ongoing political conflicts and wars between settlers and indigenous peoples were masked by the adoption of generic war acts in the staged performance. The battles fought by Native Americans could seem unconnected to colonial struggles in Australasia, except that the depiction of hostilities provoked violent responses from members of the audience. War re-enactment continued to be an extension of actual warfare as it ignited a sense of injustice and antagonism, the underlying emotional impetus.

Morbid bad taste?

As Wirth's circus travelled to perform and tour in southern Africa in 1893 and 1894, a newspaper debate arose in New Zealand over the big cat act and its head-in-the-mouth stunt touring with Frank Fillis' circus and menagerie from southern Africa, which additionally reignited controversy about female presenters. Fillis' circus had toured through South-East Asia to Australia, and on to New Zealand, where it was on a second tour of major towns during 1894. Floris van der Merwe's biography of Fillis remarks that he was called 'the "Barnum" of South Africa' because he was an extremely adventurous large-show entrepreneur.[65]

Fillis was born into an English circus family and became an equestrian like his father and his uncle, working at Hengler's Circus in England before travelling to South Africa to join Bell's circus in 1880. There, he performed the longstanding staple riding acts of the English circus, such as 'Dick Turpin's Ride to York' and 'Mazeppa'. By 1884,

---

64   Werry 2011, 125. Performances with Maoris downplayed warlike dimensions.
65   van der Merwe 2007, 130.

Fillis was running his own circus, billed as the largest in the southern African colonies, and by December 1884 it included an auxiliary zoo tent and an African elephant named Jumbo looked after by a keeper named Funny Francis. The next year Fillis bought an Indian elephant, Bob, for £580 in England. Although he admitted to resorting to what can only be considered severe force, using chains and starvation techniques, eventually the elephant would ride a bicycle, play a mouth organ, stand on his head, and walk on his hind legs. Fillis' memoir, *Life and adventures of Frank E Fillis* (1901), is republished in van de Merwe's biography of him.

Expanding on his Zulu war re-enactments, Fillis took his show 'Savage South Africa' to London in 1899, and in 1904 he created the Anglo-Boer War re-enactment show in the USA for the St Louis World's Exposition (see Chapter 6).

Newspaper coverage in England during the 1870s and 1880s suggests that although there was criticism of menagerie acts, they were widely accepted. However, specific controversies arose in Australia and New Zealand between 1892 and 1894 regarding female tamers and big cat stunts in Fillis' circus. Although Fillis conceded to the protests and removed female tamers from his acts in Australia in 1892 and in New Zealand in 1894, he continued presenting the big cat act with the controversial head-in-the-mouth feat in both Australia and New Zealand. The stunt became the topic of extended debate during the second 1894 tour of New Zealand, specifically about the handler, John Cox, putting his head in the big cat's mouth and other handling stunts which critics believed made his act demeaning to humans. Fillis' memoir exposed a thinly disguised opportunism in relation to publicity that corresponded with Barnum's style of promotion, raising the possibility that Fillis might have relished publicity gained from these controversies.

The 1894 newspaper debate was precipitated by a small attack during a performance in Christchurch, New Zealand, that drew increased public attention to the presence of the lion- and tiger-handling acts in Fillis' circus. On 10 January 1894, the big cat handler, Cox, was in the process of putting his head into the mouth of a Bengal tiger named Scindia when she closed her jaws and bit his face.

The circus program was predominantly equestrian displays, acrobatics and aerial acts, but it also included acts with elephants, lions, tigers and bears, and monkeys as jockeys. In Christchurch it was very

5 Head in the colonial lion's mouth

well received, except for the head-in-the-mouth stunt, which was described as 'needlessly repulsive' and degrading to both, in a considerate acknowledgement of the animal.[66] A review of the performance supported the appearance of the big cats, but not that particular stunt; it does seem to have been omitted in some subsequent performances.

While Cox's wound was not serious – he performed later – 'the incident caused considerable consternation among the audience'.[67] As well, a 'young lady was to have entered the lion's cage, but the police prohibited her doing so'. It is unclear if this woman was another circus performer. The full routine for the cage act in Fillis' circus must be surmised in the absence of further explanation, but it was probably performed in a confined small menagerie cage on a wagon wheeled into the circus performance space rather than in the larger arena cages that came into use during the 1890s.

Although a tamer was able to detect any muscle movement of the jaw, as Conklin explained, the feat required the trainer to exercise bodily strength and agility when handling the animal. How experienced was Cox when he undertook the feat with a tiger? Although there seemed to have been a turnover of tamers with Fillis', Cox, who was probably initially the elephant presenter, had been billed as a big cat tamer by March 1893 – so he had at least a year's experience before the incident in Christchurch.

The controversy in New Zealand may have surprised even Fillis, who had toured there the year before with a season in Wellington between 17 and 27 May, and in Auckland between 14 and 26 June 1893.[68] But there may have been a less developed big cat act on the first tour. After the shows in Christchurch in 1894, Fillis' very large circus was in Wellington by 13 January, with special trains organised to take people to and from where the circus tent was mounted in the city area. In a short extract quoting the theatrical newspaper *Lorgnette*, the Fillis show was described as being 'decidedly the best circus' that New Zealand had had since the 1879 Chiarini circus tour. The elephants and big cats pass unmentioned among comments that

---

66   *New Zealand Mail* 1894, 19 January: 27.
67   *New Zealand Mail* 1894, 12 January: 19, also 18.
68   van der Merwe 2007, 113. The 1893 program for Fillis Great Circus and Menagerie Wellington season Grand Debut Performance, 16 May 1893.

the 'company is a very strong one' and the acrobatic 'Feeley [sic] family are the great draw'.[69] A preference for acrobatic acts by humans may well reflect older circus tastes and their dominance of the equestrian circus before the 1890s. Alternatively, it might have indicated a wish to avoid controversy.

A writer with the nom de plume Scrutator refused to call Cox's act a performance and demanded it be banned, claiming, 'it is high time that such exhibitions were forcibly stopped by the authorities', since they cause 'the degradation of a noble animal' with 'the proprietor and the performer [being] equally and alone to blame, and not the lions'.[70] The strongly worded statement calls a handler entering a big cat cage 'idiotic', and questions why Fillis would continue to allow an act in which Cox 'mauls' the animals. It continues that if the presenter were seriously injured, the horrified public might be spared further 'insensate and degrading' displays and meanwhile the putting of heads in animal mouths should be 'forbidden forthwith' by law. Scrutator condemned the human handler for holding the animal's jaws open and explained that his views were confirmed by newspapers in Christchurch. A succession of big cat presenters with Fillis' circus suggested that Scrutator was mistaken in his belief that an injury would finish the act.

Fillis wrote letters to the editors of the *New Zealand Times* and the *New Zealand Mail* in response. He writes in defence of 'the dangerous practice of performing with wild animals' since those in his circus were born in captivity, and no longer posed the dangers of 30 years before, when animals were taken from the wild and entry to the cage required 'sheer pluck' on the part of the trainer.[71] He may have been mistaken about greater compliance from those born in captivity (see Chapter 6). Further, Fillis' defence claims he provides adequate care for the animals and space to move around in. He continues that they could be let out of the cage up until two years of age, were caressed, and did not really pose a risk to handlers or to the public. Fillis' tone is measured, but indignant, and unwittingly reveals that the wild animals

---

69   *New Zealand Mail* 1894, 19 January: 2.
70   *New Zealand Mail* 1894, 19 January: 21.
71   *New Zealand Mail* 1894, 26 January: 19, includes the folllowing quotation about rousing lions.

5 Head in the colonial lion's mouth

in his circus were increasingly placid, and needed to be roused 'to create the certain measure of excitement necessary to entertain the public'. Fillis compares the act to the risks of injury associated with those in sports, including horseracing, and explains that Cox's small accident was unusual, and entirely his mistake, rather than an unprovoked attack by a vicious tiger.

While Fillis does not directly counter the 19th-century view that it was demeaning for humans to handle animal bodies, his defence suggests that he might well have been aware of the broader concerns about animal welfare and longstanding debates over menagerie exhibitions in England and the rest of Europe. The anxiety that was directly and defensively addressed by Fillis was about the dangers of attack when wild animals were close to humans, which was perceived as a display of human bravery and fearlessness.

Scrutator replies in the same edition to Fillis' letter, and, claiming to speak on behalf of the majority who were the 'reasonable-minded public', he disputes Fillis' claims about harmless docility, explaining, 'it does not in the least shake my contention that for a performer to stick his head in a tiger's or elephant's mouth is a repulsive and disgusting sight'.[72] He reasons that if the tigress was so placid, why had Cox not continued with his feat? Scrutator's commentary continues, '[a]s to the effect upon the public I noticed that out of about fifteen ladies and children in my immediate neighbourhood, fully ten turned their chairs a little to one side ... and on all sides I heard expressions of fear and disgust', contending that the public does not wish to witness dangerous sports. In arguing against shows that pander to morbid public tastes, Scrutator outlines a belief that the authorities should regulate family animal entertainment.

It might be tempting to view Scrutator's position as an indication of socially progressive values, but his criticism arises primarily from an anthropocentric position, rather than from concern about animal wellbeing. The handling of the animal was part of the reason for his rejection because it implied no separation between humanity and animality. The entertainment undermined a 19th-century vision of the advancement of human society with the spread of imperial culture

---

72 *New Zealand Mail* 1894, 26 January: 23.

that relegated close contact between humans and non-human animals to the primitivism of the past. Physical handling made humans seem animal-like, closer to nature. It was the threat to the moral standing and distinctiveness of humans within an implicit hierarchy that came to the fore in Scrutator's comments. The debate also suggested that there were probably additional insecurities in the British settler colonies that arose from their geographical distance from the British and European centres of culture. If animal stunts were popular as entertainment, their degrading effect only reinforced the status of the colonial settlement as not yet civilised.

By the 1890s a prudish protestation about a tiger stunt may arguably have been belated and hypocritical. There had been a tiger den and performer billed in New Zealand 20 years earlier.[73] In an extended review of the 1894 New Zealand tour with Cox, there was also an indication of the popularity of Cox and his act when he 'received quite an ovation on coming forward', although 'the spectator breathes more freely when he is again out of the cages in safety'.[74] Here was evidence of audience support for the big cat act; the head-in-the-mouth stunt may have been omitted. Any reactions of fear and disgust would have been outweighed by the applause and no doubt lucrative box-office income.

Fillis claims that his circus had been 'well-received everywhere in Australia' the year before, in 1893.[75] He omits mention of negative publicity in Sydney about the appearance of a woman, Madame Jasia Scheherazade, in the lion act in 1892, and also in Melbourne in 1893 when the handler, Captain Russell, was attacked – Russell seemed to have replaced Captain Humphrey. Pre-show publicity in Sydney in 1892 promised Madame Jasia would 'tackle the gory carnivora in their lair'.[76] It would have been the first act with a female presenter to be seen in Australia. But only Captain Russell appeared in Sydney after

---

73 Downes argued that circus had become accepted from the 1850s. *New Zealand Mail* 1879, 29 November: 3. Chiarini's Royal Italian Circus and Performing Animals Bill advertised: 'Among the Wild Animals – the finest and freshest ever submitted for the public approval and appreciation – will be found a Den of Performing Royal Bengal Tigers! which will be introduced to the audience by Charles Warner, the intrepid Tiger Tamer, who handles these ferocious beasts without the slightest fear.'
74 *New Zealand Mail* 1894, 19 January: 27.
75 *New Zealand Mail* 1893, Fillis circus, 12 May: 32.

a newspaper report of a scandalised protest led to the intervention of the premier of New South Wales, Sir George Dibbs, who banned the woman from appearing in the act. In Sydney, Fillis presented a water pantomime instead of a female tamer, and the show ran from 19 November 1892 until mid-January 1893. It met with a favourable reception and humorous praise for the 'larrikin' lion, Pasha (also spelt Pacha), who was perceived as an equal of Fillis.[77]

In January 1893, the 'excellent' show opened in Melbourne with an act in which an elephant and a pony had supper, and were served by a monkey waiter. The program included a performer named Bertie on high trapeze with a 50-foot dive to a net, a trainer putting his head into an elephant's mouth, and the final act involved the tall Captain Russell, in a 'red Hussar costume' carrying a whip, in a cage with four lions, culminating in the lions jumping through blazing hoops.[78] Russell was billed as a decorated soldier.

A January review in the *Argus* commented that at one point Russell lost his footing and had a lion standing over him until Fillis fired a rifle and the lions scattered. The next edition of the newspaper reports that 'though the affair caused alarm, probably few people considered that Captain Russell had been in serious danger ... [although he] had been very severely bitten by the lion Pacha'.[79] Below the report was a letter to the *Argus* editor that contradicted the statements that spectators thought it was a minor incident. The letter describes how a lion 'jumped' at Russell and 'no words can depict the groan of horror that escaped the frightened audience'. 'It is repugnant to civilised feeling that

---

76   *Bulletin* 1893, 19 November: 6. The show promoted 'two lion-tamers – one of them a lady'. The female presenter may have appeared in one show. *Sydney Morning Herald* 1892, 21 November: 6. The evening concluded with 'Captain W.E. Russell – a man born to command, rule and subjugate beasts' ... [that is] 'four huge Nubian lions on Saturday evening no-one would begrudge the three medals for valour whilst in the army, and seven gold medals for courageous displays' with 'ferocious brutes' and getting them to skip, run and leap in the act.
77   *Bulletin* 1892, 26 November: 8, reviewed. *Bulletin* 1893, 28 January: 6, Russell 'fell down in the den, and Pasha the larrikin lion, all but ate him'. *Bulletin* 1892, 4 February: 9, 'next to Pacha in public estimation comes Fillis' and this edition includes an extended description of the event as a poem.
78   *Argus* 1893, 23 January: 6.
79   *Argus* 1893, The lion act at Fillis's circus, 24 January: 6.

such exhibitions should be given', especially as the defence provided by Fillis was that 'such feeling ceases' after repeated viewing, which was tantamount to becoming 'effectively brutalised'.[80] The letter argued that familiarity accustomed observers to brutish behaviour and thus destroyed the morally upright human values that, the author implied, underpinned civilisation.

Clearly spectators were disturbed to witness an attack. There is a further retort of 'unadulterated nonsense' and memory loss to Fillis' claim about the lack of danger, especially as the performer was hospitalised for weeks after lion Pasha attacked.[81] Certainly the full houses in the 1893 Melbourne season attested that attendance was not affected by newspaper reports that a lion knocked down Russell on opening night. Even if there were some exaggeration, Russell still required recovery time from his injuries in January 1893, while Fillis' circus played to full houses, introducing the Bengal tiger in the next week, and later presenting a re-enactment of the Zulu wars.[82]

Cox was named as presenter by week five; a turnover of handlers for the big cats was apparent in several years. A 'daring young gentleman' spectator, Mr JF McMillan, also entered the cage.[83] The last 1893 Melbourne performance was a major event on the social calendar, with the acting governor and naval and military personnel in the audience, all respected members of the establishment.[84] Their attendance again reinforced the convergence of an experience of military service and socio-political authority with support for animal shows and war re-enactments.

---

80 *Argus* 1893, The exhibition with lions at Fillis's circus, 24 January: 6.
81 *New Zealand Mail* 1894, 26 January: 23.
82 *Argus* 1893, 30 January 1893: 7; *Argus* 1893, 6 February: 7; *Argus* 1893, 13 February: 7; *Argus* 1893, 21 February: 6. These staged wars were probably based on shows first staged in England.
83 *Argus* 1893, 6 March: 6.
84 *Argus* 1893, 13 March: 6.

5 Head in the colonial lion's mouth

Publicity dares

The removal of Madame Jasia Scheherazade in Sydney from a cat act and of an unnamed female big cat presenter in Christchurch was a concession to colonial anxieties and raised the question as to why a female tamer was considered more unacceptable in the two colonies than the controversial head-in-the-mouth stunt. Ironically perhaps, women in New Zealand led the world in achieving suffrage at that time. Paternalistic values clearly affected social attitudes, since the female tamer was removed in 1892 in Australia due to the intervention of politicians, and in New Zealand in 1894 when expressions of public concern brought in police. The prohibition in Christchurch was not overturned until 1902, when female spectators undertook dares to appear in the big cat cage or drive a chariot pulled by trained lions.[85] Yet this was not a uniform rejection of female tamers in the British colonies, as they appeared elsewhere on tour with Fillis' circus before and after the Australasian tour.

The lions in big cat acts came from Europe, although Fillis' circus toured southern Africa, where lions originated. Fillis presented an English style of circus there in 1885, including a staging of English hunting,[86] a version of the act called 'The Royal Stag Hunt'. He would have known it from Hengler's circus, where it was performed from 1857 to 1888. The act involved a stag chased by riders on horses, accompanied by hounds. There were probably lions in Fillis' menagerie accompanying the circus by 1887. These were widely seen, judging by an anecdote that quotes Cecil Rhodes; Rhodes later acquired a pet lion, Fanny, who featured in political criticism of Rhodes.[87] The publicity-seeking Fillis was presenting African animals, including the so-named Jumbo, when he organised festivities in Kimberley, in southern Africa, in 1887 for Queen Victoria's Jubilee, with the continent of Africa represented by an indigenous presenter 'with a real leopard by his side'.[88] Apparently this 'perfectly tame' leopard was restrained only by a chain while riding aboard a wagon through a large crowd, and a 10-year-old

---

85   *Lyttleton Times* 1902, 18 February: 5.
86   van der Merwe 2007, 81.
87   van der Merwe 2007, 53; Malherbe 1999, 27–32.
88   van der Merwe 2007, 54.

boy who got too close was 'scalped'. Fillis would have been aware of the huge risk with an uncaged big cat in a crowd, but could have been emulating Sanger's tableau with a lion.

Fillis sought to attract public attention with his acts. The first imported lion act in a small cage with Fillis' circus included cubs; it arrived in southern Africa in January 1888 with the tamer Salvator Bugeja.[89] Bugeja had worked at BB, Folies-Bergères in Paris, and at London's Alexandra Palace. The lead act in Fillis' circus program in 1888, however, was Lazel's human cannonball projectile stunt, imitative of Farini's patented Zazel cannonball act.[90] Eliza (Elise) Mayol was Lazel, who was shot from the cannon with a new spring mechanism, to be caught mid-air by Miss Alexandra, hanging upside down from a trapeze. Mayol became Fillis' second wife. Despite the considerable risks of a dangerous projectile act, it may have been a more reliable top act. Just 11 months after he joined Fillis' circus with his lions, Bugeja was attacked and badly injured. The replacement act with husband-and-wife tamers Carlo and Idola Popper had four lions acquired from Salomonsky's circus in Russia.[91] The act arrived in Africa on 21 March 1888 with Idola performing.

In 1890 Fillis claimed that the menagerie zoo travelling with the circus did not generate sufficient income to feed all the lions, cheetahs, leopards, wolves, baboons, hyenas and the elephant, and he seemed to have engineered newspaper publicity by falsely reporting that an escape had caused mayhem.[92] Fillis resorted to publicity stunts on an ongoing basis, and to improve flagging box-office income in April 1890 he persuaded a boxer from southern Africa to agree to enter the lion's cage in a convergence of fighting entertainments. As this did not improve the financial situation Fillis relinquished some animals and travelled abroad with a much smaller number. It was with this reduced menagerie that Fillis embarked on the tour of India, Singapore, Australia and New Zealand in October 1890; the circus remained on tour until November 1894. Even so, accompanying Fillis' on the 1893 to 1894 tour of Australia and New Zealand were four lions, a black

---

89   van der Merwe 2007, 84–85.
90   Peacock 1996, 227–37; Tait 2005, 48–51.
91   van der Merwe 2007, 87–89
92   van der Merwe 2007, 88.

panther, a Bengal tiger, a leopard, a bear, monkeys, gorillas, zebras, 50 to 60 horses, a kangaroo and five elephants.[93]

After surviving a railroad accident in India in 1892, Fillis returned to Singapore to open his show on 28 May 1892. The lion act included Madame Jasia Scheherazade, probably in a partnership with a male tamer. When Madame Jasia (possibly Mrs Russell, although she is also named as Mrs Humphreys) appeared, a noticeable number of female spectators moved nearer the exit.[94] This may have reflected a fear that a woman might not be able to maintain control of wild animals, but spectator unease was not the same as official intervention to remove her from the act. The tour travelled south and reached Sydney, Australia, where Madame Jasia was banned.

The issue of wild animal handling proved more contentious than even the atypical extreme athleticism displayed by muscular female acrobats in other circus acts. Philippa Levine summarises how the colonies were a pioneering masculine-dominated culture and, towards the late 19th century, 'celebrated a very particular vision of white maleness as physical, responsible, productive, and hard-working', qualities denied to women and indigenous peoples.[95] Thus Levine suggests femininity was characterised by a 'lack of physical prowess', 'delicacy' and 'nervousness', and at the same time, 'women's place in society stood as an index of civilization'. Femininity was indicative of cultured gentility and thus emblematic of how colonial development brought civilisation. Its contravention undermined colonial rule – leaving aside women's labour in the domestic sphere. In that framework an expectation of the social dependence of women was measured against the physical prowess of men, and in frontier colonial settlement those physical displays included the dominance of other species, and activities such as hunting. Accordingly, women needed to be protected from large animals capable of hunting humans.

Female circus performers, like theatre performers, evaded some of the restrictions on social behaviour. For example, Australia's renowned high-wire walker, Ella Zuila, also performed in southern Africa before travelling to the USA in 1880 to become a lead act in Forepaugh's

---

93 van der Merwe 2007, 118.
94 van der Merwe 2007, 112–13.
95 Levine 2004b, 7.

circus.[96] But a female handler of African wild animals, rather than of domesticated species like horses, directly confronted social propriety in Australia and New Zealand. She seemed to challenge more than vague sensitivities about what constituted the limits of socially respectable behaviour in public, though the norms were routinely breached in entertainment. There were no aggressive animals like lions in Australia and New Zealand, so that the human–big cat act with a female presenter directly disturbed the gendered premise within a fledgling colonial society.

It seemed, however, that a female tamer or a woman entering the cage of a big cat was more acceptable in the African homeland of the lion. Back in the southern African colonies in 1895, where Fillis' circus promoted Herr Winschermann wrestling a tiger, it was acceptable for the newly wed Mrs Winschermann to enter the cage alone, and another unnamed woman even danced in the cage.[97] In further publicity stunts, Fillis offered prize money to anyone willing to enter the lions' cage.

By 1900 the practice of encouraging a spectator, and especially a young woman, to enter the wild-animal cage for publicity was also followed by Wirth's in Australia. A barmaid from Ballarat, Miss Graham, who was 'fleshy, fair and fascinating', entered the tigers' cage with the trainer and the tigers Pasha and Prince, and drank a glass of champagne.[98] The stunt became a topic of newspaper discussion, and a humorous fake funeral business advertisement in the same newspaper edition offered to embalm Miss Graham. The advertisement explains that if she were 'assimilated by one of the tigers, of course, it will be difficult to separate you [her], in that case we will bury the animal at reduced rates'. The presence of women in big cat acts continued to offer sensationalist value in the remote colonies long after it ceased to have novelty value in Britain, mainland Europe or the USA.

While Wirth's circus returned to Australia and New Zealand with an expanded program, the company was also determined to

---

96 Tait 2003, 80–92. Zuila has recently been identified as Catherine Isabella Webber, b. 30 October 1854 in Sydney, by Erica Ryan, Manager, Printed Australiana, National Library of Australia.
97 van der Merwe 2007, 90, 94–95. Captain Russell was performing with the lions, although Winschermann seems to have later taken over this act.
98 *Bulletin* 1900, Sundry shows, 1 December: 8.

make the menagerie financially viable, and it now included the elephant Ghuni Sah (or Gunnesah). Ghuni Sah was acquired from a menagerie in Surabaya, Indonesia, owned by a Dutch 'sportsman', Herr Von Grosser. Ghuni Sah also proved able to work, loading the circus equipment.[99] The circus included elephant-riding tigers trained by Johnny Rougal, a riding bear trained by Wineherman [sic], and riding and somersaulting baboons. A feat with two or more different species became characteristic of trained acts during the 1890s and Wirth's rival, the Fitzgerald Bros. circus, was touring an imported Hagenbeck-trained lion in an elephant-riding act by 1896.[100] Eventually Wirth's made the menagerie viable by opening the animal feeding to the public and charging patrons to hear the bear trainer Wineherman's lectures on menagerie animals.[101]

The prevalence of feeding and tamer acts in menageries in Britain, mainland Europe and the USA meant that spectators could readily encounter performances by the second half of the 19th century. Such entertainments were rarer in the colonies in the 1890s, as the controversies in Australia and New Zealand reveal. Therefore Scrutator's opposition in the 1890s to the tamer act and the head-in-the-mouth stunt might have been indicative of late 19th-century anxieties about the loss of human dignity, but it confirmed additional sensitivities in colonial settler society. The style of fighting in shows with animals and in circus war re-enactments may have expanded in circuses with menagerie entertainments that toured globally during the 1890s, but the acts still seemed to reproduce British and American precedents. Yet there were differences in responses to these shows among imperial countries and their colonies. Re-enactments of local wars were only acceptable away from the colony that experienced the war.

The tamer act controversies cannot be attributed to concern about the treatment of animals and their rights. The loss of animal dignity did become a preoccupation in England as the century progressed, but the head-in-the-mouth stunt in the colonies was troubling because it undermined human identity in new settler societies that sought to

---

99   Wirth no date, 103–106; Wirth 1925, 132.
100   Poster, Fitzgerald Bros. Circus, Cabot Collection, Alexander Turnbull National Library, New Zealand.
101   Wirth no date, 105–106.

uphold a hierarchy of culture over the natural world and indigenous cultures. The removal of women from tamer acts emphasised lasting concerns, derived from beliefs about innate divisions in nature pertaining to gender and ideas of a human–animal species hierarchy (see Chapter 7). Domesticated, but not large, exotic, or wild animals were acceptable in acts with women. Regardless, the 1890s was a decade of transition in big cat stunts throughout the colonies, and in Britain, Europe and the USA, menagerie feeding displays and head-in-the-mouth stunts were largely relegated to the 19th century as they were superseded by trained acts with complex feats.

6
War arts about elephantine military empires

Menagerie animals provided a backdrop to groups of indigenous peoples who were transported in increasing numbers from colonial regions for exhibition in Britain, Europe and the USA. This chapter introduces a range of shows from the 1880s to the 1900s that presented indigenous warriors and fighting scenarios together with animal displays that implicitly suggested the violence of colonialism perpetuated on humans and animals. The entertainment genre of performances depicting battles was expanded with demonstrations of fighting by the cultures resisting the British army and rule, and eventually these formed part of one huge spectacle in which all existing types of militarised animal acts and travelling museums and menagerie displays converged.

A military outfit on a male presenter had become standard in lion and tiger acts by 1900; the stereotype was a large man in a Hussar uniform carrying a pitchfork and a whip. Although costumed orientalism persisted, especially in elephant acts, most big cat presenters demonstrating the new science of animal training wore imitative uniforms as they proclaimed gentler treatment in ironic contradiction of a soldier's attire. Trained big cat and elephant groups would be fully integrated into the circus ring program by 1900 with human performance identities spanning military conquest and faux native origins.

Ethnographic warrior shows

The exhibiting of humans and animals was a well-established practice before the 1870s, when the exhibition of human groups began to increase greatly in scale and geographical scope. Janet Davis notes that PT Barnum popularised the term 'human menagerie', and entrepreneurial exhibits of both exotic humans and animals intensified following the advent of social Darwinism in the 1860s.[1] At the time, processes for the acquisition and transportation of menagerie animals and indigenous people converged.

The species trade of Hagenbeck's encompassed both humans and animals by the 1870s, and its zoological exhibition continued to contain ethnographic displays. Initially the presence of indigenous attendants was intended to enhance Hagenbeck's animal exhibition. A Hagenbeck show in 1877 presented a 'Nubian Caravan' that included dromedaries, rhinoceroses, giraffes and four 'playful' elephants; it toured to Paris and London with 14 'native attendants' from different tribes who did 'sham fights' as hunters and hung hunting trophies on their dwellings.[2] Carl Hagenbeck had to agree to send the hunters home within a set time. The animals were the main exhibit and the hunters contributed to the atmosphere, but this balance began to shift in shows during the 1880s.

William Coup writes revealingly of American circuses with menageries that also exhibited human groups in an exotic village setting. As he explains: 'But it is not always animals that make the success of a circus. An unfamiliar type of the human species will occasionally make the fortune of a showman.'[3] Indigenous Australian groups were toured in 1883 in Europe, and a group of nine were taken on tour in 1884 to the USA.[4] In 1885 Forepaugh's circus presented its assembly of nations in the ring, including 'Australia's Real Native Boomerang Throwers', and combined this with the viewing of 'Kangaroos, Emus,

---

1   Davis 2002, 10. See Goodall 2002; Rothfels 2002a.
2   *Era* 1877, The Nubians at the Alexandra Palace, 16 September: 4; *Lloyd's Weekly Newspaper* (London) 1877, Alexandra Palace, 16 September: 5.
3   Coup 1901, 163.
4   See Poignant 2004. Also *Adam Forepaugh's Courier* 1885, Billy Rose Collection, New York Public Library of Performing Arts; Fox & Parkinson 1969, 81, 39 (posters).

6 War arts about elephantine military empires

Birds, Reptiles in the Menagerie'. In turn, a diverse range of menagerie animals could enhance human distinctiveness. Such ethnographic and animal shows culminated in the staging by Barnum and Bailey Circus The Greatest Show on Earth (BB) of the 'Great Ethnological Congress' of humans and animals.

John MacKenzie summarises two developments in the later decades of the 19th century in England that delineated an expansion of human exhibiting within a convergence of reality and entertainment spectacles:

> The 'native village' became a central part of imperial exhibitions and, at times, a familiar sight in seaside entertainment. Colonial wars were swiftly represented on the theatrical stage or in the circus ring, and the sting of black opponents was drawn by their appearance at shows acting out the resistance which had so recently been bitterly fought out in reality.[5]

Animals were an integral component of the larger type of ethnographic enactment since they provided an atmospheric effect, although the menagerie was increasingly relegated to the position of subservient attraction in such shows.

One aspect of the presentation of a 'native' way of life proved particularly politically sensitive. The British government did not approve when Farini (William Hunt) organised a performance of Zulu war methods in London in June 1879 during the middle of the 'Zulu wars' (1879 onwards) in southern Africa.[6] Farini had hired Net Behrens, who had previously worked for Barnum, to go to Durban to bring back a group of young Zulu men. Before the arrival of the Zulu men with Behrens, Farini staged a song-and-dance show with a 'Zulu Kaffir Boy', and two women billed as '"Wild Women" from the "Dark Continent"'.[7] The first show was well attended, but there was public doubt in regards to the authenticity of the background claimed for the two female performers, who were probably not the daughters of a Zulu

---

5 MacKenzie 1986b, 11.
6 Peacock 1996, 251–54, Mr Cross, Secretary of State for the Home Department, represented the British government.
7 Peacock 1996, 253, 251–56.

chief. Therefore when the larger group of Zulus arrived in London with Behrens, Farini obtained signed statements, including one from a police sergeant, that the performers were unquestionably Zulu. Despite Farini's assertion that this group was friendly to the British government, the latter's disapproval meant that the group did not perform at the Royal Aquarium, a major venue, as planned. For the first month the group performed at St James' Hall, known for its American black-face minstrel shows, but once the show had proved highly popular, it transferred back to the Royal Aquarium. The initial publicity focused on the war arts and claimed that the Zulu fighters were demonstrating their customs: 'The manner in which they illustrate the method of killing their war victims is in itself enough to strike terror into the stoutest heart.'[8] A highly skilled show entrepreneur, Farini made the most of topical public interest in warlike displays.

The surgeon and naturalist Frank Buckland met with six Zulu travellers and described their physical features. He also observed their politeness and 'goodnature', although their '"dances were emblematic of fighting, and victory to the death"', and he specified that the Zulu men had "amazing quickness of hearing and sight"'.[9] Their assegai weapon of pliable wood was about five feet (1.5 m) in length and the Zulu thrower made it quiver before it was thrown with the speed and power to penetrate a human body fatally. Though, when the Zulu visitors were taken to London's Zoological Gardens they were apparently fearful of the elephants.

The expanded performance, complete with dances and spear-throwing, attracted large audiences. Behind the scenes, Farini's management was challenged by the Zulu performers demanding more pay and their independence, but he seemed to somehow resolve those problems.

Coup appreciated that members of the public were interested in seeing the warriors who proved a military match for British soldiers and he claimed that the show provided recognition of Zulu bravery. He outlines that:

---

8   Cited in Peacock 1996, 253.
9   Bompas 1886, 377–78, citing Buckland. He met Digandan, a chief, Possmon, Magubi, Nusan, Kikou and Oskei.

6 War arts about elephantine military empires

These Zulus had made such a bold resistance to the British government that the excitement ran high and the press of the world contained daily reports of England's conflict with this now subdued people. Their bravery in battle and gallant defense of their homes attracted widespread attention and made them objects of deep interest and curiosity.[10]

Another circus enterprise quickly copied the show and was explicit about the Zulus' defence of their freedom. JS Bratton writes that the Zulu show combined an 'interplay of triumphalism, an intellectual quasi-scientific discourse concerned with constructing a hierarchical ethnology, and the perennial attractions of pseudo-educational spectacle'.[11] She continues that, importantly, the selling point was a theatrical claim of 'authenticity, the unmediated presentation of reality'. The authenticity of the warlike display by warriors proved a successful business strategy.

It seemed that some of the Zulu warriors reaching Europe did come directly from active engagement in war. Coup's account of how those Zulu warriors reached London and then New York certainly acknowledges that Behrens went to Africa but omits mention of Barnum's business rival, Farini, and his initiative. There was probably more than one trip. Behrens went directly to the British army headquarters in Durban and presented letters of introduction and then, with his own supplies, joined an army column moving inland. The army encountered a large group under the leadership of Oham, reportedly rebelling against his brother, King Cetewayo, who had already been imprisoned by the British. The Zulu warriors who assisted the British army and were selected to go to England with Behrens proved very reluctant. Since they were 'at the mercy of their captors', 'persuasion' was used to induce them to 'yield', although the means by which this was achieved was not made explicit.[12] A traveller, Ernst Wache, and Matthias Walter, who worked for Hagenbeck's, were sent to assist. Coup

---

10   Coup 1901, 163.
11   Bratton 1991a, 3–4; Bratton 1991b, 25, Cooke's Royal Circus was licensed to stage *The grand equestrian spectacle of the war in Zululand*.
12   Coup 1901, 164, 165–66, also 167.

specified that this group arrived in London with three princesses, a baby, the leader, Incomo, and 23 warriors.

The Zulu performers presented three times a day for nearly two-and-a-half years at the Royal Aquarium. Their acts consisted of songs and dances about 'marriage, death, hunting, joy and sorrow, changes of the moon, rain, sunshine, and war' as well as assegai-throwing displays, the making of fire, methods of fighting, sports, and marriage arrangements in which a bride was negotiated for six to ten cows. In 1881 Farini took several of the Zulu performers and Zazel's human cannonball act, which he had patented, to New York to join BB.[13] In spite of the political controversy, warriors who were representative of an enemy force fighting against British rule also proved a popular entertainment troupe in the USA.

A display of indigenous fighting skills stirred social admiration while government scrutiny encapsulated an underlying unease. The prolongation of white settler rule was achieved with the enforcement of visible markers of racial difference, and a sustained belief in the superiority of the British family for the organisation of society and in the British Empire.[14] Even so, reports in England of the 'hard-drinking licentiousness of frontier living, careless of the niceties of proper relations' also generated disquiet about colonial life.[15] There were perceptions of disorder in accounts of the colonial world, and these were brought to the fore in Britain by the reports of social disturbance and outbreaks of fighting. Exhibited war arts showed indigenous cultures resisting what would, over time, come to be considered the physical, emotional and political violence wrought by colonial rule.

As indicated in Chapter 3, a hunting-style motif and action became a well-established part of staged menagerie cage acts from the mid-19th century. The addition of an African identity, assumed or not, compounded an impression of geographical authenticity in the performance and it underwent a revival in London following the success of the Zulu shows.

Menagerie proprietor Edward Bostock had started out on his own in 1883 with the Grand Star menagerie, one among three large and

---

13 See Peacock 1996 for detailed accounts of the 1881 and 1882 trips.
14 Hall 2004, 51–52.
15 Levine 2004b, 8.

6 War arts about elephantine military empires

six small touring menageries at that time in England.[16] He recounted how an African-American, William Dellah, performed in a menagerie cage lion act under the stage name Sargano (I). A replacement had to be found, and a West Indian who went by the stage name Alicamousa (John Holloway Bright), became Sargano (II). Despite a mauling, Sargano (II) worked for Edward Bostock until 1891 when he left to start his own travelling menagerie. This was short-lived and he returned to Edward Bostock's employ with a lion-wrestling act in a cage on London's Oxford Music Hall stage. The handling act's conception may have been influenced by the Greek myth of Hercules wrestling a lion. Sargano (II) twice got the lion up on his back legs and put his arms around the lion in a pretend wrestling match before pushing him away, even throwing him. The lion had to appear to win the first round. The act played for eight weeks before transferring with William Crockett to the USA to tour under Frank Bostock's management.[17] The performance of an African identity continued to revitalise the conventional animal-handling act, although a wrestling stunt was unreliable and not sustainable. The geographical performance, however, was now more likely to be shaped by human performance identity.

Savage economics

When the Mahdi people in the Sudan rose up against colonial rule (1882 to 1898), the trade in animals (and, most likely, people) transported northwards out of Africa to Europe was halted.[18] Carl Hagenbeck looked for other options by searching maps of the world. A process of procurement and transportation of 'Laplanders', the first Arctic peoples to reach Germany, had started earlier, in 1875. It proved popular, and they had been presented to Emperor Wilhelm I.

---

16   Bostock 1972 [1927], 97, and photograph, also, 101, 110, 127–28. Captain Rowley replaced Alicamousa.
17   Turner 2000, 29; Turner 1995, 91, 117. Crockett returned to Scotland with an elephant, Nancy. Turner has listed both Sarganos dying in 1892, with Sargano (I), as Dellah Montana, attacked by bears on 14 March, despite his rescue by Frank Bostock, and Sargano (II) dying on 16 December.
18   Hagenbeck 1956, 16, also 19–21, 25; Rothfels 2002a, 143. The identities cited here are as they are given in the historical sources.

Hagenbeck's subsequent ethnographic shows involved 'Eskimos' and 'Somalis', 'Indians', 'Ceylonese' (Sinhalese) and other ethnic groups, including Indigenous Australian people. The exhibition of humans in village life associated with animal exhibiting compounded ideas of physical difference in nature in the later decades of the 19th century. Native Americans from the Bella Coola River region were brought from Canada and Kalmyk people from the Russian Volga. Years later, in 1956, Lorenz Hagenbeck remembers: 'The reason for all this was that in Europe an interest in colonial expansion had suddenly been awakened, and exhibitions of exotic living races drew enormous crowds.'[19] He claims that in Berlin 93,000 people turned out to see the 'Folk Exhibition of Kalmyks and Singhalese' and this was followed by the 'Grand Ceylon Show', the latter including 25 elephants and their keepers. The size of the crowd may have been confronting for the elephants.

Lorenz Hagenbeck travelled in India in 1902 to transport elephants to Europe; he later remembers, interestingly, that 'newly caught elephants cannot stand the smell of Europeans ... But everywhere the drivers are the same, whether we know them as mahouts, oozies or kornaks.'[20] The animals might have been an indistinguishable species to Lorenz, but here he seems to attribute a common identity to the indigenous riders. Yet he observes that the training methods for elephants in agricultural or tree-logging work in North India, Ceylon (Sri Lanka), Sumatra, Assam and Burma (Myanmar) did vary, as did the commands.

An ex-soldier with experience in a colonial region and even of a colonial war seemed to have the credentials to manage the transportation of animals and humans from a colony.[21] Joseph Menges had been part of the Khartoum Sudan campaign (and the siege of 1884 and 1885) fought by General Gordon, and he was contracted by Carl Hagenbeck to travel to India to obtain animals. In 1893 Menges was put in charge of the Hagenbeck animal park in Neuer Pferdemarkt, Hamburg, and two years later he organised for a group of Somali people and their leader,

---

19   Hagenbeck 1956, 16.
20   Hagenbeck 1956, 42–43. Those regions continued to provide elephants for the circus in the first half of the 20th century.
21   Hagenbeck 1956, 16–17, also 25, 36, 67; Mangan & MacKenzie 2008, 1218–42. Also see Rothfels 2002a.

Hersy Egeh, to travel to Hamburg from Abyssinia (Ethiopia), and to London for the Somaliland show. This was a career transition from safari hunting and military service to zoo and ethnographic management and logistics. The Hamburg animal park was shifted to Stellingen in 1896 with a Hagenbeck patent for the provision of a specially created artificial environment with fake nature for the viewing of the animals. The plan to build a utopian sanctuary from what Nigel Rothfels calls 'a violent world', however, and its struggle for survival with an illusion of freedom was not properly realised. Rothfels writes that 'however much Hagenbeck and his followers wanted to put a positive spin on the company, it remained difficult to represent an enterprise that thrived on the capture, trade, and exhibition of animals and people as some kind of conservation organization.'[22] The combination of human and animal exhibiting had popular appeal, but also met public resistance.

Scientific interests, political events and social curiosity in the 19th century supported the proliferation of ethnographic and zoological spectacles. In particular, the success of Farini's Zulu shows inspired imitations through the years, including in the British colonies. In 1893 Fillis' circus in Melbourne presented an enactment of the Zulu wars to capacity houses.[23] When Wirth's circus reached southern Africa from Australia that year with the Wild West segment in their show, the additional Zulu war re-enactment was stopped. Wirth's then hired a group of Zulu warriors to leave southern Africa with the circus and to continue to South America with the tour. George Wirth explains: 'We had on board with us as novelties a number of fine, big upstanding Zulus, a couple of Cape boys, a Hottentot, and a Bushman.'[24] But the appearance of the Zulu warriors in Wirth's show were thwarted. The company reached South America, whereupon a theatre manager, telephoning long distance from Buenos Aires, told George that he had heard about 'a troupe of black people' walking around 'nearly naked', and warned him that they needed to be fully dressed or there would be trouble with the authorities. George explained that the group were wearing their preferred 'native' dress and objected to wearing trousers

---

22 Rothfels 2002c, 212–13.
23 *Argus* 1893, 30 January: 7; *Argus* 1893, 6 February: 7; *Argus* 1893, 13 February: 7; *Argus* 1893, 21 February: 6.
24 Wirth 1925, 83, also 85.

and boots. No doubt this had the advantage of sensationally advertising the show. The Zulus, however, suddenly disappeared from the entourage before they appeared in the show, and George suspected that they may have been enticed or abducted to become cattle ranch workers.

Shows opportunistically presenting topical colonial themes increased in scale as they brought together practices in traded commodities, fighting demonstrations, and animal exhibition. Fillis later toured 'Savage South Africa' to London for the Greater Britain Exhibition of products from the colonies, organised by Imre Kiralfy in 1899 and 1900, following the great success of one-and-a-half million people attending his 'India' production and exhibition from 1895–96 with Indian and British officials.[25] At the venue in Earls Court, Fillis' spectacle in the evening included a re-enactment of the Matabele (Rhodesia/Zimbabwe) wars of 1893 and 1896 for English audiences. The huge outdoor exhibition included 200 indigenous Africans in 35 'kraal' (village) huts against a painted veldt, as well as Boer families, and lions, tigers, leopards and baboons; elephants could be seen in an artificial dam, and three of the lions had the names of political figures: Cecil Rhodes, Oom Paul and Lobengula.[26] Fillis' show was very successful. The program's racially demeaning commentary explains that this was 'a sight never previously presented in Europe, a horde of savages direct from their kraals'.[27] Ben Shephard proposes that the sheer size of the show partly explains its success.

The inclusion of African recruits in the show had been opposed in southern Africa, and the campaign continued as the troupe reached England. A representative of the British government explained it could not force Fillis' troupe members to return home. While there was public criticism of 'the action of the organizers in bringing over a large number of natives to be stared at', there was praise for the realism of the dances and 'methods of warfare'.[28]

---

25 van der Merwe 2007, 131, running from 8 May 1899 until 29 October 1899; Gregory 1991, 150–78; Assael 2005, 77–79.
26 van der Merwe 2007, 121–22. Van der Merwe lists the Zulu, Swazi, Matebele, Khoi, Malay and Coranna peoples included in the exhibition.
27 Cited in Shephard 1986, 97.
28 *Times* (London) 1899, The Greater Britain Exhibition, 9 May: 14.

6 War arts about elephantine military empires

Before leaving southern Africa, Fillis had advertised for participants, listing humans and animals together, requesting 'horned animals, baboons, zebras, giraffe, koodo, springbucks, hartebeests', and 'Afrikander girls' who needed to be light-skinned and 'good-looking'.[29] Shephard notes that an 'expensive replica of the "Kaffir Kraal"' that presented a view of the 'savages' at home for sixpence was only one part of the entertainment, and the full spectacle included circus war re-enactments. Alongside the horseriding and firing of rifles was the inclusion of a Maxim gun that allowed British spectators to recognise its 'deadly' effectiveness in colonial wars, although the spectators would not have appreciated the process of guerrilla warfare from this display. While the circus enactment of the 1893 First Matabele War involved the warriors preparing for war, it had Fillis playing the role of the military leader on horseback, and in the 1896 enactment there was an attack on a stagecoach and a white farmhouse by warriors – supposedly of Ndebele identity – which ended with the colonial farmer's daughter committing suicide to avoid capture. The 19th-century ethnographic war act had acquired a narrative with close parallels to an American Wild West 'cowboys and Indians' war show, and the blend of genres did not escape contemporary observers. But the *Times* includes an interesting digression about the audience reactions to an episode in which 'a native prisoner, who refuses to tell which way his chief had fled' is shot by soldiers. The scene aroused loud sustained cheers of support for his bravery and the plot was changed because 'our race has never been slow to recognize and respect courage in its foes'.[30] (Note that even this episode needed to be framed as an indication of racial superiority.) In another show, however, when the 'native dancers' proved reluctant to end their performance, a galloping horseman was sent on to hasten the act's finish.

A diverse range of African animals provided a picturesque, although not necessarily a realistic, addition to a display of human village life inclusive of methods of fighting. The menagerie animals in Fillis' 'Savage South Africa' were background exhibits. They might have been exhibited in larger numbers than ever before, but such accompanying exhibitions were having less impact. The considerable success of

---

29 Shephard 1986, 97, also 98, 99.
30 *Times* (London) 1899, The Great Britain Exhibition, 8–9 May: 14.

the live show meant that an early film was made of it, which was shown widely throughout the colonies.[31]

Fillis' spectacle with war re-enactments in London represented an enlarged and blended version of the menagerie and circus entertainment forms that had originally been exported out of England. It coincided with political revisions in the melodrama presented in spoken-word theatres about the English colonies. Penny Summerfield argues that dramas about the liberation of colonial regions, centring on a populist figure, that were staged in the music hall in the 1870s, were superseded in the mid-1890s by melodrama with a class bias to the victory – a change reinforced by an increasing disappearance of music hall venues.[32] For example, 'Cheer Boys Cheer', written in 1895, depicted a group of upper-class English women warning British soldier heroes of the Matabele war preparations. Even colonial battle defeats had to appear triumphant on the stage, but by the 1890s the villains might also be other Europeans. Those later dramas depicted the victors as having social rank in England and being capable of defeating resistant colonial native peoples in 'military spectacle and patriotic expression'; while these performances depicted indigenous inhabitants as the enemy, other characters from rival European nations could also not be trusted.[33] It had become evident during the Sudan War (1882–98) that a simplistic narrative of the British or Europeans arriving to liberate colonial peoples could not accommodate sustained wars of resistance or territorial disputes among European nations, even after the 1885 Berlin division of colonial geography. The popularity of shows with Zulu warriors in Britain interestingly preceded the later spoken-word theatre emphasising military rank and overt class values.

John Springhall writes of campaigns against 'Zulus, Ashanti, Afghans, Boers, Burmese and Sudanese' as being initially 'small-scale military campaigns' leading to 'the recurrent forcible and bloody suppression' of local resistance.[34] The war correspondents for newspapers included artists illustrating events. Artists in studios also created artworks that were reproduced cheaply, and Springhall argues that

---

31 van der Merwe 2007, 131.
32 Summerfield 1986, 32, 34.
33 Holder 1991, 34.
34 Springhall 1986, 49, also 51, 62, 69.

increased availability of such images was likely to romanticise such wars. Springhall continues that, while it is difficult to claim 'cause and effect in the popular culture of imperialism ... it is quite possible to speculate that popular art was just as important as war reporting or popular fiction' in garnering support for government policies.

The large, all-encompassing 1899 to 1900 show presented by Fillis may or may not have encouraged popular support for British military ventures in Africa. To some extent its narrative undermined a message about the validity of courageous indigenous people engaging in warfare, which may have been more straightforward with Farini's earlier show. But events surrounding Fillis' show did bring to the fore issues of race and violence in the colonies that revealed a range of responses to the indigenous inhabitants. The complications of an interracial marriage by one of the Zulu performers working with Fillis revealed a social division between racist attitudes and racial tolerance towards the end of the 19th century. Fillis' show included Peter Lobengula, billed as the son of the Matabele king, who had been taken prisoner during the Matabele War. While the show was successful, newspaper coverage increased noticeably once it emerged that the well-mannered and English-educated Lobengula, who may or may not have been from a royal family, was to marry an English woman, Kitty Jewell, whom he had met in southern Africa.[35] Recognition of the nobility and bravery of indigenous warriors resisting British rule might have become acceptable by the 1890s, but the issue of interracial marriage with a warrior proved controversial and divisive, and made Lobengula and Jewell celebrities – and no doubt gave Fillis a publicity bonus. There was an impression that Lobengula achieved a quasi-hero status among female spectators in particular, suggesting that social attitudes to race in England were complicated – and possibly made more so by the popularity of theatrical depictions. Fillis went on to create a far bigger war spectacle with the 'Anglo–Boer War' re-enactment show in St Louis in the USA in 1904 (see later in this chapter). Colonial wars might have taken place in remote geographical regions, but involvement permeated

---

35   van der Merwe 2007, 127–28, 130; Shephard 1986, 99–100. Shephard provides an analysis of Lobengula and Jewell's marriage and its breakdown under economic and racial pressures of life in England, and mentions questions as to whether Lobengula was really the son of the Matabele king.

most aspects of social life in the colonising nations. Certainly the figure of the fighter had become ubiquitous in animal acts.

Training aesthetics

In 1900 when Hagenbeck's trainer, Julius Seeth, appeared with 21 lions at the long-awaited opening of the London Hippodrome, he was costumed in quasi-military dress.[36] Hagenbeck trainers rose to prominence wearing evening dress, so even their acts had succumbed to the prevailing aesthetic of army dress by 1900. They were well known in London for a succession of complex multiple-species animal acts that demonstrated precision and reliable obedience by exotic wild animals. With the advent of well-trained animal acts during the 1890s, largely from Hagenbeck's and Frank Bostock's menagerie businesses, a big cat act in particular manifested both direct and indirect associations with the military. The costume conveyed dual, but paradoxical, impressions of implicit force to achieve submission and well-regulated discipline to maintain it.

While Seeth's act was completely different to earlier menagerie cage acts, it could be aligned with a topical allusion to current events in several ways. There is a review of Seeth's act in the *Times*, which also contained news about the Boer War and African colonies where European nations had deployed their forces. It was difficult to overlook how territorial acquisitions by Germany and Britain in east Africa encompassed areas with large numbers of wild animal species such as those in Seeth's act. The reviewer praises the whole program for excellence, but Seeth's 'forest-bred lions' are said to be 'the sensation of the evening', and received very enthusiastically.[37] The review continues that he brings on 21 lions 'and with a quiet confidence which compels admiration, which though the situation excites some trepidation,

---

36 Speaight 1980, 83, poster.
37 *Times* (London) 1900, 16 January: 4. '[S]teel grills' enclosed the ring but were lifted with 'hydraulic rams' to let the lions into the ring. The same newspaper edition covers the events of the Boer War and has a brief note on food shortages among the 6000 inhabitants of the 'German Colonies' in east Africa on the same page as the review.

makes the great beasts do his bidding with perfect docility'. The lions are compared to dogs answering to their names. 'If occasionally one snarls or claws at his trainer, Herr Seeth smiles and pats his nozzle, or if kindness is wasted, chases it round the ring with the whip.' The trained animal act was so well controlled that antagonism from African lions received kindly gestures of understanding; the movement sequence and the use of the whip would have been part of the rehearsed show.

While the costume was indicative of broader wardrobe trends in the circus, the image of the soldier also underpinned the newer trained animal acts by 1900. The thick material of the uniforms usefully provided the trainer/presenter's skin with some protection from incidental scratches. But perhaps this militarisation of human identity in big cat acts was also a covert response to political events, if not also implicitly responding to the popularity of war shows, including those featuring indigenous people. Certainly it reiterated the social esteem of the 19th-century soldier and firm beliefs about the social value of militarisation, as well as the century's legacy of war dramas on theatre stages and war re-enactments with animals.

In reflecting on the advancements of the 19th century, and its successes and failures, social thinker Alfred Russel Wallace vividly criticises what he terms 'militarization' as a curse that held his society back, and although duelling wars between individuals were abolished in Britain and disappeared once these were officially forbidden to military men in the first half of the century, 'the vampire of war' among nations did not.[38] The 'war-spirit' prevailed and escalated in the second half of the century. He described Europe as a vast military camp with greater numbers of military personnel than ever before.

Performance aesthetics reflected this militarised society. Towards the end of the 19th century the potential for some species of large exotic animals to be reliably trained for performance like horses had been achieved, and with comparable rhetoric about gentleness in training, although the animals were put through regimes of conditioning that seemed like quasi-military training.[39] This was a transition from taming

---

38 Wallace 1898, 324–25, 331.
39 Kober 1931, 109, circus historian AH Kober oddly nominates Paul Batty working with big cats in 1874 with Renz's circus as 'one of the first of the modern school'. Thétard 1947, 48, 231, for acts in 1850s Paris.

to training; from a generalised hit-and-miss and physical handling and pushing to the strictly regulated, complex routines of obedience with minimal handling that would become central to big cat and other acts from the 1890s. Importantly, the principles of training removed any physical shoving of the animals during the best of these acts; the trainer carried sticks, poles and other props for visual effect and to cue animals, but only made contact when absolutely necessary. Trained animals responded to verbal and visual cues and to the body position of the presenter and the other animals.

Older menagerie cage acts with a willing but inexpert handler who often had to provoke a relaxed group of lions to react were replaced by shows in which animal groups predictably moved on a cue that was often not seen by the spectators. The animals seemed to willingly take their seats on pedestals in a graduated pyramid formation at the beginning of an act. A small number of the trained animals coached to sit on pedestals proved capable of executing a sequence of complicated movements to deliver impressive physical feats on cue. Animals were reasonably cooperative and their movement was guided by a standard set of cues that could be learnt and given by different presenters. The animal performers learnt the routine so that it was often delivered by them with minimal instruction, and they might take their cues from other animals. While the dominant businesses by 1900 were exemplified by Hagenbeck's and Frank Bostock's shows in Europe and the USA,[40] it was the Hagenbeck trading business, directly connected to an entertainment business and to Carl in particular, that eventually became synonymous with milder methods of conditioning the movement of exotic animals with rewards and coaxing; a training breakthrough possibly happened after Hagenbeck's employed an ex-Bostock employee.[41] The point here is that those trained gentler acts were created within a small interconnected network of trainers and it is likely that specialised knowledge was passed on. This was not so apparent for the earlier tamer acts.

In the Hagenbeck business, Carl and Wilhelm began developing circus acts after 1887 with male presenters wearing formal attire. The

---

40   Kober 1931, 104.
41   See Tait 2012. This is a history of trained big cat and elephant acts in the 20th-century circus and opposition to them.

6 War arts about elephantine military empires

Hagenbecks would become highly successful by selling or hiring out to other circuses the complete finished act during the next 50 years. Initially Carl was able to select a small number of animals who proved especially cooperative and suitable for training to achieve what were understood as gentler and caring methods. Other trainers had less choice and had to work with the available animals, although there was far greater knowledge about big cat species, which made it easier to avoid the use of forceful methods in the initial training.

Because trainers passed on knowledge to each other, rumours abounded regarding how training was achieved. The rumours included notions that a trainer had to enter the cage for the first time naked in order to be smelt, or that the lions were drugged or hypnotised.[42] But the 'secrets' to animal training were positive reinforcement with food and improved methods of animal care due to closer observation and greater understanding of a species' physical attributes and of animal personalities. The successful menageries had the financial resources to support training and improved care. Nonetheless, in training after the 1880s, a lion was often restrained in an iron collar and chain while he or she became accustomed to having a human presence in the cage. A chain was needed as lions could bite through rope, and Conklin even put gloves on a lion's paws and used a muzzle. While whip cracking could be discarded, Courtney Ryley Cooper notes that big cats were given a strong tap on their sensitive noses with a light stick or buggy whip if they misbehaved; he used a broom.[43] It was trainers who also mentioned some of the subterfuge used in older menagerie acts, such as employing the smell of ammonia to rouse lions.[44] Trainers responded to public scrutiny and changing social expectations by advocating training with rewards, but they generally avoided mention of punishments and the initial use of bodily restraints.[45]

---

42 Eipper 1931, 115. This was a longstanding accusation; see Le Roux & Garnier 1890, 146.
43 Cooper 1928, 17–18, 31.
44 Beatty & Wilson 1946, 131–33.
45 Accusations that big cats were declawed or otherwise deformed seemed to be avoided, rather than addressed, as if mention of this unacceptable practice to the public might raise suspicion of its existence.

Trained animal acts increased in number once training techniques were standardised. For example, Willy Peters worked for Frank Bostock's during the 1890s and trained 36 tigers and 100 lions.[46] Peters presented them running around and, for the act's finale, the big cats jumped over him and blocked each other's passage. Bostock's training protocol first let animals play around the trainer. Next Peters had them 'begin to run around the ring at top speed, but at his word of command they pulled up suddenly on their haunches, turned around and set off running in the opposite direction'. The chasing of a hunting act in a small cage was replaced by such controlled fast movement in a larger cage, and it was repetitively rehearsed. Peters trained a tiger to shake his hand, a second tiger to embrace him and a third to roar and snarl. He trained some to perform as if fighting him or as if obediently submissive and this dual division in trained styles continued. Trained fighting acts, however, were often perceived as a continuation of menagerie cage acts. Fighting acts with trained animals in the circus after the 1890s were, in most instances, highly orchestrated routines.

Within the program in the circus ring there was an increasing number of other trained animal acts from the menagerie by the early 1890s. For example, there were white doves that landed on an apparatus held by an elegant female trainer in evening dress, and instrument-playing shiny seals balancing objects on their noses. Seals and sea lions were first trained by Captain Joseph Woodward in the 1880s and the acts were further developed by the Judge brothers.[47] John Tiebor coached a sea lion for two years before exhibiting it, and Albert Rix from Hagenbeck's took three years to teach a seal to stand on one flipper.[48] Big cats were not necessarily the most dangerous animal performers to train. Bears were considered extremely difficult to work with, although street acts with brown bears long preceded the invention of the early modern menagerie and circus. Polar bears were introduced into acts, and Wilhelm Hagenbeck may have been the first to develop this act as a speciality. The popularity of novel animal acts created demand, but highly trained animals were expensive to acquire because training was

---

46   Kober 1931, 103, also 104.
47   Hagenbeck 1909, 144, 145.
48   Bradna & Spence 1957, 209.

time-consuming and only some animals had the personalities to cooperate in the presentation of complex feats.[49]

A range of costumed identities in the act did continue, in keeping with the diverse aesthetics of the circus. The precedent set by 19th-century pantomimes and processions with large menagerie animals meant that some leading presenters perpetuated orientalist fancies by wearing more theatricalised costumes of baggy trousers, glitter and turbans. A fantasy persona evoked an imaginary world and an exoticism shared with the animals. Fantasy identities perpetuated the earlier 19th-century belief that the presenters had special abilities that made wild animals obey them.

Richard Sawade was a leading trainer with Hagenbeck's, performing until 1919 in a signature fanciful costume of an Indian rajah, suggesting mysterious powers, as he cued tigers to leap from pedestal to pedestal and to pose in tiered groupings.[50] Trainers heightened the excitement of the act through their delivery, and Sawade reportedly became such a celebrity in Russia that, after a performance, a crowd even pulled his sleigh, and he received numerous presents from the tsar and aristocratic spectators.[51] Born in the Prussian town of Drossen, Sawade toured internationally and extensively promoted Hagenbeck's 'gentling' method of training. Sawade's act, although not his costumed persona, went without him to the USA with his student Rudolf Matthies, who instead wore a military-style costume.[52] Sawade retired to become the general manager of a travelling circus. He was accorded honorary membership of the Royal Society for the Prevention of Cruelty to Animals in Britain, and Matthies was the first animal trainer to be awarded the German Animal Protection Medal.[53] Thus, Hagenbeck's reputation for a gentler approach was legitimised.

---

49 Coxe 1980a, 145–46. Coxe specifies that Hagenbeck's 1890s mixed-species act cost nearly £3000, and that in 1897 an untrained polar bear cub would fetch £30 to £35 and a trained bear £100, but costs increased ten-fold after World War II.
50 Eipper 1931, 112–14.
51 Hagenbeck 1956, 85, and accompanying photograph.
52 Culhane 1990, 209–10. Matthies was one of several acts in Ringling Brothers Barnum and Bailey Circus The Greatest Show on Earth (RBBBC), which in 1924 had the largest display of trained animals to that date; he returned for the 1948 to 1949 seasons.
53 Kober 1931, 112; Hagenbeck 1956, 92.

Official recognition that the newer training approaches were encouraging humane methods in animal care was indicative of a major shift in social responses against the way 19th-century animal acts in the menagerie were staged and interpreted. Big cats could now be viewed by the public away from small cages. The animal acts that left behind the menagerie precincts gave a distinct impression that they had moved beyond the harsher treatment of captive animals during previous decades.

Regardless of whether a presenter adopted a softer exotic costume or a uniform, by the early 20th century animals were trained in similar ways to be either quietly obedient or noisily confrontational. The aesthetic of a military costume heightened the impact of the animal act and gave it a particular slant, with trainers often adapting the military dress worn in warmer climates and by safari hunters. Since some trainers were ex-soldiers, the costumes had the added effect of eliding the distinction between animal training for performance and military training for battle. The presumption of violent action was displaced by the display of preparatory discipline.

Hero of the military

Admired for his control of a record number of 27 lions, Captain Jack Bonavita wore a military-style costume in a comparatively quiet act by 1900. He was called a 'hero' by the American vice-president, Theodore Roosevelt, at the Pan-American Exhibition in 1901 and was praised for his 'pluck'.[54] The exhibition included a display of buildings lit by electricity as well as the sideshow entertainments, which included the Frank Bostock lion act and exhibited elephants. Working for Frank Bostock, ex-acrobat John Gentner, who took on the stage name Captain Bonavita, had the largest group of lions in one act by the turn of the 20th century. He was photographed c. 1903 completely surrounded by lions, with only his head and shoulders visible. General Miles, impressed by the act, wrote to Frank Bostock commending Bonavita's

---

54   Bostock 1903, 218, also 37–40, 43–44, 78, 136, 196–98, 200, 211, 217–20, 238; Turner 2000, 12 (Gentrer); Joys 1983, 30, 28–32. For the list of Bonavita's films, see www.imdb.com/name/nm0093844/.

6 War arts about elephantine military empires

control over the lions as 'truly remarkable'. Bostock agreed, commenting that Bonavita gave the impression of 'a refined and courteous gentleman', one 'peculiarly reserved'.[55] Bonavita's stoic demeanour and military costume meant that he appeared to manage the lions with minimal effort, and his dress and manner were assumed to be the indicators of manly virtue.[56] The trainer's stoicism might have suggested that the act's big cats were docile, and the assumption was that Bonavita had induced this placid behaviour. He began his performance by getting the lions to assume their positions on their pedestals, and he walked among them; apparently verbal commands were minimal. It is likely that the trained lion performers followed the visual cues provided by Bonavita's bodily position and gestures. A male trainer calmly confronting potentially aggressive animal performers was clearly socially esteemed.

In a 1911 account, Bonavita describes training animals through a very slow, gradual process of familiarisation with him, the equipment and other animals, including other species, as he worked each day for months to get them ready to be included in an act. He started by reaching into the cage, snapping a collar around the lion's neck and using an attached rope to pull the lion over to drinking water so the lion understood that there was a reason for the treatment. He carefully observed the temperament and behaviour of an individual animal, and created a pattern of movement to suit. For example, action on the ground for a lion that would not climb steps or get onto a pedestal with food inducements, or sitting action if one would not lie down. An animal was gradually coaxed into position, one paw at a time, until he or she accepted an action such as balancing. He writes: 'they realize they must go through the routine of their tricks before they can eat'.[57] Bonavita discloses that after training a lion to ride an elephant, he earned US$500 a week, which reveals how human trainers were motivated by the considerable financial rewards.

In one photograph, Bonavita appears carrying a large lion across his shoulders in awkward prominence, as if a lion could be a pet or an

---

55 Bostock 1903, 218.
56 Mrozek 1987, 220–21, for a discussion of manly qualities and anxieties in relation to the military in the USA.
57 Bonavita 1930 [1911], 13–14.

object. The live animal worn like a fur piece demonstrated supreme obedience to a human master. Bonavita became well known in the USA after appearing there, and he had at least 50 accidents in the ring, eventually losing an arm in an attack by the lion Baltimore, who nonetheless remained in the act.[58] Bonavita died in 1917 when he was attacked by a polar bear while working in films for Selig's menagerie in Los Angeles.

The animal trainer had acquired a status akin to that of a military hero by 1900. The dominance of large animals was underscored by a presenter's military identity, including a title.[59] In a studio photograph, Bonavita posed in jackboots and thick leather gloves to the elbows, the uniform of a calvaryman or a lion tamer. Similarly the Hagenbeck trainer Julius Seeth's appearance in an act with obedient wild animals made him seem to be 'the hero of it, whose frame is certainly cast in the heroic mould', and he 'was recalled again and again' at the end.[60] Even though this was performance, ideas of heroism were manifest in the control of live wild animals, providing a presenter could look the part of a hero. Donald Mrozek explains that the outward appearance and style of a military man was crucial, since 'Victory was central but so was the manner of its attainment. Gentlemen officers did not "fake it", nor did those few who were promoted to the ranks of heroes'.[61] Trained acts benefited from such expectations irrespective of fake identities in performance.

A trained act was a display of self-control by the animals. But it was understood as a display of control over the animals. An extended description of Bonavita's management of the lion performers outlines how his 'self-possessed' calm and mastery overcame their hostile behaviour.[62] The spectators, too, were responding to a visual impression of a soldier as if a truly 'manly' hero simply communicated self-discipline to the animals who followed his example.

---

58   Bostock 1903, 217, 220; Kober 1931; Velvin 1906; Robeson & Barnes 1941, 240.
59   Joys 1983, 45. Colonel Daniel Boone and Miss Carlotta presented the first American-trained animal act. Also, see Joys 1983, 25. Frank Bostock's sideshow acts included two Englishmen, Colonel Francis A Ferari and Captain Joseph G Ferari, who acquired their titles 'from battles with wild animals'.
60   *Times* (London) 1900, 16 January: 4.
61   Mrozek 1987, 231.
62   Velvin 1906, 51.

6 War arts about elephantine military empires

Training animals did align with regimes of military training to develop and maintain the habitualised patterns of movement for performance, while the costumes helped confirm their control for audiences. Particular businesses used the skills of individual trainers who disseminated processes of training. For example, Hungarian-born Louis Roth made his debut as an adolescent animal presenter with Frank Bostock's in the USA, dressed as a French army general, and after working with Hagenbeck-trained animals went on to become a seminal influence on animal training in the USA through his training of leading acts and presenters at the Al G Barnes circus.[63] The animal act depended on orchestrated routines combined with animal care, but it built on shared specialist knowledge developed over time that was attuned to basic requirements for the good health and survival of increasingly expensive animals. The human performance identity reassured the public about animal control and care.

As specialised trained big cat acts flourished and the more ad hoc 19th-century menagerie cage entertainments gradually disappeared, the trainer's costume, which might be a horseriding outfit with knee-high boots, or a soldier safari hunting suit, was a central visual sign of control over animals. The big cat act became enmeshed in a type of hyper-masculine display that upheld social ideals of obedience. At the same time, away from small cages, assumptions of gentlemanly self-restraint also allayed fears about how the animals were treated and implicitly confirmed a socially admirable behaviour extended to horses and to wild animals. Regardless of twists in faked national identity, the standard costuming affiliated these acts with the social esteem accorded national armies and the cavalrymen, while it also indirectly continued to prefigure the conquest of colonial regions and the ensuing displacement of the inhabitants, including the animals. Imitative uniforms continued to be part of trained animal acts until the mid-20th century.

In complete contrast to the quiet, 'manly' militarism of Bonavita and Seeth were the trained acts that staged confrontational fight scenarios. Courtney Ryley Cooper provides a detailed, if emotionally embellished, account of an anonymous trained lion routinely performing in a fighting act.

---

63   Robeson & Barnes 1941, 56.

The lion is let into the arena, roaring and bellowing the minute he leaves the cage. He chews at his pedestal. He turns and claws and thunders at the attendants outside. To all intents and purposes, he is a raging, vengeful thing that really doesn't begin to get along with himself until he's killed a trainer or two a day. He seeks to climb the bars of the big den; he claws at the netting; from outside the trainer throws him a crumpled piece of cloth and he tears it to shreds even before it has had time to strike the arena floor. Meanwhile the audience shivers and shakes, hoping the trainer won't try to go in there, and then hoping that he will, inasmuch as they've never really seen a trainer killed. Then the trainer opens the door and leaps within. The battle is on!

Revolvers flash, whips crack. But the lion will not be tamed. Gradually he forces the trainer backwards, closer, closer; now he has him in a corner and crouches to leap; now the trainer edges forth into a new chance for life, only to be re-cornered by the bloodthirsty beast; to be almost chewed to pieces, and finally, in a desperate rush, he escapes through the steel door just as the lion comes crashing against it!

Thrilling! But only an act, after all. For every moment of that battle is a rehearsed thing.[64]

The lion was trained to play the role of an attacking animal, completely rehearsed to appear ferocious on cue – the trained action was different to menagerie acts. The acts were typically expected to show a contrast between a ferocious effect and graceful movement and trainer triumph. The quieter act conveyed a more subtle ideal of military manliness that competed with brazen fighting acts, but both aligned with longstanding cultural ideas of human triumph over nature.

Elephant drills for Wonderland

Elephants were a particularly popular part of the larger spectacles by the late 19th century, and because they were caught up in a penchant

---

64 Cooper 1928, 157–58.

for military-like movement in animal acts. But there was an insidious underlying violence behind trained elephant acts. RW Thompson writes that 'the fashion in animals was always changing', and in the 'nineties elephants were the popular fancy'.[65] The consequence of this popularity was that increasing numbers of elephants were acquired from the wild and brought to submission. The process of elephant submission remained physical and often harsh, and elephants who did not submit were deemed unreliable for performance. If retained, they remained in the menagerie with a wide variety of other species.

Early in his working life George Conklin taught four elephants to do a military-like drill as a group. The drill involved marching movements before they stopped and turned together on command. Elephants were expected to contribute to acts for an admiring or comic response. Conklin eventually became the head trainer with BB and toured throughout the USA and to London's Olympia Hall and grounds in 1896 and 1897. He had more than 30 years' experience working with and teaching tricks to elephants by the time BB opened in London with a grand parade and three separate herds of elephants. These 'wonderfully educated' elephants included Conklin's 'herd of large elephants in new and novel dances, feats and tricks of all kinds', William Newman with baby elephants performing tricks, and George M Bates presenting elephants in 'difficult and intricate feats'.[66] Later in the program, the circus promoted 'cleverly trained animals' as a 'children's number', and one act with 'Comicalities and Humorous Feats' with Juno, the baby elephant. Whether it was overtly signalled in the act or not, all feats involved a type of drill to achieve co-ordinated elephant movement.

Conklin learnt a basic approach to managing elephants by observing Stuart Craven at work for more than two years c. 1868, when Craven visited O'Brien's circus to assist with the elephants (see also Chapter 5). The first elephant Conklin worked with was Queen Annie, who was 35 at that time and weighed 4.5 tons (4.6 tonnes). For the performance, Conklin wore a black velvet suit with vertical gold stripes down the trousers as he trotted and walked Queen Annie

---

65 Thompson 1934, 31.
66 BB Official Program 1896–97, Joe E Ward Collection, Harry Ransom Library Special Collections, University of Texas at Austin, Box 55, items 63–68.

around the ring. He instructed her, with a whip, to lift each of her legs high and to move to the beat of the stick in a Spanish trot, and to the tune of 'Coming Through the Rye'.[67] Since the circus music was played live, it could be adjusted to suit the elephant's movements.[68] Conklin taught Queen Annie to walk as if she had a lame foot, to vary the limping foot, and to untie a handkerchief from her leg. The act's climax involved Conklin lying down on a carpet, and Queen Annie stepping over him and then slowly kneeling down sideways over his body. Conklin taught her these tricks using an elephant hook; her movements were learnt to avoid the hook, and she would react quickly to the hook in her skin. During the final kneeling feat, Conklin held the hook or a nail as protection.

When Conklin was starting out, he found that a trick elephant had been advertised by WW Cole's circus in San Francisco, although the circus did not have an elephant who could do tricks. Cole instructed Conklin to simply walk Tom Thumb and unusually small, 35-year-old, three-ton Indian elephant around the ring. But Conklin encouraged an unsuspecting co-performer to lie down in the ring, and he walked Tom Thumb over him several times. Conklin also taught another elephant to walk across a 'tightrope'. It took months to achieve this feat, in which the elephant learnt to walk across a low plank carrying a balance pole in his trunk. The height of the plank was gradually raised and the elephant walked up a ramp at either end. The plank was eventually exchanged for timber embedded in rope, so it looked to the audience as though the elephant was walking a tightrope. Conklin also coached an elephant to walk on a row of wooden bottles and the elephant learnt to turn the key to his stable, and to throw objects. Conklin worked with the aforementioned Lallah Rookh as well (see Chapter 3).

In the elephant group that learnt the military drill at Cole's circus, there was an elephant who was taught to sit on a chair at a table opposite Conklin. The elephant held a fan and rang a bell insistently until a clown waiter returned with a water bottle containing water sweetened with molasses. Conklin, wearing a top hat and tails, would stand up and leave his hat on the chair, and the elephant would then sit on Conklin's chair, squashing his hat, which invariably received loud laughter from

---

67 Conklin 1921, 115–19, also 120–24, 144–45.
68 Baston 2010.

6 War arts about elephantine military empires

the audience. An elephant was taught to sit by fastening his or her back legs and being forced into the chair, and by having an elephant hook put into his or her skin folds.

Elephants were initially prepared for performance with forceful equipment and with extreme force to achieve a head stand. Through his experiences of teaching individuals, Conklin became effective at training groups. He used an elephant's aversion to the elephant hook to make him or her move as required. A rope sling through a pulley lifted the hind quarters in order to get an elephant into a head stand against a brick wall until the elephant could do the trick on a verbal command without the equipment or the wall. There was a reward of a carrot at the end of that extremely brutal initial conditioning. Similarly an elephant was taught to lie down by being pulled down on command. Conklin devised or at least adapted most of the harnesses, hobbles and tackles used with elephants in late 19th-century American circus.

Elephants and other animals were divided between those who could be trained for the circus ring and those who were untrained and remained in the menagerie exhibition. By the early 1900s, in complete denial of the force used behind the scenes, the BB menagerie was called 'Wonderland of Mystery and Delight', presenting a space of imaginative fantasy that included the 'grand vestibule' in which 'Animal Land' required an hour to view.[69] This was where 'wild beasts of every clime are exhibited in a condition as near to nature as the exigencies of travel will permit'. Two pages of the BB program in 1903 and 1904 present an educational format with an informative diagram that has a wide range of animal species drawn within two circles, and additionally grouped in bands across the circles according to their geographic and climatic zones, from the Arctic to southern temperate regions. The BB menagerie claims to be comprehensive. 'It may also be remarked that, with a very few exceptions, the [BB] exhibit comprises every beast, bird or reptile mentioned in Natural History'.[70] The exceptions were probably those that could not survive in the menagerie. Descriptive entries

---

69 BB Official Program, 'Circus Day' 1905 (BB Program), 1, also 2, 3, 7 (John and Mabel Ringling Museum Archives). Sections of the program covering the menagerie overlap with those in previous years. For a discussion of cynicism about wonder applied to Hagenbeck's animal exhibition, see Rothfels 2002c, 199–223.
70 BB Program 1903, 22, 23, also 25.

summarising animal species and their behaviour were still in programs in 1915 along with narrative embellishments.[71]

On tour across the USA in 1903, models of American warships were promoted in conjunction with the BB menagerie, which proclaimed itself a menagerie of 'superexcellence' with the largest and best animals, in a strange juxtaposition of military tribute and circus animal advertising. By 1905 the menagerie had become 'a congress of wild beasts', but the 1905 program also directly instructs the reader about what the menagerie meant to viewers and how animals were captured.

The 1905 program reinforces how a visit to the BB menagerie provided educational stimulus, whether the spectator was an adult seeking to broaden his or her general knowledge or a child familiar with nursery rhymes. But the program description also outlines the violence in hunting as though it is considered part of the educational information and explains in detail how giraffes were hunted and caught. Once a group was found, long fences coming to a point at one end were erected and '[s]everal thousand natives were then sent to form a semicircle around the copse where the giraffes were browsing, while the white men of the expedition got behind the animals and drove them in toward the corral'.[72] It describes how the so-named 'natives' prevented giraffes from escaping sideways by 'wildly yelling' and 'waving their spears'. Eventually, four so-called 'specimens' for the BB menagerie were driven into the point of the corral while another two were killed. The commentary explains that the four giraffes in the BB menagerie had recovered from their homesickness and had even adapted to 'American' food such as hay and vegetables, so it was no longer necessary to import African foliage.

Larger-bodied animals were promoted as very good-looking specimens of their species. The black African male rhinoceros displayed by BB in 1905 was called a particularly good-looking representative of the species – presumably he was deemed ugly in comparison with other animals. When he was in a bad mood, a keeper entering the cage would be unlikely to escape alive. The hippopotamus was still identified as the Bible's 'blood-sweating Behemouth [sic]',

---

71 BB Program 1914 and 1915.
72 BB Program 1905, 3.

6 War arts about elephantine military empires

although he or she did not sweat blood but a protective fluid.[73] But no animal was more majestic than a male lion such as Prince, a 'perfect specimen', captured from the African jungle, rather than born in captivity. It was also possible to see Nelly, a well-behaved lioness who had raised 40 cubs in captivity, two herds of elephants that would perform feats, the finest specimens of tigers, claimed as the equal of any seen in the wild, and numerous other animals.

While the BB program contained extensive information about menagerie animals, its zoological department also appears to have contained human ethnographic displays. Yet the BB menagerie was presented as being indicative of the American democratic ethos according to which the human spectators in the crowd – if not the exhibited indigenous people – were all equal . The 1905 program explains that the 'laborer [could be] glad that in this representative American crowd each man is as good as his fellow', with the same capacity for enjoyment.[74] The BB 1905 program describes the crowd waiting for the menagerie to open:

> Outside the big circus the crowd restlessly surges to and fro. It is a typically American crowd. Rich and poor, young and old, all rubbing elbows and waiting with laughing good nature.

The crowd visiting BB's Wonderland, however, had to be regimented. The program informed the spectators how to behave and what to do once the whistle signalled that the menagerie was open. In a revealing description in 1905, there was a hint that the size of the crowd could intimidate, as 'the ocean-like roar of the throng' suggested an experience that was potentially bewildering and overwhelming. Reassuring descriptions of the social types to be found in the crowd were offered, possibly to offset the poor reputation of travelling shows. As long as a spectator focused on the exhibited animals, his or her visit could not go

---

73 BB Program 1905, 4, 5. 'Leopards, polar bears, great grizzlies from the Rocky Mountains, curious kangaroos, horned horses, dainty little gazelles, and, not least, a great cage filled with a hundred jumping, chattering, playful monkeys, from almost every tropical country in the world. Then there are great droves of camels and dromedaries, the zebras, the zebus, the alpacas, the llamas.'
74 BB Program 1905, 1.

amiss. It was the guidance of the 'polite attendants' that would facilitate movement in one direction, 'instead of being tossed from side to side like a boat adrift in the sea'.[75] It is interesting that the program provided reassurance about distress caused by the pressure of the crowd. It suggests this was a problem, and that clearly a visit to Wonderland was not quite as magical as the name implied. By 1905 the BB audience was organised to follow a structured and managed circuit, and spectators had limited freedom to wander as they once did around menageries in the mid-19th century. The path through the menagerie ended at the seats for the circus ring, and the music of the Carl Clair Military Band encouraged spectators to hurry and take their seats for the circus spectacle. Even circus music evoked the regulated order of a military parade ground.

'War elephants'

An imposing African or Indian elephant became an indispensable part of the circus spectacle and, costumed for a fantasy act, they created a grandiose impression of indomitable strength. The BB circus developed 'The Durbar of Delhi' procession as a feature of the circus show after 1904.[76] The 1905 BB program describes the crowd's progression through the menagerie to a seat at the circus in order to see the preliminary spectacle of magnificent 'war elephants capped with mammoth howdahs, bearing the viceroy and vicereine of India', the representatives of the royal family in this 'land of mystery'.[77] There were also performers in the costumes of British officers on horseback in Horse Guards uniforms and maharajahs on elephants in the 'costliest of silks and satins and cloth of gold', and 'a troop of native soldiers' riding camels followed by 'mystic priests'. The procession included the re-enactment of Indian princes and a Siamese prince making a ceremonial tribute to the viceroy and vicereine, who represented 'Imperial power'.

---

75   BB Program 1905, 2.
76   Davis 2002, 218. 'Durbar' is defined here as a royal court, although it was originally a gathering of indigenous rulers.
77   BB Program 1905, Entertaining features, 7; The Durbar of Delhi, 8.

6 War arts about elephantine military empires

The entertainment was based on events in India in January 1903, when Edward VII of England had become Emperor of India. The British expanded on the longstanding practice of creating durbars in India by developing a special durbar ceremony for the occasion, and invited all the regional rulers within British India and the extended empire to attend and to recognise the king as emperor. King Edward VII was represented by his viceroy, Lord Curzon, who was accompanied by his wife, Mary.

The Delhi Durbar re-enactment was ideal for a turn-of-the-century circus animal show. Additionally this re-enactment suited American audiences because Mary was American. The political event fully justified a spectacle combining military and orientalist fantasy costumes and costumed elephants and horses together. An illustration accompanying the 1905 BB magazine article depicts a performer as Lady Curzon in a long dress and wide-brimmed hat, climbing onto a seated elephant to take her place between an Indian mahout driver and a servant holding a large sun umbrella. Her status was raised in the American circus version of the Delhi Durbar ceremony to a starring role.

In exploring the negotiation of American identity in the context of the British Raj, Nicola Thomas outlines how Mary was deemed an 'American Queen in India' in 1899, possibly to the annoyance of her husband. The Curzons arrived in India in 1898 and left in 1905, and from the outset Mary received widespread newspaper coverage that identified her as the most important woman in colonial Indian society. Thomas explains that 'Mary was positioned at the pinnacle of society within the Raj, a culture that was obsessed with precedent, ceremony and hierarchy'.[78] As the wife of the viceroy she was constantly involved in official duties and hosting formal social events. These duties included entertaining military leaders and accepting the views of her husband that Britain needed to maintain a military presence throughout the empire. Mary acted as a 'conduit for ideas', including that Indian and other troops from the British colonies should be sent to fight in the Boer War in South Africa.

The BB re-enactment of the Delhi Durbar procession and ceremony lasted more than 15 minutes, with the stand-in for Mary and other

---

78   Thomas 2006, 295, also 290, 298, 302. Mary was born in 1870 and died in 1906.

historical figures sitting on elephants, although it obscured the political purpose of the occasion. It expanded the longstanding 19th-century circus practices of depicting historical figures, romantic couples and a victory parade, and followed BB's depiction of 'Oriental India' in 1896. The latter claimed to show Ceylonese and Indian life, but Janet Davis calls this an 'immutable cultural landscape'.[79] The circus spectacle might have reduced the Delhi Durbar event to a fantasy of rich dress fabric and exotic animals, but it did implicitly validate royal power and authority in colonial contexts. This type of pageant with elephants conveyed an impression that the USA could be aligned with Britain and the rest of Europe in their control of other regions of the world.

Deadly punishments

The glorious orientalist spectacle with a large number of elephants was achieved at considerable physical cost to the animals in captivity. The inclusion of an increasing number of elephants in all levels of circus show belied how their management was fraught with difficulty. Brutal punishments continued to be practised throughout the 19th century and into the 20th century towards elephants, some of whom fought back, resisted captivity or became violent. There seemed to be an assumption in the later decades of the 19th century that once an elephant reached a mature age it might need to be killed. Elephants were expensive for circuses, so the animals were punished by methods that seem like torture, and an elephant was only killed as a last resort. Paul Chambers details how elephants, including Jumbo, were physically punished for misbehaviour at London's zoo.[80] At the time of Jumbo's exhibition in the USA in 1883 and 1884, WW Cole's circus presented an even larger elephant, Sampson, used for children's rides with up to 20 on his back at one time. Sampson went on a rampage in the menagerie, throwing cages of animals around the tent until George Conklin shot the elephant in the trunk.[81] Sampson started to chase Conklin, who was, at the time, in his lion tamer costume and riding a horse with

---

79 Davis 2002, 216–17.
80 Chambers 2008, 100–3.
81 Conklin 1921, 138–42, also 125, 141–42.

6 War arts about elephantine military empires

a Mexican saddle. On Cole's instruction Sampson was tied up and severely beaten with tent stakes as punishment, although he survived. Sampson died in a menagerie fire at Bridgeport in 1887.

Elephants that became unmanageable were often shot. Conklin, however, devised an alternative process by which he choked an elephant to death in about 10 minutes as 'the easiest and most humane way'. When Don the elephant escaped BB's in 1889 in England, James Bailey, the owner of BB, ordered him killed. Conklin explains that he had three stakes driven into the ground around Don:

> Then my men brought a couple of ropes an inch and a half in diameter. On one end of each of them I had made a strong slip noose and thoroughly soaped it so it worked freely and easily. These nooses I put round the elephant's throat and carried the ends of the ropes to the stakes at either side of him. The one on the left I put round the stake, drew up snugly, and fastened. On the right I secured a snatch block to the stake, and, passing the rope through the block, carried the end back to where I had another elephant waiting, and fastened the rope to his harness. When all was ready I gave the word, and the [second] elephant began to pull on the rope, which caused both nooses to close round Don's throat with tremendous force. As he felt the ropes tighten, instead of trying to pull away he threw the whole of his weight against them.[82]

Conklin believed that this caused less suffering than other methods such as poisoning and shooting, in which an elephant took longer to die or was maimed but did not die. Conklin's method, however, involved using an unsuspecting second elephant in the process of the killing.

Fritz was another elephant whom Conklin strangled in this way. While onstage for BB in New York at Madison Square Garden, Conklin perceived that Fritz was about to attack him with his tusks, and so he ran quickly through Fritz's legs and offstage without bowing. Conklin had taught Fritz to sit up, hold up his front legs and trunk, and then let Conklin climb onto his back and head and hold up his trunk. The finale of the act involved the elephant group standing in a row and putting

---

82 Conklin 1921, 126, also 127, 129, 130, 131. James Bailey added to the animals in BB by buying out Forepaugh's in 1890 and Cole's in 1896.

their front legs on the hips of the elephant in front, while Fritz at the front of the row lowered his head for Conklin to step onto his tusks. While the other elephants exited, Fritz took a bow with Conklin by lowering and raising his head. After the performance in which Fritz had seemed ready to instigate an attack, Conklin tied Fritz up and gave him 'a good punishing', to which the elephant submitted. In France several years later Fritz bolted and had to be chained. Bailey ordered that Fritz be killed, although this was against Conklin's wishes. The body of Fritz was skinned and stuffed, and placed in the local museum at Tours for scientific study.

Also at BB, when the elephant Mandarin killed a keeper who was cleaning up, Bailey instructed that Mandarin's crate be duly dropped into the ocean. Some elephants retaliated against their treatment, but their capacity to fight back was restricted. In another incident an elephant threw off a human rider and tore his body in half. If an elephant reacted out of fright, startled by unexpected elements in their environment, their head or trunk might accidentally crush a human to death.

Elephant death usually took place away from public view. In an exception at Coney Island on 4 January 1905, Topsy was electrocuted in a publicised event that was also filmed by Thomas Edison.[83] She was accused of killing three keepers, one of whom had, earlier in her life, burnt her with a lit cigar. It is difficult to know if the keeper's deaths were accidents or whether Topsy was taking revenge for an earlier offence. Circus annals record a number of situations that provoked extreme reactions and accidents between elephants and humans, resulting in a fatality.[84] The domination of elephants in order for humans to achieve close proximity to them continued to require brutal physical methods of control and punishment.

---

83   For a fuller account see, for example, Scigliano 2002; for a discussion of complications arising from ethics and elephants including Topsy, see Rothfels 2008, 101–19.
84   Campbell 1957.

6 War arts about elephantine military empires

'Elephant etiquette' and war veterans

In the early 20th century Hagenbeck's sent its largest contingent of elephants and animals to date to the USA, only to have its new animal show with innovative painted backdrops outdone by a war re-enactment mounted by Frank Fillis. In 1904 Reuben Castang supervised and presented the 20 elephants in an act for Carl Hagenbeck's trained animal show performing at the Louisiana Purchase Exposition, known as the St Louis World's Fair. By then the world leaders in trained animal shows were reported to demonstrate humane animal acts as the result of gentle training that led to well-behaved and cooperative animals. In 1904, however, the trained animal act was completely overshadowed by Fillis' realistic full-scale Boer War re-enactment with hundreds of animals and thousands of specimens. Even Hagenbeck's penultimate show could not equal the interest generated by the immense scale of Fillis' war spectacle, which attracted up to 25,000 spectators per performance. The staged event not only demonstrated the global spread of the war re-enactment genre, but also revealed how increasingly larger war re-enactments had become inseparable from other types of animal entertainment.

Castang travelled with Lorenz Hagenbeck and the Hagenbeck elephants as part of Hagenbeck's shipment of 150 animals and 30 trainers sent from Hamburg to New York in 1904.[85] This was the largest group of exotic animals transported that year across the Atlantic, and Carl gave the responsibility for the safe sea transportation of the animals to his son, Lorenz, instructing him not to lose a single elephant.[86] The shipment included 36 elephants, some of whom went to Ringling Bros Circus, some to the menagerie at Coney Island's Luna Park, and the rest to the St Louis show. Luna Park at Coney Island had the world's largest fixed-venue menagerie at that time. Once landed, the elephants were transported from the dock in wooden boxes on top of carts, which had to be cut down to get under rail bridges, so the elephants who stuck out of the top of each box had to bend down. The arrivals attracted considerable newspaper publicity and crowds lined the streets to see the

---

85   Thompson 1934, 82.
86   Hagenbeck 1956, 48, 49; also see Kasson 1978, about Coney Island entertainment within modernity.

elephants pass by. The elephants destined for the St Louis show then travelled by train with Castang accompanying them.

While elephant performances pandered to misconceptions of ease in human–animal relations, behind the scenes even the most experienced keeper approached a familiar elephant with caution, first calling out the elephant's name. Castang, who conditioned the elephants sold by Hagenbeck's to circuses, explains that 'elephant etiquette' was premised on coming close to an elephant and standing quietly still, while the elephant inspected the person with his or her trunk and then permitted stroking.[87]

Castang's first act with six trained elephants debuted in Vienna. He later toured with Hagenbeck's circus in Europe, where he gained a reputation as an elephant trainer and all-round 'animal man'. Castang's father and grandfather were London animal dealers, and the family, of German-Swiss origin, seems to have had a menagerie shop in London from the mid-18th century. Family members definitely assisted when Chuny, the elephant who was later killed by firing squad in the Exeter Exchange building, apparently developed toothache in London. In 1893 Carl Hagenbeck took the then 13-year-old Castang back with him to the Hamburg zoo theme park to undertake his adolescent apprenticeship. RW Thompson reports that Castang found elephants graceful and 'not only beautiful but sad'.[88] He nursed a sick female elephant, Bedelia, and began learning elephant care under Julius Wagner. Castang learnt the verbal instructions derived from Hindi for Indian elephants, such as 'come here', 'kneel' and 'move quickly', as well as the elephant's physical ways of communicating hunger, happiness and anger. He described learning how to be the first human to sit on an elephant brought from the wild, and through a range of emergency situations he learnt how to avert disaster and to stop a stampede.

The 1904 St Louis World's Fair, opened remotely by Theodore Roosevelt through the telegraph system, had pavilions showing geographical features and people from around the globe in a travel

---

87   Thompson 1934, 40–42, also 16, 26, 31, 37. Castang's most famous co-performers would be the chimpanzee stars Max, Moritz and Akka, appearing at Bertram Mills Circus in 1931 and 1932 and in Hollywood films, and touring internationally and even to the Australian Tivoli stages.
88   Thompson 1934, 31.

6 War arts about elephantine military empires

extravaganza that included an exhibit derived from Jules Verne's novel, *Around the world in eighty days*.[89] The lions and tigers in the Hagenbeck's menagerie entertainment proved especially popular, with an exhibition space designed for spectators to look down on them from above. A joint American–Hagenbeck business venture, the Pavilion was a complex with a circus arena and fenced-off viewing areas called 'jungle, primeval forest, fjord and pack ice landscapes', created with painted backdrops developed by Hagenbeck's. The 'Arctic Ocean Panorama' appeared on the cover of *Scientific American*.[90] The painted backdrops of scenes that had long been used in theatres to depict major events, such as battles or disasters, had also been developed for other venues, including menageries and museums. In St Louis, painted panoramas and live animals staged ideas of the geographical diversity and encapsulated landscapes in remote places.

Castang led the elephants up to a platform, where he sent them down a chute into a tank of water.[91] The Hagenbeck's show was positioned next to the Japanese village and in front of a Wild West Hotel that had riding displays by 'Apaches, Sioux, Winnebagos and Senecas', which Lorenz describes as the most genuine shows he had seen.[92] Other attractions included buffalo dancing by Native Americans, mail-coach hold-ups and shooting displays. Forewarned about a fire threat by a letter 'from an animal-loving gangster' fond of elephants, Lorenz moved some animals and had others ready to move, managing to save them when fire did break out towards the close of the fair, although the newspapers mistakenly reported the destruction of the animal show by fire.

Hagenbeck's St Louis animal show went on tour and Lorenz and Castang became part of the 'Giant Circus and Wild Animal Show'. Castang would later appear at the New York Hippodrome with a troupe of elephants in the autumn of 1907. The act with 12 elephants was the first time such a large herd had appeared on a stage, although they worked on a 120-foot (36 m) section in front of it. Castang, in top hat

---

89 See Parezo & Fowler 2007 for analysis of ethnographic shows.
90 *Scientific American* 1904, 6 August: cover image.
91 Thompson 1934, 113. The two main trainers in the circus arena were Charly Judge and Castang.
92 Hagenbeck 1956, 53, also 55–56.

and tails with lavender gloves, rode the lead elephant at the end of the act. He added gimmicks such as two elephants seeming to waltz, and painted one animal, Patsy, green for St Patrick's Day.[93]

Perceptions that elephants have a greater individuality compared with other animals from the wild, and claims that elephants were human-like in their responses, were reinforced with human-like action and framing in such elephant acts. While trained elephants had become entrenched in modernist entertainment and dominated animal shows in the USA, strong competition came from escalated fighting displays and war re-enactments.

Frank Fillis had been approached to stage an event with war veterans led by Captain Arthur Waldo Lewis from St Louis, who had fought in the Boer War and wanted veterans to enact aspects of the war for audiences at the 1904 Fair.[94] The shareholder company that financed and organised the show for US$195,000 on 10 acres (4 ha) in St Louis approached Fillis to re-create the Anglo–Boer War. Fillis obtained a large amount of artillery, three machine-guns and 600 horses and recruited 50 indigenous people from Africa, reportedly with Sotho identity. He was urged to represent the war victories of both sides.

The outdoor re-enactment space was large and allowed the horses and riders to move around as if on a battlefield. In a substantial stunt, Fillis taught 50 horses to lie down and lie still as if shot dead, to simulate battlefield carnage, and this became a celebrated feature of the St Louis show (Plate 7).[95] The circus trick of teaching one horse to limp or play dead dating from Philip Astley's original feats had been greatly magnified in the early 20th century with the coaching of such a large number. The visual effect was a realistic battlefield to scale, with 'dead horses'.

The record-breaking size of this spectacle was unparalleled. The amphitheatre for 25,000 spectators contained a Boer encampment, a British military camp, a kraal for an indigenous leader, Chief Umkalali, and representatives of 60 different African nations as well as an enormous exhibition of artefacts. The live equestrian battle re-enactment happened in conjunction with a display of dead animal

---

93   Thompson 1934, 165–66.
94   van der Merwe 2007, 134–35, also 136–39. van der Merwe reproduces original posters, bills and photographs.
95   See Hyland 2010 for more about horses in the Boer War.

6 War arts about elephantine military empires

specimens that included 47 lion skins, 100 leopard skins, 400 kaross skins, buffalo horns and ivory. The specimen exhibition alone almost seemed like a major museum collection. By the turn of the 20th century, the museum, menagerie, circus and war re-enactment had converged into one huge spectacle, and a version subsequently went on tour in the USA.

The main show, the re-enactment of the Boer War, was described in the bulletin of the World's Fair as a hit.[96] Turning away 10,000 spectators at the opening on 17 June 1904, the war re-enactment proved highly successful with two shows daily; the season ran until 2 December 1904. The program opened with British war veterans, followed by Boer veterans and the artillery display; part one concluded with horse races in which the Australian Boer war veteran contingent from the New South Wales Lancers did a sword demonstration. Part two involved the enactment of the Battle of Colenso – a key battle between British and Boer soldiers in 1899 – with gunfire and cannons. The horses falling down dead as casualties of war and laying motionless were particularly praised, and one even limped off.

Floris van der Merwe notes one interesting deviation in mid-August from the main program. In a revealing cultural convergence of hunting and war re-enactment, the British contingent staged a fox hunt with 50 dogs (probably under Frank Fillis' direction). There was also a regular circus program presented during November.

The bulletin of the World's Fair describes the main show of the Boer War re-enactment as the largest spectacle staged in the USA, 'ahead of all predecessors', 'a triumph of genius, its setting a work of tragic art', and a 'fascinating and captivating entertainment'.[97] Those attending the whole St Louis World's Fair could move from colonial battlefield, war re-enactment and indigenous village displays to seeing lion, tiger and elephant acts and other animals in circus and menagerie collections. The struggle to achieve animal exhibition converged with the violence that displaced people and led to war. Any distinctions between event and venue, circus and menagerie, war re-enactment and ethnographic show, live and dead specimen were obviated as all known

---

96 Cited in van der Merwe 2007, 149; see also 139, 142–50.
97 Cited in van der Merwe 2007, 149.

elements of entertainment with animals had been brought together, side by side, in the one mammoth exposition.

Popular spectacles of this type, if not of similar scale, were also evident in Britain and Europe. The regular use of entertainment spaces that could accommodate larger numbers of people delivered an insidious slippage between military parades and other spectacles held at the same venues. At London's Agricultural Hall, with its history of fairground entertainments, and later at the Olympia, it was possible to see the reproduction of a military tournament one day and, on another, to see a menagerie and circus. Venues that spanned the menagerie to the military potentially also reached the same audiences, but it is difficult to evaluate whether attendance at those shows indicated regular habits, tacit support for imperialist ventures, or simply a publicised event that everyone wanted to see.

In the convergence of popular entertainments, colonial exhibits became embedded in the wider context of fighting shows. For example, the shows produced by the English performer, manager and show entrepreneur Charles Cochran, marketed to a wide audience, ranged from conventional theatre and musical theatre to circus and menagerie, from wrestling matches to boxing contests.[98] As well, Cochran and Frank Bostock co-leased a moving-picture theatre, pointing to the strong connection between show animals and film production from the outset. When Cochran first presented his circus at Olympia with fair booths and a menagerie, he contracted Biddall's menagerie to present the animals.[99] In 1913 Cochran organised a tour of the Hagenbeck menagerie zoo and circus to London with ethnographic shows. Hagenbeck's created acts for 'The Wonder Zoo' and 'Big Circus' at London's Olympia, which Cochran calls a 'stupendous event'.[100] The Wonder

---

98 Cochran 1929, 135, also 136, 139, 191, 193. But it was his involvement in the promotion of wrestling displays that revealed the convergence in popular entertainment, 110, 112–14. Boxing was the domain of the National Sporting Club and Wonderland and even in 1914 boxing could not fill the 5000-seat venue at the Olympia easily without much publicity. For a discussion of wrestling as a traditional sport and in pre-colonial Africa, see Paul 1987.
99 Cochran 1929, 136, 139. One of the menagerie bulls was named the Sacred Bull of Benares, and was costumed with gilded hoofs and an Indian rug. He was exhibited in a booth decorated as an Indian temple with attendants doing rites that had not been seen before. This free exhibit received considerable publicity.

6 War arts about elephantine military empires

Zoo's hits were 500 Barbary apes presented with a trench between them and the spectators, and lions who moved against backdrops of mountains. By comparison, the 5000-seat circus presented only a handful of select animals in trained acts, and included BB's leading star, the Australian equestrian May Wirth, as well as Richard Sawade with tigers and Rueben Castang, who had been Carl Hagenbeck's apprentice, with the chimpanzees Max and Moritz. Cochran writes that Castang 'carried out a theory of [Carl] Hagenbeck's, that anthropoid apes might, by a systematic education from earliest youth, become accustomed to live like human beings.'[101] Their performance involved standard tricks as well as comic ones, such as bicycle riding, and Cochran recounted that Castang rewarded Max but chastised and punished Moritz for responding to audience laughter and applause, and for doing the same tricks repeatedly for more applause.

By the early 1900s, the trade and exhibition of humans and animals had become inseparably linked to military identity, formalised fights and large-scale shows about war. The majority of the thousands of exotic wild animals who were acquired from the colonies were by then consigned to an anonymous large group, with only the exceptional few becoming star performers and being treated as such. The extensive displacement of the original inhabitants of colonial lands included animals, who had no means of returning to their countries of origin. But most animals became displaced further within the much larger entertainments developed towards the end of the 19th century, relegated to the background to create an authentic atmosphere. The presentation of species diversity had been replaced by displays of hundreds of anonymous animals of the same species. Spectators might have been generally better behaved, but capacity audiences gave tacit approval to the brutal process of shipping thousands of animals, dead or alive, across the world for gigantic entertainment spectacles.

---

100   Cochran 1929, 186–89; Hagenbeck 1956, 98.
101   Cochran 1929, 187, 188–89.

7
Nature's beauties and scientific specimen contests

This chapter considers big cat acts trained by women in the 1890s and early 1900s in relation to the acts of male trainers, and to the broader context of values in the natural sciences. Live animal acts now competed for audiences with other types of exhibitions, including museum collections of dead specimens. Female trainers remained anomalous within an alignment of training and the natural sciences as they continued to be evaluated by older 19th-century ideas of animal responsiveness to kindness.

The imperative to hunt, collect, study and preserve animal specimens for museums, zoos and menageries remained a thoroughly masculine activity and competitive ideas of scale and species numbers surreptitiously became incorporated into contests between nations. An admirer of trained lion acts and taxidermied display, American president Theodore Roosevelt went on African safari on behalf of the natural sciences. Meanwhile, in trained acts, women in particular conveyed a misleading impression of gentleness in artificially naturalised poses with wild animals who had been trained out of their natural behaviour.

Feminine care

The female animal trainer constituted an unconventional social identity, and recognition of her training achievements was undermined by prejudice. Social beliefs about an innate nature forestalled recognition of women as trainers of fierce animals. Instead, their acts received mixed reactions and were viewed with suspicion, even by male trainers. The animal act thus displayed contradictory human gender identity values.

Madame Louise Morelli was a well-known trainer working with a leopard act for Frank Bostock c. 1897 in Europe, and in the USA by the early 1900s, performing at Luna Park, Coney Island.[1] She was probably the trainer of the leopard act, which had five or six animal performers. A studio photograph suggests that there might have been a mixture of leopards and jaguars. Morelli wore a full-skirted, long white dress indicative of the fashion of the 1890s, and she was seated, her feet resting on one animal lying down, surrounded by five leopards on pedestal seats of varying heights. The presence of the pedestals provided the act's apparatus and the calmness of the seated leopards in their respective and varied poses indicated a new type of trained animal act.

Frank Bostock describes Morelli as:

> a small woman and rather frail, but her nerve and quiet self-possession are truly wonderful. Leopards, panthers and jaguars are noted for their stealthy, sly ways, and their deceit and treachery. They are most difficult to train and subdue, and can never be relied upon. These cringing big cats are the most alert fiends by nature; they have none of the nobility of the lion, none of the aloofness of the tiger.[2]

The emotional qualities attributed to Morelli were polarised with those accorded the leopards; frail femininity was contrasted with animals deemed 'fiends by nature'. While admiring of her daring and self-control, Bostock did not expect a woman to subdue leopards who were judged as an enemy within nature. According each species a temperament, Bostock admits that it was wonderful to watch leopards doing feats: 'to see four or five do so with one small woman is a

---

[1] Velvin 1906, 144–45. Velvin saw Morelli's act at Luna Park.
[2] Bostock 1903, 220, also 221–23, 255. Photographs of Louise Morelli. One has the caption 'jaguars, panthers and leopards' but there do not seem to have been panthers in the act, although one animal appears to have a larger head like a jaguar.

marvelous sight'. He seemed surprised that a woman could work with them. Morelli spoke to the leopards in French and Bostock attributed her management of the act to their responses to the tone of her voice – he implied that it was soft. If female interaction was gentler and softer, the female trainer was perceived as weaker and less heroic.

Although female performers had worked with trained horses and other animals throughout the 19th century, and in circus from its earliest days, some animal acts remained acceptable for female presenters while others drew a degree of criticism. In the 1880s domesticated animals in dog and pigeon acts appeared in circuses everywhere, presented by female trainers such as Alice Fontainbleau, Madame Felix and Madame Eliza (Elise) Fillis, Frank Fillis' second wife.[3] Female presenters routinely appeared in novelty acts with a mix of performing dogs and monkeys; for example, Mademoiselle Carlini at London's Royal Aquarium and Crystal Palace in 1886 and 1887 and at the Agricultural Hall. By the mid-1880s, Leoni Clarke's 'Happy Family' act consisted of cats, monkeys, rats, mice and canaries. In that act, the cats walked over the other performers sitting on a cord, and the rats travelled in a miniature train. At one time Clarke's business also presented a wrestling lion.

In contravention of gendered restrictions on dangerous activity, women had appeared in cage acts in family-owned menagerie businesses for 50 years, and they continued to work with a full range of animals. For example, in the 1890s Mademoiselle Sherizade [sic] appeared briefly with the Bostock and Wombwell's big cats, and Madame Telzero appeared for the menagerie with wolves.[4] By the 1890s, however, such acts with women were no longer simply part of family enterprises, and individual performers moved between menageries. For example, a performer known only as Thora presented monkeys for Frank Bostock's, was also associated with Hagenbeck's and with Julius Seeth in 1912, and worked with horses for Edward Bostock in 1915.

Morelli and other female trainers indicated a new type of independent female trainer emerging during the mid-1890s who presented a succession of complex tricks by big cats and remained with an act

---

3 Turner 1995, 46–47, 48, also 21, 28.
4 Turner 2000, 103, 106, 107.

for years. Yet the same act with a male presenter such as Captain Jack Bonavita or Seeth was considered an innovative display of control over the animals, and Morelli probably worked in the same programs as Bonavita. A public perception that an attack was more imminent in an act with a female presenter remained.

The social implications of such an act extended beyond the dangers of proximity and fears for Morelli's safety. For Frank Bostock, Morelli's most dangerous trick involved allowing one of her leopards, Cartouche, 'to place the weight of his prostrate body on a stick held horizontally in her hands and over her face, while she looks up into his glaring eyes'.[5] The extent of the presenter's control of the animal performers in the execution of such a feat was at stake since loss of control might place spectators at risk. Even Frank Bostock, who was familiar with Morelli's skills, perceived that she was more at risk of attack than male trainers because of her small build. Further, the closeness of the animal to the woman in the feat held other connotations. The animal was standing up full-length on back legs, face-to-face, eye-to-eye with the woman – Morelli had to look up to see the animal – which evoked notions of partnership. A feat whereby an animal performer became a substitute partner placed a female performer beyond notions of protection, rescue and manly chivalry as it also potentially sexualised the interaction.

A contrast between ideas of active wild nature and passive feminine beauty might have enhanced the appeal of the act. Morelli performed with bare arms and neck, so the meshed scars from scratches across her neck and shoulders were visible.[6] If it were assumed that a female trainer could not impose the force that a male trainer might bring when problems arose, the examples given by Bostock confirm that it was quick thinking and fast, agile reactions that protected a performer when something untoward disturbed the animal performers. Morelli moved quickly. In one incident the lace of Morelli's dress brushed against a leopard who was moving towards a pedestal and, surprised, the leopard sprang forward. Bostock says that there would have been a serious accident if she had not caught the leopard with the whip as she jumped away. Bostock seemed to attribute her prevention of the attack to good

---

5 Bostock 1903, 223, also 252, 255.
6 Velvin 1906, 145.

luck, rather than rapid reflex reactions and experience. There was another incident, however, when a leopard did not leave the cage at the end of the act and, released, sprang onto Morelli's neck and shoulders. It was Captain Bonavita who rushed into the cage to assist an injured Morelli. Bostock said that considerable effort was made to persuade Morelli to give up her act, but she refused and returned to the act as soon as she had recovered. Whether or not this indicated that women were assumed not to have freely chosen exotic animal training, Bonavita experienced numerous problems with uncooperative animals and there was no similar assertion that he should give up amid the admiration for him.

The details of an act's content and the sequence of tricks by Morelli and other female performers are scant, and the elements of the routine must be surmised from accounts arising from its disruption. Madame Pianka (Charlotte Bishop) also worked for Frank Bostock and toured in the USA. A photograph, 'Mme Pianka and her class', shows five lions placed in a graduated pyramid formation, standard for a trained act at that time (Plate 8). The caption implies that the animals were like pupils. They sit on high pedestals of varied height behind Pianka, standing with her back to the lions, dressed in a full-length elegant white dress. There are five lower pedestals, suggesting that the lions moved between these pedestals during the act. Pianka's act started with the lions walking in and climbing on to pedestals – she may actually have been working with animals that Bostock trained. In one part she fired a gun with blanks and in another part she put her arm around a lion's neck in a 'natural pose'. Of course it was a completely unnatural pose, but the familiarity and casualness of the human and animal posed together suggested interspecies friendship and implied that the lion had become like a pet.[7] Bostock includes another studio photograph showing Pianka without the lions and wearing a large hat and a white dress with a train at the back, and carrying a white parasol – that is, dressed to the standard of socially respectable apparel. In one incident when a swipe from a lion's paw tore Pianka's long dress and cut into her skin so that she was bleeding, she continued with the act to the end. At the beginning of the act, she had taken into the arena cage

---

7   Bostock, 1903, 157–58, also 85, 229. The detail of Pianka's act comes from a description of an attack on Frank Bostock.

a bunch of red roses given to her by an audience member, and a lion who had not reached his pedestal sprung forward at the roses, catching Pianka with his paw. The roses were a new addition to the cage environment, and attracted attention possibly because of the smell or the colour. Pianka threw the roses down; the other lions sprang to look and then went back to their pedestals, and she continued with the act. She fainted from her injury once she was offstage.

The full-length, full-skirted, fashionable dress of the female presenters may have put them at greater risk of incidental accidents than male costumes, but what each wore was also of special interest to the lion performers. An account of the preparation for Pianka's photographic session to produce the aforementioned photographs, including the one with the lions sitting on their pedestals, revealed that the session had to be extended over three days. Before the photographic session began, Pianka had made a new dress of white that Ellen Velvin describes as 'organdy, pretty and dainty enough for a fashionable tea-party'.[8] When the photography was due to start, the lions did not want to enter the arena, as if they knew that it was not a regular performance. Velvin continues, 'Trying to rouse them the trainer [Pianka] touched one lion lightly with the whip. He struck at the whip gently with his paw, as though to put it out of the way, his claws caught in the light dress and the whole skirt was nearly torn to shreds.' The dress was repaired, and the posing resumed, except that this time a lion reached out to touch a new bow that Pianka had added to her hair. An attendant or trainer outside the cage flicked a longer whip at the curious lion, who took this as his cue to get down off the pedestal, as happened in the routine towards the end of the act. The other lions followed him and they would not return to the pedestals, assuming that they had done the act for the day. When the photographic posing was resumed on the third day, the lion at the top of the pedestal pyramid again tried to reach out with his paw to touch Pianka's new bow, and this was captured by the camera (Plate 8).

Female performers experienced the same problems as men in training when an element of the environment was varied even slightly and the animals reacted adversely or with curiosity. On another

---

8   Velvin 1906, 63.

occasion, the cage for Pianka's act had been lost, and she had to perform in a smaller one. The change upset the lion performers and a lioness, usually compliant, refused to go into the performance cage. Pianka 'coaxed, ordered, and flicked her whip' without effect, and Bostock intervened to 'insist on obedience'.[9] The lioness obeyed and went through her routine, but Bostock admitted that his confidence made him careless and when he flourished his whip the mate of the lioness leapt 20 feet (6 m) and jumped on him. The lion proceeded to lift Bostock up in his mouth. Pianka was holding a revolver with blanks and fired two blanks close to the lion, who fortunately responded out of habit to the sound and dropped Bostock from his teeth hold. Firing blanks was the cue for coming closer and, combined with Pianka's other cue when she draped her arm around the lion's neck, the lion's resistance dissipated and he took up his accustomed sitting position. As a regular feature of a trained lion act with female presenters and trainers, this naturalising pose on cue had been usefully instigated.

By the last decade of the 19th century the role of a female presenter who ran quickly in and out of a menagerie cage, while attendants stood ready outside, had been expanded to include a routine with dancing action in front of lions sitting up on pedestals. A dancing act was still far simpler for the presenter than concurrent acts with trained feats. La Belle Selica danced and pirouetted in among four lions sitting on pedestals. Bostock claimed that she was only at risk when the lions descended from the pedestals,[10] and they were trained to only come down on cue. Once down, however, their behaviour was less predictable. In one performance La Belle Selica was halfway through the dance routine when a lioness climbed down and lay on the ground. Selica continued to dance and verbally instructed the lioness to return to the pedestal, but she only growled and did not respond even to the flick of Selica's whip. A second lion climbed down and sprang forward, knocking Selica to the ground. She jumped up and rushed for the cage door, avoiding more serious injury. Bostock writes that, curiously, the lions appeared to have forgotten all about the incident the next day. Others gaining prominence within the next decade included Mademoiselle Adgie and her

---

9   Bostock 1903, 157.
10 Bostock 1903, 194, also 197

five lions performing with Barnum and Bailey Circus The Greatest Show on Earth (BB), c. 1913.[11]

A woman who married a male trainer in the 1890s or who took over the presentation of an act worked with trained animals habituated to their routine, although she might later train feats of her own. For example, Hermann Haupt's first wife, Marguerite, joined his act – he was taught animal training by Claire Heliot (see below).[12] Marguerite was reported to have treated the lions kindly, as if they were pets, and she worked in the act until 1912 when she was attacked and fatally wounded. Haupt's family acts included one with a horse-riding lion.[13] The same act with a female, instead of a male, presenter could be viewed differently and some performers accentuated the distinction for effect.

A female presenter who was part of a family or married into a business could be assumed to do the existing act out of love for the male trainer – whether she cared about the animals or not. But women did train animals into routines. The bear trainer Mademoiselle Aurora trained her polar bears to appear and take up positions on stands in the arena, but she kept their exertion to a minimum, so as not to exhaust and distress them.[14] Bears had a reputation for being less nervous than other animals, and as Bostock explains, find 'pleasure in acting and showing off before others', undertaking the routine whenever there was a spectator. This also made them more unpredictable. In a photograph Aurora stands in front of five large polar bears perched on an arch behind her. She wears a cap, thigh-high jackboots, and a military-style jacket belted at the waist reaching down as far as the top of her thighs – this was a far safer costume than a dress. If Aurora's presence in the act in the early 1900s contravened gender roles, her costume exposing her thigh tops would definitely have challenged social propriety. The appeal of her act extended beyond the accomplishment of the bears to the burlesque costuming that emulated a male military uniform.

---

11 Jackson 2008, 64–66
12 Kober 1931, 109–10; Stark & Orr 1940, 42.
13 For a fuller discussion of this type of feat, see Tait 2012.
14 Bostock 1903, 53, also 160 about Aurora.

7 Nature's beauties and scientific specimen contests

A psychology of kindness

Lion trainer Claire Heliot was described as being 'frail but fearless', and 'mild and gentle' in a 1905 *New York Times* feature article,[15] although she was actually physically strong enough to carry a fully grown lion, Sicchi, in the act, and to manage a rebellious one. Such descriptions reveal illogical responses to a female performer working with lions. In the *New York Times* article about Heliot's appearing at the New York Hippodrome, she was also labelled a 'timid sentimentalist'. The lions, however, were deemed murderous and the article begins by saying that the lions will not hesitate to kill her. The article describes the instincts and sentiments of the lions at length so that, by association, Heliot's gentle, mild 'sentiments' are made to seem instinctive. An act with a female trainer was not appraised as a calculated demonstration of human will exercised over animals, who had been conditioned to overcome their instincts and behaviour. Instead Heliot was, like the animals, attributed with instinctive reactions.

Heliot was perceived as being kind to the lions and they complied accordingly. Was it simply the expectation that female trainers and presenters would be kinder or were they actually more nurturing? Heliot explains that lions have effective memories and '[i]f you are good to lions, they will be good to you. Be positive with them, dominate them, but do not strike them.'[16] She did not use force to train for feats in keeping with the ideals of the new training practice.

Heliot was the stage name of Klara Haumann (Huth) from Leipzig, Germany, the daughter of a government post office official and the granddaughter of a minister of religion.[17] In April 1897 she created a sensation in Leipzig when she performed at the zoo, assisted by two male attendants, and she later toured widely. The presence of the male attendants may have been socially protective of Heliot's reputation, as much as a standard defensive watch for sudden or subtle movement pre-empting attack. She was on tour in England with 10 lions and two large hounds by 1901. The touring act included a simulation of a dinner party scene with the lions seated at a table to be served raw

---

15   Pendennis 1905 (SM)1.
16   Heliot 1906, 466, also 463–68; her article includes diary entries.
17   Tuner 2000, 55; Kober 1931, 109.

meat by Heliot. The meat-feeding scene was less mentioned in the USA although Heliot explained in detail how she started training lions by hand-feeding them and that practice definitely continued.

Heliot was unusual because there is no apparent link to someone even indirectly connected with Hagenbeck or Bostock's until later in her career. She expressed a love of lions, explaining that they were beautiful to look at, and she had been encouraged by a zoo director who observed her regular visits to the zoo gardens as a teenager. Her ambition in 1906, however, was to save enough money to retire to a country property in three years, suggesting economic reasons for undertaking the act, although her retirement was also attributed to an attack in Copenhagen when a lion bit through her leg. In 1905 her act had as many as 14 lions and they performed behind a 12-foot-high (3.6 m) spiked arena barrier to music from *Carmen*. Heliot was described patting the lions and lightly touching the nose of one with a leather whip, although she also carried a steel rod. Three photographs accompanying the 1905 *New York Times* article, however, reveal Heliot encouraging two lions to walk on a raised platform and a third female lion to mount a rolling barrel, and she poses with her arm around the neck of a lion with a mane. Again the pose undermined any impression of the regimented training used over time to achieve it.

The climax of Heliot's act involved a feat in which she carried Sicchi, a 10-year-old lion, on her shoulders as she left the performance. It was certainly part of the act in 1905 in New York and in 1906 in Chicago with 'A Yankee Circus on Mars'. It involved draping the 350-pound (159 kg) Sicchi across her back and shoulders, which was probably achieved by lifting the animal performer off an elevated platform onto her shoulders. Heliot was physically strong, although she explained that she started with the young Sicchi, and her strength grew as he gained weight. The feat was new, although it was also pioneered by Captain Bonavita for Bostock's and Julius Seeth with Hagenbeck's.[18]

The image of Heliot carrying Sicchi is particularly striking because the weight of the lion envelops her body (see cover). The 19th-century notion that wild animal species could be thoroughly tamed by culture, with human sympathy and feminine kindness, is grotesquely enacted

---

18 Tait 2012, 108–46.

in the passivity of the lion in this awkward pose. This demonstration of harmonious interspecies relations belies the considerable conditioning of one unique lion personality to achieve it. The addition of a flag held in Sicchi's mouth, however, highlights how even Heliot's trained animal act reinforced ideas of militarised colonial rule at the end of the 19th century, but here as if the animal were supporting the nation-state.

The actions and feats in Heliot's act demonstrated physical control and she was compared to Seeth; she was also billed as 'The Lady Daniel' in a biblical refrain. She performed in the long dresses that were the fashion of the time, including one made of white satin. In one incident when a lion named August bit her and her blood spurted over the white dress, Heliot drove the lions back to their cages, bound the wound with a handkerchief, and waited for a doctor to arrive to clean the wound to prevent poisoning. In New York in 1905 a lion's claw became caught up in the lace of her dress and when he became disturbed that he could not extract it, she was wounded.[19] Velvin includes an account of how Heliot made a clear distinction between a deliberate lion's bite and accidental scratches, which were frequent, and observes that her skin was covered in deep scars from these. Heliot claimed that a lion in her act would not bite her because she hand-fed them, and even a particularly antagonistic lion did not bite her. Velvin observes how Heliot 'would take a small piece of meat, and telling each lion to open his mouth would put it inside with her fingers'.[20]

Statements attributed to Heliot suggest that she felt responsible for the welfare of animals. They were not accorded subjective agency, and Heliot is quoted in the *New York Times* article explaining that animals such as an elephant revealed how 'a divine order of things has given his soul into the keeping of man'. She was being attributed an established belief that it was a human moral duty to provide for animals and to improve brute natures. But Heliot's diary entries explain that while she loved the lions in the act, she was creating performance, contradicting perceptions of an instinctual female nature. Her protective strategies during the act were a steel rod, a whip and a quick exit through the cage door. She once had to delay a performance when the whip went missing because one of the dogs had removed it to a kennel.[21] She continues that

---

19   Velvin 1906, 57.
20   Velvin 1906, 74–75.

during a performance when the lion August was in a bad temper, she had to threaten him with the steel bar, and a 'pretty curly-haired little girl in the front row cried, "Why don't you push him, lady?" It made me laugh.' The expectations of handling arising from simpler 19th-century tamer acts lingered, carrying misleading assumptions that lions could be easily touched.

Heliot's act was trained and the lions were not pushed around the cage. It took Heliot two years to develop a fully trained act by first spending hours in the cage with them, and then teaching them to respond to names and eventually to performance cues delivered in French. A troublesome lion on tour was often omitted from the act for a time. Heliot was more concerned that they would hurt each other in fights, and Sicchi had a habit of taking the mane off any other lion put into his cage. But in the 1905 *New York Times* article, Heliot's capacity to work with the lions is attributed to nurturing sentiments, and a quote from Heliot about the accidental scratches on her skin being due to the playfulness of the lions supports this notion. The lions are described in emotive language as embodying 'violence, rage, fearlessness, hatred, power, a wicked shrewdness, the impenetrable expression of a sphinx, and the instinct for murder . . . [and having] no virtues that are without passion'.[22] They snarl and put their ears back in reaction to Heliot, and her conciliatory response is interpreted as being coquettish. The article claims that aggressive lions did not appreciate her adoration of them, but they are, however, involved in a 'beautiful psychology'. While recognising how human psychologies might manage human–animal relations, the statement reinforced notions about management with kindness and a polarisation between animal aggression and human trust and moral responsibility. James Sully writes that although 'Animal or Comparative Psychology', as the study of animal minds had become known, had become a separate field by the 1890s, emotional ambiguity in animal expression and the 'region of animal instinct' was still 'a psychological puzzle'.[23] Nonetheless a human psychology of emotions prefigured the contradictory status of the female trainer, since kindness

---

21   Heliot 1906, 463, 464.
22   Pendennis 1905, (SM)1.
23   Sully 1892, 21.

and caring could be attributed to women and calculated manoeuvres went unrecognised.

Heliot raised the profile of female big cat trainers in the USA. She returned to southern Germany when she retired from performance, and was reported working as a hairdresser in 1930.[24] Heliot stood out from her contemporaries for the feats in her act. For example, about 1905 in the USA there was an Austrian woman presenter working with five adult lions in an act that supported her widowed mother and sister; there was also a Frenchwoman who worked with a large brown bear who carried her by the neck with his or her mouth.[25] The bear act ended quickly as audiences did not favour it; apparently the performer was grieving over the death of her child, and by implication had a death wish.

Even though trained acts were recognised to use aspects of psychology through care and kindness, the women were not attributed an ordered repetitive approach to physical training. A female trainer's interactions with the animals were based on intangible, socially ascribed emotional attitudes, rather than careful observation and knowledge of species behaviour that might constitute a so-named scientific approach.

Married to the act

The reputation of female presenters who were part of a family business or who married into an act was to some extent socially protected, even though appearing with exotic animals was highly unconventional. For unmarried female performers, a capacity to undertake this work was deemed to be a negation of domestic duties and was interpreted as the dismissal of conventional morality. It denoted 'unnatural' female behaviour.

A notion that an animal act had become a substitute for a marriage partner emerged in reports about Tilly Bébé – commentators seemed troubled that her animal act might be diverting her from family life. Bébé was well known for her work with lions in Europe at

---

24   Turner 2000, 55. The likely source of this information is Kober 1931, 109.
25   Velvin 1906, 119–21, 158–59.

the beginning of the 20th century, and in one commentary she reportedly took over an act at Sarrasani's circus in which her predecessor had been killed. She travelled with a German circus in Western Europe, including to Sweden. Bébé was described as being unable to 'tear herself away from her lions' to marry a 'Viennese confectioner'.[26] Even though she was clearly a professional animal trainer working with more than one species, the notion of Bébé's fascination with working with lions was turned into a description of how lions in her act behaved like partners towards her. In a description repeated in circus histories, her friend Roman Proske writes, 'When she entered the steel arena, her lions would behave like lovers paying court to a reigning beauty, rushing to her side and vying with one another for a caress'.[27] Proske was admiring of Bébé's professional accomplishment and reputation, but he also describes meeting Bébé in old age and finding her ill and poor, defiantly making every effort to see lions. If Bébé's biography provided a moral warning about the fate of socially adventurous females, affection from those wild animals confirmed a woman completely motivated by care and love, which also functioned as an irreconcilable psychological trap. Social precepts that an unmarried woman should be orientated to domesticity and human companionship were undermined and yet, at the same time, a display of affection suited claims of gentle approaches to animals. Perhaps because female presenters were commonly associated with an animal act through marriage, it was Bébé's own psychology that had to be explained, as if she could not marry because she loved the lions.

Bébé remained somewhat of an outsider, even in the life of the menagerie and circus. Proske acknowledged her reticence with other humans, which possibly added to a perception that she had rejected male suitors, possibly fans. In another account of Bébé, her lions understood her words, but she was made to seem foolhardy as she stretched her hands into the lions' cage, seemingly to caress them, and was bitten. Paul Eipper reports her saying, 'Shame on you, what haven't I already put up with for your sakes! I've gone hungry.'[28] The lion responded to

---

26   Kober 1931, 128, also 109. Charles Cochran lists Bébé presenting a polar bear act with 20 bears in 1913 at his 'Wonder Zoo and Big Circus' at the Olympia in London, Cochran 1929, 187.
27   Proske 1956, 81, also 41, 82–88.

7 Nature's beauties and scientific specimen contests

her comment by licking her wound. The description of the encounter implied that Bébé was devoted but naive, and needed to be more cautious. Bébé may not have been able to continue working with lions or bears because of political upheavals, including World War I and other disruptions to the circus business historically, and the costly economics of trained acts meant that she could not maintain the animals herself. But was there perhaps also an issue in that younger female presenters were more appealing and hired more easily?

A tendency to recount the stories of escaped big cats and minor attacks may have been magnified with female trainers, but there certainly were risks. In a continuation of 19th-century menagerie ethos, the big cat act with a woman in the early 20th century was still about the greater risk. The perception that the animals obeyed in response to female kindness camouflaged that individual animals were amenable to training regardless of the trainer's gender, and female performers working with trained animals demonstrated the same techniques as men. Male presenters could adopt adventurous action-based costumed identities evoking settings from safari hunting to military battle to visibly demonstrate that they were suitably experienced and in charge of the act. Moreover acts with female trainers in everyday dress camouflaged the direct connection with violent acquisition in colonial lands, whereas the male costumes perpetuated 19th-century references to a covert fighting ethos. In addition they aligned with scientific collecting practices in the early 20th century.

Virile hunter-naturalists

At the turn of the 20th century a sizeable number of animals were still captured from the wild to undergo training, and touring menageries and circuses continued to offer the public an opportunity to view a diverse range of live animal species that corresponded with what was offered by zoos in larger metropolitan centres. The connections between menageries, circuses and the zoos included the movement of animals, supporting the perception of an educational function in all

---

28 Eipper 1931, 116.

three. From the 1890s a thoroughly reasoned rejection of menagerie 'wild-beast shows' and the claim that their captive animals enjoyed their lives because they were fed included the longstanding accusation that the shows did not advance human knowledge.[29] Menageries and zoos presented living 'specimens', as did trained acts, but both faced competition from natural history collections of dead specimens that proclaimed a more scientific and therefore elevated educational purpose.

The observation of live animals was not the same process as viewing dead specimens. Even though the preservation of living animals logically seemed to offer more scope for the study of animals, large collections of dead specimens came to represent advancement in science. Public interest in taxidermied animal bodies also expanded with increasing viewing opportunities, formerly the prerogative of scientists and private collectors. Throughout the 19th century London's Zoological Society members expected to be able to dissect a dead lion, kangaroo or elephant once the animal was deceased, and to practise 'the art of taxidermy' with any wild animal, irrespective of where they were held.[30] Visitors could be influenced by the rhetoric surrounding an exhibition, but this type of knowledge contained emotionally ambiguous attitudes to the life and death of animals.

The dead species displays in museums of substantial size reconfigured longstanding patterns of exhibition and colonial expansionist activity – museums also stored countless numbers out of view. In his history of the museum as an institution, Tony Bennett points out that, similarly, the disordered jumble of the fair and the exhibition, intended to produce wonder and surprise in spectators, was a precursor to the museum that evolved into an institution that invited admiration for its display, its modernist order. Although the 'exhibitionary complex' that culminated in museum displays of taxidermied species modelled rationality, its trajectory reached back to the days of ad hoc curiosities on display.[31]

The protective sentiments now widely proclaimed by animal trainers offset scrutiny over cruelty, and can be contrasted with an absence of empathetic sentiment evident in the hunting of animals in the natural

---

29 Salt 1980 [1892], 49–50.
30 Bartlett 1898, 6.
31 Bennett 1995, 72–73.

7 Nature's beauties and scientific specimen contests

sciences. The latter seemed to perpetuate the uncaring attitudes of imperialistic trade in contrast to the change in animal act values from forceful menagerie handling to careful training. The 19th-century philosopher Henry Salt rejected the way big-game hunters indulged in 'murderous masculinity', and the way hunters deemed themselves to be civilised.[32] James Anthony Mangan and Callum MacKenzie point out how a hierarchy of masculinities developed in relation to different and earlier types of hunting. The late 19th-century hunter in Africa or Asia provided an ideal of virile masculinity, tested through the contradictory notion of a pleasurable danger of sport and military duty.[33] The grouping of hunters emerged out of the expectation that colonial military service would also involve big-game hunting. Regardless, a lack of sentimentality about animal deaths in the process of hunting specimens, alive or dead, transferred to early modernist 20th-century scientific collecting.

The identity of hunter and professional scientist became partially fused by the early 20th century.[34] As indicated, books helped to expand interest in hunting in Africa or Asia for anyone with the opportunity or financial means, while the results facilitated collecting. Geographical adventure travelogues with hunting episodes of the 1850s to 1860s were superseded by hunting publications that also contained increasingly larger appendices of species knowledge and scientific categorisation.[35] It was hunting as a narrative of dangerous adventure, though, that marked a man as 'virile'.

The scale of hunting expeditions continued to increase. In India, the British emulated the practice of tiger hunting, associated with Mughal emperors from the 18th century, and Joseph Sramek explains that 'tigers also represented for the British all that was wild and untamed'.[36] Sramek continues that the visual record of photographed British royals beside dead tiger carcasses conveyed assumptions of authority, and were symbolic of the overcoming of fear that made

---

32 Mangan & MacKenzie 2008, 1220, also 1218, 1219.
33 Mangan & MacKenzie 2008, 1219.
34 Haraway 1989.
35 For example, compare Baker 1868, dedicated to the Prince of Wales, with Baker 1890, in which chapters take the names of animal species.
36 Sramek 2006, 659, citing MacKenzie on virile masculinity.

'British imperial and masculine identities'. The emotional struggle was implicit to the maintenance of power. As William Storey summarises in his analysis of lion hunting in east Africa:

> On the one hand, big-game hunting had clear symbolic overtones concerning humans' relation to nature, and the colonists' relation to the colonized. On the other hand, the massive *Shikar* and *safari* of some colonists demonstrated their power to obtain large labour forces to suit their recreational desires.[37]

Some large animals required more hunting skill and there was a hierarchy of masculine achievement in overcoming fear in the big game safari hunt, and it could now be captured by the camera.

Opportunities to participate in the safari adventure attracted influential figures with public profiles and political power. This was exemplified by the expeditions of Winston Churchill and Theodore Roosevelt, who seemed unperturbed about the consequences of hunting. The young Churchill rode the Kenya-Uganda railway that epitomised modern achievement in the east African British protectorates to meet with district officials, and Theodore Roosevelt provided specimens for a natural science collection. As was standard, Churchill was photographed standing with dead animals, including a rhinoceros that was not found immediately on the grasslands where the train could be stopped. Instead, it had taken the party more than an hour's walk to find the grazing animals. Churchill explains, 'killing a rhinoceros in the open is crudely simple . . . you walk up as near as possible to him from any side except windward, and then shoot him in the head or the heart'.[38] If the hunter missed and the rhinoceros charged, it took a volley of shots to kill, and the photographed one beside Churchill had charged. In reference to a white rhinoceros causing 'excitement', Churchill later explained that 'to shoot a good specimen . . . is an event sufficiently important in the life of a sportsman to make the day on which it happens bright and memorable'.[39] The hunter felt good about his achievement; as if the animal's life was of no importance.

---

37 Storey 1991, 137.
38 Churchill 1990 [1908], 14–15. Also see the chapter 'On safari' in the same book.
39 Churchill 1990 [1908], 112.

7 Nature's beauties and scientific specimen contests

As a high-profile spectator of trained lion acts and an ex-military man, after serving his two terms, the now ex-president of the USA, Theodore Roosevelt, went on an African safari promoted by a justifiable scientific purpose. Departing on 23 March 1909 he was undoubtedly the most famous of the safari hunters in the first decade of the 20th century. He ostensibly travelled to Africa to obtain specimens for natural history displays at the Smithsonian National Museum, following his father's example, who had used the family money to fund New York's Natural History Museum. Theodore had a reputation as a naturalist, and major national parks were created under his presidency in the USA; his own commentary centred on preserving the habitat of wolves and pumas.[40] In preparation for the African safari Theodore read a number of the available books on safaris and game hunting in Africa.[41] He funded his trip and his son's with a publishing advance for a series of magazine articles that later became his 1910 book, *African game trails*. Crucially, Theodore also sought to meet with experienced hunters for advice before embarking on the journey including notably the taxidermist-hunter Carl Akeley, and the most famous hunter of specimens of fauna at the time, Fredrick Courteney Selous, who described some of his hunting experiences in his books.[42] Selous visited Theodore in 1905 and his 1908 book *African nature notes and reminiscences* was dedicated to Theodore, who provided the foreword. Theodore asked Selous for practical information about where to go and what to take on safari hunt and, like Selous, identified himself as a 'hunter-naturalist'.

An ethos of freedom espoused in relation to frontier regions was associated with Theodore, and frontier hunting that linked notions of manliness with dominance of the environment also identified nations as virile entities. Reminiscent of Farini taking Sam Hunt on his expedition, Theodore took his son, Kermit, who also had a camera. They travelled to Mombassa in British East Africa (now Kenya) by boat from

---

40   Velvin 1906, 187, 204.
41   Thompson 2010, 5. These books included JH Patterson's *The man-eaters of Tsavo*, Abel Chapman's *On safari*, Richard Lydekker's *Game animals of Africa*, and Major PGH Powell-Cotton's *In unknown Africa*.
42   Thompson 2010, 6, 7. See Selous 1893; Selous 1896. The latter gave an account of the Matabeleland uprisings and problems with cattle.

Italy, and the ensuing 73-tent entourage and 200 porters became the largest expedition of its kind at that time. The Roosevelts went inland by train and stayed at well-established colonial properties in east Africa, before venturing southwards for seven months, camping in relative style. The large safari group was reduced in numbers as they continued on to Uganda by train on 18 December 1909 for two months of hunting white rhinoceros and giant eland, and then through the Sudan and Egypt down the Nile.

The animals that Theodore sought were, 'in order of priority: lion, elephant, rhino, buffalo, giraffe, hippo, eland, sable [antelope], oryx, koodoo [kudu], wildebeest, hartebeest, warthog, zebra, waterbuck, Grant's gazelle, reedbuck, and topi'.[43] Specimens of all these species were acquired on the safari hunt. Three naturalists were employed by the Smithsonian to go on the expedition so that, Thompson explains, what might have been considered a 'private junket scheme was transformed into a full-fledged scientific expedition'.[44] The preparation and preservation of dead specimens was carried out by Major Edgar Mearns, a retired army surgeon; Professor J Alden Loring, a small animal and bird expert; and Dr Edmund Heller, working on big game. They did not always go on the hunt and most of the expedition's live specimens came from the private zoo of William and Lucie McMillan.

To warrant the label of 'naturalist', a hunter needed to observe exotic wild animals in their habitat – alive. There was some criticism of the impact of hunting on wildlife numbers, which led Theodore to justify his position in private communication. He denies that he is a 'game butcher' when he proclaims 'the chief value of my trip to consist of the observations I was able to make upon the habits of the game, and to a lesser extent, of the birds, smaller animals and the like'.[45]

In exacting detail Theodore writes about killing a lion:

> I was sighting carefully ... he galloped at a great pace, he came on steadily – ears laid back, and uttering terrific coughing grunts ...

---

43   Thompson 2010, 14, 34, shot with three big-game rifles, also 10, 29. See McCalman 2006.
44   Thompson 2010, 10, also 29.
45   Thompson 2010, 10, citing a letter, 25 June 1908, to Edward North Buxton, President of the Society for the Preservation of the Wild Fauna of the Empire.

7 Nature's beauties and scientific specimen contests

The soft-nosed Winchester bullet had gone straight through the chest cavity, smashing the lungs and the big blood vessels of the heart. Painfully he recovered his feet, and tried to come on, his ferocious courage holding out to the last; but he staggered, and turned from side to side.[46]

A hunter's right to kill large numbers of animals was being questioned at that time, if not a hunter's right to shoot with, as the graphic description reveals, full awareness of the internal damage, but not the suffering, of the dying animal. The animal was viewed like an enemy who needed to be killed.

The process of observing animals in their habitat did not inhibit killing nor did it arouse empathetic regret, and instead attested to the strength of an assumed right to hunt. Among a number of Theodore Roosevelt's other contradictions was the paradox of an American president, who was a former colonel from the Spanish-American War and who instigated a stronger, larger, American navy, being awarded the Nobel Prize for Peace.[47] A meeting in Kenya with the taxidermist-hunter Akeley, who was hunting elephants for New York's American Museum of Natural History, involved Theodore and his son Kermit in the shooting of at least three adult elephants and a young one for this museum collection. The pair later watched as several Nandi people were wounded while hunting lions with spears before one male lion was killed. It is recorded that Theodore was pleased that only two Nandi were injured by a rhinoceros and a leopard in the British East African section of the safari trip. The expedition seemed more focused on the quantity and competitive size of the collection, and there was a noticeable lack of sentiment about dead animals and the extreme cruelty of hunting.

As indicated, Theodore had been impressed by Captain Bonavita's act with lions. It was evident that acts with live animals were an influence on this milieu, encouraging diverse masculine activities out of quasi-scientific safari practices. In lopsided emotional responses, there was praise for bravery and courage, but the expectations of gentleness in the treatment of animals in captivity did not transfer to hunting,

---

46   Roosevelt 1910, 190–91.
47   Thompson 2010, 21, 23, also 64–67, 70–71.

which was without similar emotional impositions. Since entering a cage with lions was not really an option, someone with the resources backed by skilful hunters and locals set out to test himself carrying a state-of-the-art gun to come face to face with a live wild animal, where possible, in nature.

Patriotic services

The Roosevelts' expedition claimed to have found new specimens, perturbing the British colonials who expected that the British Museum should take precedence – 'an international race of sorts developed'.[48] National interests were extended to collecting dead specimens. The way that museums competed was reminiscent of competing 19th-century menagerie collections.

The dependency of menagerie trade, animal acts and ethnographic exhibition on the colonial empire became transparent as trainers, in turn, joined patriotic missions of animal acquisition for military campaigns. When Lorenz Hagenbeck returned to Germany following the 1904 St Louis World's Fair and circus tour, he was instructed by his father Carl to supervise the acquisition of 1000 dromedaries for the German army in South-West Africa (Namibia).[49] There, Germany was suppressing a rebellion by the Herero people (1904 to 1907), who, trying to avoid the violent conflict, died in their tens of thousands from starvation. Joseph Menges purchased the dromedaries for Hagenbeck's in ports on the Red Sea, assisted by Grieger, who loaded them onto the ships. The German government doubled the request to 2000 dromedaries. At considerable cost, the group shipped 2000 dromedaries plus saddles and 80 Arab camel-handlers on five ships to the German colony and landed them by pontoon onto the shore.

Lorenz writes that with this expedition his father believed he 'had achieved something momentous in cultural history'.[50] Such animal

---

48   Thompson 2010, 65.
49   Hagenbeck 1956, 65–69, also 71–72. A traveller, Ernst Wache, and Matthias Walter who worked for Hagenbeck's, were sent to assist.
50   Hagenbeck 1956, 72, also 77, 79.

7 Nature's beauties and scientific specimen contests

acquisition business was directly serving the colonial nation's military strategy. At that time Lorenz visited the Somali leader Hersy Egeh in Somaliland, and was the guest at a riding, fighting and dancing display: 'Egeh rose to his full chieftain-like height in his picturesque stirrups ... [and as] the whole village yelled: "Aya hovoh," spears flew into the air'.[51] Egeh became an intermediary in the bargaining for dromedaries, receiving his own cut of the purchase price. He was a guest for the opening of the Stellingen Animal Park on 7 May 1907, appearing in full war paint on this official occasion. He brought along a prospective marriageable daughter for Lorenz, who declined the offer, later noting that she had hair dressed with mutton fat. In 1908 Emperor Wilhelm II visited Stellingen wearing a naval uniform. The crowd at the animal park awaiting the royal cavalcade included school children and war veterans from the 1848–51 and 1870–71 campaigns, who were greeted by the emperor. He said to Lorenz, 'I already know your animal park so well from the cinematographs ... my brother has told me that I really must have a look at the real thing.'[52] The brass band played Saro's 'Battle potpourri', punctuated with rifle and cannon fire, and Fritz Schilling presented an act with a mixed group of big cats. It was a conjurer from India who was especially favoured by the royal spectator. But then, the animal park was also a type of fantasy presentation.

The Hagenbeck animal show functioned like a national emissary. After the 1904 St Louis World's Fair, Hagenbeck's was invited by Argentinian government officials to stage a show with animal acts in Buenos Aires in 1909, for the anniversary of the republic's centenary of nationhood.[53] 'Exposición Carlos Hagenbeck' combined circus, menagerie and ethnographic shows. The circus presented an 18-piece brass band, Richard Sawade's tiger act, Fritz Schilling with 20 polar bears, elephants, sea lions, chimpanzees on bicycles, horses and zebras. There were Somali performers, and masked dancers from Ceylon (Sri Lanka).

The trained animal act, which had become emblematic of modernist innovation and cultural improvement and progress additionally provided a symbol of national achievement and diplomacy and was

---

51   Hagenbeck 1956, 67–68.
52   Hagenbeck 1956, 79, also 80.
53   Hagenbeck 1956, 85, also 88–89.

therefore worthy of inclusion in a celebration of nationhood in the new century. During one performance, Sawade was attacked by a tiger, Nik, who generally behaved like a pet dog.[54] Rudolf Matthies fired gun blanks at Nik. The tiger, hit by the cartridge cap, stopped, and Sawade finished the performance injured in the shoulder and upper arm; despite blood-poisoning, he recovered. The accident in trained animal action within a larger performance of nationhood provided a reminder of an inherent suppressed violence in both. An inclination to attack in a confined space with other species was controlled through the training regime, and it became disrupted if an animal performer decided not to cooperate.

Claire Heliot was on the ship accompanying Sawade to the centenary celebrations but seemingly not as a performer. Her presence at a celebration of nationhood confirmed trainers' pre-eminence within modernity, but also her inability to represent such ideals. A perception of kindness might not have generated the appropriate solemn tone for an occasion in which the animal act was expected to be a modernist symbol of scientific progress, as well as the controlled improvement of nature. The dominance of wild animal species remained a male prerogative on an official occasion.

A capricious science

Training encouraged animals to suppress fighting instincts. Was training scientific or did this association arise from an alignment of animals within the broader scientific sphere of activity? The idea that caged large exotic animals could be effectively managed by knowledgeable care and fair treatment formed part of the training ethos developed from the 1880s and 1890s. This was no longer a vague notion that animals might submit to handling if they were treated kindly; there were clearly defined behavioural approaches to training. Some could be trained against their natural inclinations, and rhetorical claims about gentle training and unnatural poses that seemed benign appeased criticism. Those animals who were not obedient and could not be

---

54 Hagenbeck 1956, 91.

7 Nature's beauties and scientific specimen contests

coaxed, according to human understanding of species behaviour, were no longer handled in public view. If an animal were capricious and confrontational, he or she was simply removed from an act.

Frank Bostock explains that 'the trained animal is a product of science; but the tamed animal is a chimera of the optimistic imagination'.[55] He explains that trained animals were not tamed animals. The training of live animals in the first decades of the 20th century was assisted by the animal training manuals of Carl Hagenbeck and Frank Bostock, which contained information about animal husbandry. The manuals do not fully explain how knowledge of species movement and reflex reactions was applied in training and contributed to the claim of scientific training. It was the application of systematic approaches based on accumulated knowledge and practices, often undisclosed, that facilitated training.

The trained big cat act was fully integrated into the 20th-century circus ring, removing visible evidence of forceful containment, which parallels how orientalist fantasies with elephants belied their treatment. Performance hides the physical consequences for animals from the public. Yet Paul Eipper needed to defend animal acts in circus by rejecting trainers who lacked control, and he reiterates apologist statements about self-regulation with the standard argument that the cage life of animals was not cruel because most zoo animals have the same amount of space.[56] Judging by this defensiveness, animal acts were still being criticised. He continues that in the circus, cages are very clean and the animals immaculately groomed. Interestingly, Eipper's commentary focuses on the circus acts in which the animals displayed what could be interpreted as recognisable emotions, and he gives comparatively briefer accounts of the impressive balance of sea lions and the skills of bears.

The public perception may have been that any animal of a species was fully trainable, but in reality some individuals were more cooperative than others and amenable to doing complex feats – an uncooperative animal was a liability to an act. Animals could also be accidentally startled out of a trained routine. Eipper describes his observation of Matthies' act with Carl Hagenbeck's circus. In one

---

55 Bostock 1903, 185.
56 Eipper 1931, 17, 19, also 59.

incident a sudden running movement by two spectators had upset a Bengal tigress about to undertake a leap, so she slipped from her pedestal. The tigress' nervousness provoked a Sumatran tiger to attack a third, Ulla. Matthies took control of the situation and achieved obedience from the 15 tigers, getting them to return to their routine. At the start of the day in rehearsal the tigers were given free time to do as they pleased before Matthies called softly, 'That's enough, children! Take your places!'[57] Matthies scratched each between the ears and they sniffed his hand, as he explained that the Sumatran tiger was well behaved during rehearsal to avoid being punished with endless repetitions.

In another incident in performance, however, as the band played the 'Triumphant march' from *Aida*, it took 20 seconds for the same Sumatran tiger to grab Ulla, who swiped him out of the way, causing him to leap onto her back, sending them both to the ground. Eipper writes, 'The audience is frightened. Women begin to scream, panic is in the air.'[58] However, Matthies intervened and the tigers took their places. The uncooperative Sumatran tiger was banished from performance, and was eventually sent to a zoo. Banishment from his peers and familiar way of life might well have been another type of cruelty.

The trained animal act did retain a mystique that echoed that accorded to Van Amburgh, except that by the 20th century the mystique had been extended to the animals. John Clarke claims that while there was 'fear and distrust of animate Nature', a trainer's 'power over animals' was a 'gift'.[59] Alternatively, in their innocence, animals 'know' or sense the emanations of human emotions and can become like mind-readers, but should be approached as 'equals' in friendship. Since animals were outside culture, they had a sensory purity and innocence that allowed them to see through a trainer's social guile or guardedness.

By the second decade of the 20th century the touring menagerie accompanying the circus had become the lesser business. The shift from exhibition and simple feats to the complex tricks of trained animal performances meant that these became synonymous with traditional circus, as if they were part of the ring show from the beginning. The

---

57 Eipper 1931, 13, 16, citing Matthies.
58 Eipper 1931, 32, also 79.
59 Manning-Sanders 1952, 213–14, citing Clarke.

heyday of trained elephant and big cat acts happened during the first half of the 20th century and these acts continue in circus today.

The modernist circus became synonymous with an act in which a lone man or woman holding a stick and/or whip entered the arena inside a tall barrier spanning the space of the circus ring to present a group of big cats in human-like action. The animals, including elephants, seemed to move freely in the arena during the 20th century, masking how the performance was underpinned by regimented discipline and highly practised routines. But the animal act displayed cooperation, submission and obedience. A circus trainer or presenter's approach combined training with specialist knowledge, but not in a way that revealed a suppression of the defensive fighting behaviour of other species. The rhetoric about the science of training, underpinned by the necessary financial resources, was consolidated into three human principles: careful attention, patient perseverance, and the watchful selection of animals with the potential to become performers.

Conclusion

Fighting nature explores performances that reflect human fascination with conflict and war and a human capacity for fighting and aggression; that is, aspects of human nature. The question as to why staged conflict and war were popular prompts a range of speculative responses, from spectator interest in political events to the attractions of viewing (and participating in) fights. Fighting and conflict consistently remain central to entertainment through cinema, although the staging of war re-enactments no longer needs animals after the 21st-century success of the theatre production *War horse*, with puppets for horses. The re-enactment of battles fought with live animals was a historical phenomenon. The war perpetuated on other species continues.

In examining 19th-century menagerie animal performance history, the brutal excesses in the treatment of animals are revealed as inseparable from the predatory behaviour of humans. The cruelty of depriving exotic wild animals of their habitat and of their freedom became compounded by the process of caging and restraining them so that they could live and travel among humans for their entertainment. The extent of that animal exploitation and the scale of the numbers captured becomes almost inconceivable.

Throughout the 19th century lion-tamer cage acts depicted physical handling, confrontation and fighting action in a progression towards animal submission. The possibility of animal attacks on human tamers attracted spectators, even though some expressed apprehension and conflicted reactions. The public attended menageries in large numbers in order to see shows that staged tamer fearlessness and bravery against a hostile nature that was embodied by the animals. By the mid-century leading menagerie acts had female lion tamers enter small cages to heighten an impression of danger and by the late 1850s, a hunting identity had been added to male tamer acts. Even in the instances where individual lions and tigers in leading acts showed qualities that suggested friendliness, these were overshadowed by a generalised perception of species aggression. It is this attitude that seems to have made the large-scale hunting of large animal species permissible.

The viewing space of the menagerie was one of suppressed violence and camouflaged human aggression. The open area occupied by transient menageries and the informal arrangements for viewing animals in cages or tied up seemed to facilitate spectators behaving in unpredictable and aggressive ways. Menagerie workers and exhibited animals became a stimulus for antisocial behaviour as locals taunted animals, caused fights, and even turned into violent mobs. Human societal problems and issues of cruelty to animals were difficult to separate from menagerie viewing, so the atmosphere was one of vigilance against attack, and animals resisting keepers as workers adopted defensive strategies. It was very large crowds that may have eventually forestalled spectator mistreatment. If ideals of kindness suggested the aspirations of those working with animals, the larger an animal the bigger the confrontation and struggle to keep him or her in the menagerie. The menageries treated some animals like prisoners of war and imposed physical tortures.

Menagerie animals travelled extensively. Species came from diverse locations in expanding colonial empires, shipped along global trade routes to colonial ports and transported over land to major centres. The transported elephants that appeared on British or European stages brought together ideas of colonial governmental and royal rule and the military occupation of far-flung regions. Individual animals implicitly embodied imperial connections and even a brief appearance legitimised the exoticism of a show's location and theme. Depictions of foreign royals with exotic animals spanned socio-political hierarchies, and staged battles and wars in particular could make explicit power relations and global strategies of European dominance. Military identity in British popular entertainments delineated how the dominant

Conclusion

values became embedded and circulated across entertainments. Thus individual animal appearances influenced larger cultural beliefs about militarisation and power that extended to other species.

Accounts of aggression towards other species, however, have a counter historical narrative by the late 19th century. Colonial authorities had implemented some protective legislation for animals by 1879 when it became evident that the slaughter of roaming animals through hunting practices was bringing about species extinction in some areas. In 1900 there was a conference in London of those concerned about the decline in the numbers of wild animals in Africa.[1] By 1903 an alliance of hunters had been formed as the Society for the Preservation of the Wild Fauna of the Empire.[2] Perhaps it was ironic that hunters should be the ones championing preservation and conservation, but they did at least appreciate the scale of animal disappearance, and it was in their interests for roaming animals to survive.

Hunter and hunting party guide Denys Finch Hatton brought this issue to widespread public attention in England in 1928 when he provoked discussion with an extended article in the *Times*. The first part of the article describes the innovation of driving by motor car with two trucks to find wildlife on the Serengeti plains for cinematic filming, with the camera fixed to the external side of the car. The group filmed 70 lions in two weeks and a diverse range of other wild animals. But in a final section headed 'An abuse of sport', Finch Hatton criticises the increasingly numerous '[s]hooting visitors to East Africa who are anxious to fill their bag as quickly as possible ... most of them want to get a lion, and many of them do not care very much just how it is got'.[3] While it was still arduous to venture there by car, he envisages that this motorised hunting would compound and greatly increase the process in the future. He calls on those of influence to bring about control of hunting quickly to maintain wildlife and he outlines an alternative future when 'many more people would be willing to pay for the privilege of seeing lions and other game' in the wild

---

1   Ritvo 1987, 284, see reference to the Convention for the Preservation of Wild Animals, Birds, and Fish in Africa, 19 May 1900. Also MacKenzie 1990c, 194.
2   MacKenzie 1988.
3   *Times* (London) 1928, Lions at their ease: stalking by car, 21 January: 12. For a biography of Denys Finch Hatton, see Wheeler 2007.

and 'photographing' rather than 'shooting them' from motor cars. If the hunter and the conservationist appeared to have a mutual aim of ensuring the survival of sufficient wild animals, those earning a living from organising big-game hunting tours for visitors were concerned and rightly so. Finch Hatton's prophetic future of touring safaris photographing wildlife has been fulfilled but so too has his anxiety about animal species survival.

The information that there were limits on the large wild animals acquired by hunters for live exhibition was in general circulation in the first decades of the 20th century and arguments circulated in the press and in entertainment trade magazines. By the 1920s, animal business operators and trainers were aware that they could not rely on an endless supply of wild animals from Africa. A short report in the *Billboard*, the major trade journal for entertainers and show entrepreneurs in the USA, confirmed that the export of large numbers of animals was no longer feasible.[4] The Congo Zoological Society meeting in Brussels had been informed that the 30,000 male elephants slaughtered each year in the Congo for their ivory tusks imperilled their numbers, especially as female and young elephants were also indiscriminately killed.

As uncertainty grew about the easy replacement of animals like elephants, the newer trained acts for the circus ring became more valuable. One consequence was that menagerie entertainment that simply presented the animals declined in status. It was possibly also because of the rise of photographic technologies that disseminated images. In the first three decades of the 20th century, touring menagerie businesses accompanying a circus became increasingly secondary businesses. Yet they still accompanied major circuses in Europe, the USA and elsewhere for pre-show viewing, with a diverse range of species that did not make the transition into the circus ring as performers. In Europe, Paul Eipper describes walking through Carl Hagenbeck's circus menagerie in the late 1920s and entering where the 'beasts of prey' – 'lions, tigers, the brown, polar, and Tibetan bears, the leopards, pumas, hyenas, and panthers' – lived all year in sawdust-covered 26-foot (10 m) cage wagons; there were elephants with a matriarch, and in box stalls the 'exotic creatures: buffalo, camels, donkeys, llamas, and guanacos,

---

4   *Billboard* 1925, 27 June: 62.

antelopes, reindeer, oxen, mules and goats', then horses and a central display of monkeys and large birds.[5] A hippopotamus had a water tank. 'I smell the wild-beast smell, that savage, hotly acrid reek.' He also outlines how the children of 'exotic peoples' in the circus, the Somalis and Hindus, sell postcards while the public visit the menagerie and there see the acrobatic feats of the Chinese children. Eipper's commentary confirms that an exhibition of exoticism regardless of species continued well into the 20th century, a legacy of a previous era. Circus menageries continued to serve as touring zoos to the mid-century, emphasising values of human species dominance and forceful control.

From the mid-20th century, however, a very different struggle surrounded wild animals. It concerned the preservation of species increasingly threatened by human society and decreasing areas of habitat. The effort to overcome the historical legacy of 19th-century colonialism, war, and animal acquisition and transportation had turned into a major fight on behalf of nature to ensure the survival of threatened species. The legacy of 19th-century menageries' entrenched beliefs regarding the human right to hunt and exploit nature through warlike practices against other animal species is yet to be defeated.

---

5   Eipper 1931, 19–20, also 107, 36, 81.

Works cited

Newspapers and journals

Aberdeen Journal (1838), 10 October, Issue 4735: (1843), 23 August, Issue 4989 (British Library Newspapers Database (BLN)).
Argus (Melbourne) (1893), 23 January: 6; 24 January: 6; 30 January: 7; 6 February: 7; 13 February: 7; 21 February: 6; 6 March: 6; 13 March: 6.
Belfast Newsletter (Belfast) (1882), 6 March: 5 (BLN).
Billboard (1925), 27 June: 62.
Birmingham Daily Post (1860), 31 July: 2 (BLN).
Bristol Mercury and Daily Post (Bristol) (1882), 6 March: 8.
Bulletin (Sydney) (1892), 4 February: 9; 26 November: 8; (1893), 28 January: 6; 19 November: 6; (1900), 1 December: 8.
Daily News (London) (1872), 6 January: 5; (1882), 17 March: 6 (BLN).
Derby Mercury (Derby) (1872), 17 January: 6 (BLN).
Ellis County Mirror (Texas) (1902), 9 October: no page, advertisement for Ringling Brothers Circus.
Era (1872), 14 January: 5; (1877), 16 September: 4 (BLN).
Freeman's Journal and Daily Commercial Advertiser (Dublin, Ireland) (1838), 26 September, no page (BLN).
Hull Packet (Hull) (1840), 18 December: 8 (BLN).
Illustrated London News (1843), 21 January: 44; (1861). 2 February: 90.
Jackson's Oxford Journal (Oxford) (1843), 13 May: 3 (BLN).
Lloyd's Weekly Newspaper (London) (1877), 16 September: 5 (BLN).

Lyttleton Times (Christchurch, NZ) (1901), 4 January: 6; (1902), 18 February: 5; 10 March: 5.
Manchester Times (1884), 23 August: 5; (1891), 27 March: 4 (BLN).
Manchester Times and Gazette (1845), 9 August: 3 (BLN).
New York Clipper (1872), 27 January: 339; 3 February: 347; 10 February: 355; 24 February: 371; 23 March: 408; 30 March: 415; 13 April: 12, 15; 18 May: 55; 25 May: 60, 63; 1 June: 71; 15 June: 87; 22 June: 95; 29 June: 103; 6 July: 108, 111; 17 August: 153, 161; 7 September: 179; 21 September: 199; 12 October: 223; 9 November: 225; 16 November: 263; 21 December: 298; (1873), 4 January: 316; 18 January: 335; 1 February: 351; 8 March: 391–92.
New Zealand Mail (1893), 12 May: 32; (1894), 12 January: 18, 19; 19 January: 2, 21, 27; 26 January: 23, 19; (1879), 29 November: 3.
Newcastle Courant (1847), 13 August: 3.
Operative (London) (1839), 6 January: 11.
Preston Chronicle and Lancaster Advertiser (1841), 23 January: 2, a reprinted review from Manchester Guardian (BLN).
Sydney Morning Herald (1892), 21 November: 6.
Times (London) (1838), 11 September: 5; (1882), 21 February: 10; 24 February: 10; 18 March: 5; 27 March: 10; (1883), 18 March: 5; 22 December: 8; (1899) 8 May: 14; (1900), 16 January: 4; (1928), 21 January: 11–12.

Newspaper articles and columns

Alexandra Palace. *Lloyd's Weekly Newspaper* (London) (1877), 16 September: 5 (BLN).
Burning of Barnum's circus, museum and menagerie. *New York Clipper* (1873), 4 January: 316.
Carter and his lions. *Hull Packet* (Hull) (1840), 18 December (BLN).
Circuses. *New York Clipper* (1872), 27 January: 339; 3 February: 355; 10 February: 359; 24 February: 371; 23 March: 408; 13 April: 12, 15; 18 May: 55; 25 May: 63; 15 June: 87; 22 June: 95; 29 June: 103; 6 July: 111; 17 August: 161; 7 September: 179; 21 September: 199; 12 October: 223; 9 November: 225; 16 November: 263; 21 December: 298; (1873), 18 January: 335; 1 February: 351; 8 March: 391–92.
Elephants, to the editor of *Times*. *Times* (London) (1883), 18 March: 5.
Fillis circus. *New Zealand Mail* (1893), 12 May: 32.
Jumbo, to the editor of *Times*. *Times* (London) (1882), 24 February: 10.
Lion taming. *Manchester Times* (1884), 23 August: 5 (BLN).
Lions and lion tamers. *New York Clipper* (1872), 13 April: 12.
Lions and lion taming. *Daily News* (London) (1872), 6 January: 5 (BLN).
Lions at Astley's. *Illustrated London News* (1861), 2 February: 90.

Works cited

Lion-taming exhibitions. *Derby Mercury* (Derby) (1872), 17 January: 6 (BLN).
Literature. *Operative* (London) (1839), 6 January: 10, 11.
Mlle La Rosa accidentally shot and killed. *New York Clipper* (1872), 30 March: 415.
Menageries and lion tamers. *Manchester Times* (1891), 27 March: 4.
Miscellaneous. *New York Clipper* (1872), 1 June: 71.
Mr Van Amburgh and his lions at the English opera house. *Illustrated London News* (1843), 21 January: 44.
Prince Charles Bonaparte. *New York Clipper* (1872), 6 July: 108.
Provincial theatricals. *Era* (1872), 14 January: 5 (BLN).
Sundry shows. *Bulletin* (Sydney) (1900), 1 December: 8.
The exhibition with lions at Fillis's circus. *Argus* (Melbourne) (1893), 24 January: 6.
The Great Britain Exhibition. *Times* (London) (1899), 9 May: 14.
The lion act at Fillis's circus. *Argus* (Melbourne) (1893), 24 January: 6.
The Nubians at the Alexandra Palace. *Era* (1877), 16 September: 4.
The sale of Jumbo [by telegraph]. *Belfast Newsletter* (Belfast) (1882), 6 March: 5 (BLN).
The tenting season. *New York Clipper* (1872), 13 April: 12.
The Zoological Society and Jumbo. *Daily News* (London) (1882), 17 March: 6 (BLN).
Tiger fighting in Java. *New York Clipper* (1872), 25 May: 60.
To Lalla Rookh. *New York Clipper* (1872), 30 March: 414.

Books, book chapters and journal articles

A concise account, interspersed with anecdotes of Mr Van Amburgh's celebrated collection of trained animals, including the giraffes and the performing elephant. (1841). London: JW Peel.
Akerberg S (2001). *Knowledge and pleasure at Regent's Park.* Sweden: Department of Historical Studies, Umea University.
Alberti SJMM (Ed) (2011a). *The afterlives of animals.* Charlottesville and London: University of Virginia Press.
Alberti SJMM (Ed) (2011b). Maharajah the elephant's journey: from nature to culture. In SJMM Alberti (Ed). *The afterlives of animals: a museum menagerie* (pp37–57). Charlottesville and London: University of Virginia Press.
Allen E & Kelley BF (1941). *Fun by the ton.* New York: Hastings House.
Allin M (1998). *Zarafa: a giraffe's true story, from deep in Africa to the heart of Paris.* New York: Walker & Co.
Altick RD (1965). Introduction. In T Carlyle. *Past and present* [1843] (ppv–xviii). RD Altick (Ed). Boston, MA: Houghton Mifflin Co.
Altick RD (1978). *The shows of London.* Cambridge, MA: The Belknap Press of Harvard University Press.

Amato S (2009). The white elephant in London: an episode of trickery, racism, and advertising. *Journal of Social History*, 43(1): 31–66, 251.

Arrighi G (2009). Negotiating national identity at the circus: the Fitzgerald Brothers' circus in Melbourne, 1892. *Australasian Drama Studies*, 54: 68–86.

Assael B (2005). *Circus and Victorian society*. Charlottesville and London: University of Virginia Press.

Assael B (2012). The American circus in Victorian Britain. In S Weber, KL Ames & M Wittmann (Eds). *The American circus* (pp86–105). New York/New Haven, CT: Bard Graduate Center and Yale University Press.

Astley P (1802). *Astley's system of equestrian education, exhibiting the beauties and defects of the horse; with serious and important observations on his general excellence, preserving him in health, grooming etc.* 8th edn. Dublin: Thomas Burnside.

Astley P (1826). *The modern riding-master: or a key to the knowledge of the horse, and horsemanship*. Philadelphia: Robert Atkem.

Bain A (1875). *The emotions and the will*. 3rd edn. London: Longmans, Green & Co.

Baker Samuel (1868). *The Nile tributaries of Abyssinia*. London: Macmillan.

Baker Samuel (1890). *Wild beasts and their ways: reminiscences of Europe, Asia, Africa and America*. London: Macmillan & Co.

Baker Steve (2001). *Picturing the beast: animals, identity and representation*. Urbana and Chicago, IL: University of Illinois Press.

Baker WJ & Mangan JA (Eds) (1987). *Sport in Africa: essays in social history*. New York: Africana Publishing Co.

Ballantine B (1958). *Wild tigers and tame fleas*. New York: Rinehart & Co. Inc.

Baratay E & Hardouin-Fugier E (2002). *Zoo: a history of zoological gardens in the West*. London: Reaktion Books.

Barnum PT (1926). *Animal stories*, illustrated by FW Williams. Akron, OH and New York: The Saalfield Publishing Co.

Bartlett AD (1898). *Wild animals in captivity*, compiled and edited by E Bartlett. London: Chapman & Hall Ltd.

Baston K (2010). The eye of the ear, *Popular Entertainment* 2:. Retrieved on 7 September 2015 from https://novaojs.newcastle.edu.au/ojs/index.php/pes/article/view/14.

Beatty C & Wilson E (1946). *Jungle performers*. London: Robert Hale.

Bedini SA (1997). *The Pope's elephant*. Lisbon, Portugal: Carcanet in association with The Calouste Gulbenkian Foundation.

Bekoff M & Meaney CA (1998). *Encyclopedia of animal rights and animal welfare*. Westport, CT: Greenwood Press.

Bennett T (1995). *The birth of the museum*. London: Routledge.

Works cited

Blacking J (1987). Games and sports in pre-colonial African societies. In WJ Baker & JA Mangan (Eds). *Sport in Africa: essays in social history* (pp3–22). New York: Africana Publishing Co.

Blunt W (1976). *The ark in the park: the zoo in the nineteenth century*. London: Hamish Hamilton.

Boddice R (2008). *A history of attitudes and behaviours towards animals in eighteenth- and nineteenth-century Britain*. Lewiston, SA: The Edwin Mellen Press.

Bompas GC (1886). *Life of Frank Buckland*. London: Smith, Elder & Co.

Bonavita, J (1930). Making actors of wild animals. In *The circus scrap book*, October 1930 (8) (pp7–15), republished from *New Age*, August 1911.

Bostock EH 1972 [1927]. *Menageries, circuses and theatres*. New York: Benjamin Blom Inc.

Bostock F (1903). *The training of wild animals*. New York: The Century Co.

Bouissac P (2012). *Circus as multimodal discourse*. London: Bloomsbury Academic.

Bradby D, James L & Sharratt B (Eds) (1980). *Performance and politics in popular drama*. Cambridge: Cambridge University Press.

Bradna F & Spence H (1957). *The big top: my forty years with the Greatest Show on Earth*. New York: Simon & Schuster.

Bratton JS (1980). Theatre of war: the Crimea on the London stage 1854–5. In D Bradby, L James & B Sharratt (Eds). *Performance and politics in popular drama* (pp119–37). Cambridge: Cambridge University Press.

Bratton JS (1986). Of England, home and duty: the image of England in Victorian and Edwardian juvenile fiction. In JM MacKenzie (Ed). *Imperialism and popular culture* (pp73–93). Manchester: Manchester University Press.

Bratton JS (1991a). Introduction. In JS Bratton et al. *Acts of supremacy: the British Empire and the British stage 1790–1930* (pp1–17). Manchester: Manchester University Press.

Bratton JS (1991b). British heroism and the structure of melodrama. In JS Bratton et al. *Acts of supremacy: the British Empire and the British stage 1790–1930* (pp18–61). Manchester: Manchester University Press.

Bratton JS, Cave R, Gregory B, Holder H & Pickering M (1991). *Acts of supremacy: the British Empire and the British stage 1790–1930*. Manchester: Manchester University Press.

Broome R & Jackomos A (1998). *Sideshow alley*. Sydney: Allen & Unwin.

Callaway A (2000). *Visual ephemera: theatrical art in nineteenth century Australia*. Sydney: University of New South Wales Press.

Campbell C (1957). Elephants good and bad. *Circus Review*, 5(1): no pagination.

Carlyle T (1965 [1843]). *Past and present*. RD Altick (Ed). Boston, MA: Houghton Mifflin Co.

Carnegie DW (1898). *Spinifex and sand*. London: C Arthur Pearson Ltd.
Cartmill M (1993). *A view to a death in the morning: hunting and nature through history*. Cambridge, MA: Harvard University Press.
Carus CG (1989 [1846]). *Psyche: on the development of the soul*. R Welch et al (Trans). Dallas, TX: Spring Publications, Inc.
Chambers P (2008). *Jumbo: this being the true story of the greatest elephant in the world*. Hanover, NH: Steerforth Press.
Churchill W (1990 [1908]). *My African journey*. New York: WW Norton & Co.
Cochran C (1929). *The secrets of a showman*. London: Heinemann Ltd.
Conklin G (1921). *The ways of the circus*, set down by HW Root. New York: Harper & Brothers Publishers.
Cooper CR (1928). *Lions 'n' tigers 'n' everything*. Boston, MA: Little, Brown & Co.
Cooper J (1983). *Animals and war*. London: William Heinemann Ltd.
Coup WC (1901). *Sawdust and spangles*. Chicago, IL: Herbert S Stone & Co.
Coxe AH (1980a). *A seat at the circus*. Hamden, CT: Archon Books.
Coxe AH (1980b). Equestrian drama and the circus. In D Bradby, L James & B Sharratt (Eds). *Performance and politics in popular drama* (pp109–18). Cambridge: Cambridge University Press.
Culhane J (1990). *The American circus: an illustrated history*. New York: Henry Holt & Co.
Cumming RG (1850a). *Five years of a hunter's life in the far interior of South Africa*. Vol. 1. New York: Harper & Brothers Publishers.
Cumming RG (1850b). *Five years of a hunter's life in the far interior of South Africa*. Vol. 2. New York: Harper & Brothers Publishers.
Darwin C (1999 [1872]). *The expression of the emotions in man and animals*. London: Fontana Press.
Davey G (2006). Visitor behaviour in zoos: a review. *Anthrozoös*, 19(2): 143–57.
Davis J (2002). *The circus age*. Chapel Hill, NC: University of North Carolina Press.
Davis J & Emeljanow V (2001). *Reflecting the audience: London theatregoing, 1840–1880*. Iowa City, IA: University of Iowa Press.
Dennett AS (1997). *Weird and wonderful: the dime museum in America*. New York: New York University Press.
Disher MW (1937). *Greatest show on earth*. London: G Bell & Sons.
Donald D (2007). *Picturing animals in Britain 1750–1850*. New Haven, CT: The Paul Mellon Centre for Studies in British Art by Yale University Press.
Downes P (1975). *Shadow on the stage: theatre in New Zealand, the first 50 years*. Dunedin, NZ: John McIndoe.
Durant J & Durant A (1957). *Pictorial history of the American circus*. New York: AS Barnes & Co.
Eipper P (1931). *Circus: men, beasts and joys of the road*. FH Martens (Trans). New York: Junior Literary Guild.

Works cited

Evelyn J (1908). *The diary of John Evelyn*. London: Macmillan & Co.

Farini GA (1886). *Through the Kalahari desert: a narrative of a journey with gun, camera, and note-book to Lake N'Gami and back*. London: Sampson Low, Marston, Seale & Rivington.

Ferguson OJ (1861). *A brief biographical sketch of IA Van Amburgh*. New York: Samuel Booth.

Festing S (1988). Menageries and the landscape garden. *Journal of Garden History*, 8(4): 104–17.

Finch Hatton D (1928). Lions at their ease. *Times* (London), 21 January: 11–12.

Flint K (2000). *The Victorians and the visual imagination*. Cambridge: Cambridge University Press.

Flint RW (1996). American showmen and European dealers: commerce in wild animals acts in nineteenth-century parks to 1899. In RJ Hoage & WA Deiss (Eds). *New worlds, new animals: from menageries to zoological park in the nineteenth century* (pp97–108). Baltimore, MD: The Johns Hopkins University Press.

Fox C (1960). *Pictorial history of performing horses*. Seattle, WA: Superior Publishing.

Fox CP & Parkinson T (1969). *The circus in America*. Waukesha, WI: Country Beautiful.

Frost T (1875). *Circus life and circus celebrities*. London: Tinsley Brothers.

Fudge E (2002). A left-handed blow: writing the history of animals. In N Rothfels (Ed). *Representing animals* (pp3–18). Bloomington, IN: Indiana University Press.

Gillbank L (1996). A paradox of purposes: acclimatization origins of the Melbourne Zoo. In RJ Hoage & WA Deiss (Eds). *New worlds, new animals: from menageries to zoological park in the nineteenth century* (pp73–85). Baltimore, MD: The Johns Hopkins University Press.

Golby JM & Purdue AW (1984). *The civilisation of the crowd: popular culture in England 1750–1900*. London: Batsford Academic and Educational.

Goodall JR (2002). *Performance and evolution in the age of Darwin*. London: Routledge.

Gould M (2011). *Nineteenth-century theatre and the imperial encounter*. New York: Routledge.

Gregory B (1991). Staging British India. In JS Bratton (et al). *Acts of supremacy: the British Empire and the British stage 1790–1930* (pp150–78). Manchester: Manchester University Press.

Guither HD (1998). *Animal rights: history and scope of a radical social movement*. Carbodale, IL: Southern Illinois University Press.

Hagenbeck C (1909). *Beasts and men*. Translated and abridged by HSR Elliot & AG Thacker. New York: Longman Green & Co.

Hagenbeck L (1956). *Animals are my life*. A Brown (Trans). London: The Bodley Head Ltd.
Hahn D (2003). *The Tower menagerie*. London: Simon & Schuster.
Hall C (Ed) (2000a). *Cultures of empire: a reader*. New York: Routledge.
Hall C (Ed) (2000b). Introduction: thinking the postcolonial, thinking the empire. In C Hall (Ed). *Cultures of empire: a reader* (pp1–33). New York: Routledge.
Hall C (2004). Of gender and empire: reflections on the nineteenth century. In P Levine (Ed). *Gender and empire* (pp46–76). Oxford: Oxford University Press.
Ham J (1997). Taming the beast: animality in Wedekind and Nietzsche. In J Ham & M Senior (Eds). *Animal acts: configuring the human in Western history* (pp145–63). New York: Routledge.
Hammarstrom DL (1980). *Behind the big top*. Cranbury, NJ: AS Barnes & Co. Inc.
Hancocks D (2001). *A different nature: the paradoxical world of zoos and their uncertain future*. Berkeley, CA: University of California Press.
Haney's art of training animals (1869). New York: Jesse Haney & Co. Publishers.
Hanson E (2002). *Animal attractions: nature on display in American zoos*. Princeton, NJ: Princeton University Press.
Haraway D (1989). *Primate visions*. New York: Routledge.
Harding L (2000). *Elephant story: Jumbo and the PT Barnum under the big top*. Jefferson, NC: McFarland & Co. Inc., Publishers.
Harris N (1973). *Humbug*. Boston, MA: Little, Brown & Co.
Hayes P (2000). 'Cocky' Hahn and the 'Black Venus': the making of a native commissioner in South West Africa, 1915–46. In C Hall (Ed). *Cultures of empire: a reader* (pp329–55). New York: Routledge.
Hediger R (Ed) (2012). *Animals and war: studies of Europe and North America*. Leiden, Netherlands: Brill.
Heliot C (1906). Diary of a lion-tamer. *Cosmopolitan Magazine*, 41, September: 463–68.
Herman DJ (2007). From farmers to hunters. In K Kete (Ed). *A cultural history of animals in the age of empire* (pp47–71). Oxford: Berg.
Hoage RJ & Deiss WA (Eds) (1996). *New worlds, new animals: from menageries to zoological park in the nineteenth century*. Baltimore, MD: The Johns Hopkins University Press.
Hoage RJ, Roskell A & Mansour J (1996). Menageries to zoos to 1900. In RJ Hoage and WA Deiss (Eds). *New worlds, new animals: from menageries to zoological park in the nineteenth century* (pp8–18). Baltimore, MD: The Johns Hopkins University Press.
Hoh LVG & Rough WH (1990). *Step right up! The adventures of circus in America*. White Hall, VA: Betterway Publications Inc.

Works cited

Holder HJ (1991). Melodrama, realism and empire on the British stage. In JS Bratton (et al). *Acts of supremacy: the British Empire and the British stage 1790-1930* (pp129-49). Manchester: Manchester University Press.
Hone W (1838). *The everyday book and table book*, Vol. 1. London: Thomas Tegg & Son.
Hume D (1896). *A treatise of human nature* (3 vols), LA Selby-Bigge (Ed). Oxford: Clarendon Press.
Hyland, A (2010) *The warhorse in the modern era: breeder to battlefield: 1600 to 1865*. Stockton on Tees, UK: Black Tent Publications.
JA (1872). Is 'lion-taming' a perilous occupation? *Glasgow Herald*, 16 January: 2.
Jackson D (2008). *Lion*. London: Reaktion Books.
Jackson S & Vernes K (2010). *Kangaroo: portrait of an extraordinary marsupial*. Sydney: Allen & Unwin.
Jamieson D & Davidson S (1980). *The love of the circus*. London: Octopus Books.
Jando D (2008). Strange beasts from foreign lands. In N Daniel (Ed). *Circus 1870-1950* (pp274-345). Los Angeles, CA: Taschen.
JCD (1888). Circus life behind the scenes. *Graphic* (London), 1 July: 20, 22, 24, 26.
Joys JC (1983). *The wild animal trainer in America*. Boulder, CO: Pruett Publishing Co.
Kasson J (1978). *Amusing the million: Coney Island at the turn of the century*. New York: Hill & Wang.
Kelly FC (2012). Circus swindlers and their games, reprinted in *Bandwagon*, 56(1), January–February: 30-33.
Kete K (2007a) (Ed). *A cultural history of animals in the age of empire*. Oxford: Berg.
Kete K (2007b). Introduction: animals and human empire. In K Kete (Ed). *A cultural history of animals in the age of empire* (pp1-24). Oxford: Berg.
Kober AH (1931). *Circus nights and circus days*. New York: William Morrow & Co.
Kreger M (2008). Canvas to concrete: elephants and the circus–zoo relationship. In C Wemmer & CA Christen (Eds). *Elephants and ethics* (pp185-203). Baltimore, MD: The Johns Hopkins University Press.
Kwint M (2002a). The circus and nature in late Georgian England. In R Kosher (Ed). *Histories of leisure* (pp45-60). Oxford: Berg.
Kwint M (2002b). The legitimization of the circus in late Georgian England. *Past & Present*, 174(1): 72-115.
Lambert D & Lester A (Eds) (2006a). *Colonial lives across the British Empire: imperial careering in the long nineteenth century*. Cambridge: Cambridge University Press.
Lambert D & Lester A (2006b). Introduction: imperial spaces, imperial subjects. In D Lambert & A Lester (Eds). *Colonial lives across the British Empire:*

imperial careering in the long nineteenth century (pp1–31). Cambridge: Cambridge University Press.
Landry D (2011). English brutes, Eastern enlightenment. *The Eighteenth Century*, 52(1): 11–30.
Le Roux H & Garnier J (1890). *Acrobats and mountebanks*. AP Morton (Trans). London: Chapman & Hall.
Lester A (2001). *Imperial networks: creating identities in nineteenth-century South Africa*. London: Routledge.
Levine P (Ed) (2004a). *Gender and empire*. Oxford: Oxford University Press.
Levine P (2004b). Introduction: why gender and empire? In P Levine (Ed). *Gender and empire* (pp1–13). Oxford: Oxford University Press.
Lockhart G (1938). *Grey Titan*, with WG Boswell. London: Burns Oates & Washbourne Ltd.
Lukens J (1956). *The Sanger story*. London: Hodder & Stoughton.
MacKenzie JM (Ed) (1986a). *Imperialism and popular culture*. Manchester: Manchester University Press.
MacKenzie JM (1986b). Introduction. In JM MacKenzie (Ed). *Imperialism and popular culture* (pp1–16). Manchester: Manchester University Press.
MacKenzie JM (1987a). The imperial pioneer and hunter and British masculine stereotype in late Victorian and Edwardian times. In JA Mangan & J Walvin (Eds). *Manliness and morality: middle class masculinity in Britain and America 1800–1940* (pp176–98). Manchester: Manchester University Press.
MacKenzie JM (1987b). Hunting in eastern and central Africa in the late nineteenth century, with special reference to Zimbabwe. In WJ Baker and JA Mangan (Eds). *Sport in Africa: essays in social history* (pp172–95). New York: Africana Publishing Co.
MacKenzie JM (1988). *The empire of nature: hunting, conservation and British imperialism*. Manchester: Manchester University Press.
MacKenzie JM (Ed) (1990a). *Imperialism and the natural world*. Manchester: Manchester University Press.
MacKenzie JM (1990b). Introduction. In JM MacKenzie (Ed). *Imperialism and the natural world* (pp1–14). Manchester: Manchester University Press.
MacKenzie JM (1990c). Experts and amateurs: tsetse, nagana and sleeping sickness in east and central Africa. In JM MacKenzie (Ed). *Imperialism and the natural world* (pp187–212). Manchester: Manchester University Press.
MacKenzie JM (1995). *Orientalism: history, theory and the arts*. Manchester: Manchester University Press.
Madden D (2011). *The authentic animal: inside the old and obsessive world of taxidermy*. New York: St Martins.
Malherbe VC (1999). Fanny, the political lion. *Quarterly Bulletin of the National Library of South Africa*, 54(1): 27–32.

Works cited

Mangan JA & MacKenzie C (2008). Imperial masculinity institutionalized: the Shikar Club. *International Journal of the History of Sport*, 25(9): 1218–42.

Mangan JA & Walvin J (Eds) (1987). *Manliness and morality: middle class masculinity in Britain and America 1800–1940*. Manchester: Manchester University Press.

Manning-Sanders R (1952). *The English circus*. London: Werner Laurie.

Marra K (2015). Massive bodies in mortal performance. In J Parker-Starbuck & L Orozco (Eds). *Performing animality: animals in performance practices* (pp117-34). London: Palgrave Macmillan.

McCalman I (2006). Teddy Roosevelt's trophy: history and nostalgia. In M Lake (Ed). *Memory, monuments and museums* (pp58-75, 256-59). Melbourne: Melbourne University Press.

McCulloch J (2004). Empire and violence 1900–1939. In P Levine (Ed). *Gender and empire* (pp220-39). Oxford: Oxford University Press.

Melman B (2006). *The culture of history: English uses of the past 1800–1953*. Oxford: Oxford University Press.

Mill JS (1969). Nature. In JM Robson (Ed). *Essays on ethics, religion and society* (pp373-402). Toronto: University of Toronto Press and Routledge & Kegan Paul.

Mizelle B (2012). Horse and cat acts in the early American circus. In S Weber, KL Ames & M Wittmann (Eds). *The American circus* (pp250-75). New York/New Haven, CT: Bard Graduate Center and Yale University Press.

Mrozek DJ (1987). The habit of victory: the American military and the cult of manliness. In JA Mangan and J Walvin (Eds). *Manliness and morality: middle class masculinity in Britain and America 1800–1940* (pp220-41). Manchester: Manchester University Press.

Munby AJ (1972). *Munby – man of two worlds: the life and diaries of Arthur J Munby*. D Hudson (Ed). London: John Murray.

Nance S (2012). Elephants and the American circus. In S Weber, KL Ames & M Wittmann (Eds). *The American circus* (pp232-49). New York/New Haven, CT: Bard Graduate Center and Yale University Press.

Nance S (2013). *Entertaining elephants: animal agency and the business of American circus*. Baltimore, MD: The Johns Hopkins University Press.

Nixon R (2011). *Slow violence and the environmentalism of the poor*. Cambridge, MA: Harvard University Press.

Paul S (1987). The wrestling tradition and its social functions. In WJ Baker & JA Mangan (Eds). *Sport in Africa: essays in social history* (pp23-46). New York: Africana Publishing Co.

Parezo NJ & Fowler Don D (2007). *Anthropology goes to the fair: the 1904 Louisiana purchase exposition*. Lincoln, NE: University of Nebraska Press.

Peacock S (1996). *The great Farini*. Toronto: Penguin Books.

Pendennis (1905). Claire Heliot: most daring of lion tamers. *New York Times*, 29 October: (SM)1.

Pfening F (2004). Montgomery Queen: short term circus king. *Bandwagon*, July–August: 3–14.

Plumb C (2010a). 'Strange and wonderful': encountering the elephant in Britain, 1675–1830. *Journal for Eighteenth-Century Studies*, 33(4): 525–43.

Plumb C (2010b). Reading menageries: using eighteenth-century print sources to historicise the sensorium of menagerie spectators and their encounters with exotic animals. *European Review of History*, 17(2): 265–86.

Poignant R (2004). *Professional savages: captive lives and Western spectacles*. New Haven, CT: Yale University Press.

Poliquin R (2012). *The breathless zoo: taxidermy and the cultures of longing*. University Park, PA: Penn State University Press.

Potter SJ (2003). *News and the British world*. Oxford: Clarendon Press.

Proske R (1956). *Lions, tigers and me*. New York: Henry Holt & Co.

Putnam W (2007). Captive audiences: a concert for the elephants in the Jardin des Plantes. *Drama Review*, 51(1) T193: 154–60.

Ritvo H (1987). *The animal estate: the English and other creatures in the Victorian age*. Cambridge, MA: Harvard University Press.

Ritvo H (1996). The order of nature: constructing the collections of Victorian zoos. In RJ Hoage & WA Deiss (Eds). *New worlds, new animals: from menageries to zoological park in the nineteenth century* (pp43–50). Baltimore, MD: The Johns Hopkins University Press.

Ritvo H (2002). Destroyers and preservers: big game in the Victorian empire. *History Today*, January: 33–39.

Robbins LE (2002). *Elephant slaves and pampered parrots: exotic animals in eighteenth-century Paris*. Baltimore, MD: The Johns Hopkins University Press.

Robeson D (1941). *Louis Roth: forty years with jungle killers*. Caldwell, ID: The Caxton Printers Ltd.

Robeson D & Barnes AG (1935). *Al G Barnes: master showman*. Caldwell, ID: The Caxton Printers Ltd.

Robinson MH (1996). Foreword. In RJ Hoage & WA Deiss (Eds). *New worlds, new animals: from menageries to zoological park in the nineteenth century* (ppvii–xi). Baltimore, MD: The Johns Hopkins University Press.

Rogers JW (2007). Circus-related crime and deviance: revisiting the prevalence and decline of a circus darkside. In R Sugarman (Ed). *The many worlds of circus* (pp115–25). Newcastle, UK: Cambridge Scholars Publishing.

Roosevelt T (1910). *African game trails: an account of the African wanderings of an American hunter-naturalist*. London: John Murray.

Rothfels N (2002a). *Savages and beasts: the birth of the modern zoo*. Baltimore, MD: The Johns Hopkins University Press.

Rothfels N (Ed) (2002b). *Representing animals*. Bloomington, IN: Indiana University Press.
Rothfels N (2002c). Immersed with animals. In N Rothfels (Ed). *Representing animals* (pp199-224). Bloomington, IN: Indiana University Press.
Rothfels N (2008). Elephants, ethics and history. In C Wemmer & CA Christen (Eds). *Elephants and ethics* (pp101-19). Baltimore, MD: The Johns Hopkins University Press.
Rowlands M (2007). Philosophy and animals in the age of empire. In K Kete (Ed). *A cultural history of animals in the age of empire* (pp135-52). Oxford: Berg.
Russell G (1995). *The theatres of war: performance, politics and society, 1793-1815*. Oxford: Oxford University Press.
St Leon M (1983). *Spangles and sawdust: the circus in Australia*. Melbourne: Greenhouse Publications.
St Leon M (1993). *The wizard of the wire: the story of Con Colleano*. Canberra: Aboriginal Studies Press.
St Leon M (2011). *Circus: the Australian story*. Melbourne: Melbourne Books.
Salt H (1980 [1892]). *Animals' rights: considered in relation to social progress*. Clarks Summit, PA: Society for Animal Rights Inc.
Sanger G (1927 [1910]). *Seventy years a showman*. London: JM Dent & Sons.
Saxon AH (1968). *Enter foot and horse*. New Haven, CT: Yale University Press.
Saxon AH (1978). *The life and art of Andrew Ducrow*. Hamden, CT: Archon Books.
Saxon AH (Ed) (1983). *Selected letters of PT Barnum*. New York: Columbia University Press.
Saxon AH (1989). *PT Barnum: the legend and the man*. New York: Columbia University Press.
Scherren H (1955). *The Zoological Society of London*. London: Cassell & Co. Ltd.
Scigliano E (2002). *Love, war, and circuses*. Boston, MA: Houghton Mifflin Co.
Selous FC (1893). *Travel and adventure in South-East Asia*. London: Rowland Ward & Co. Ltd.
Selous FC (1896). *Sunshine and storm in Rhodesia*. London: Rowland Ward & Co. Ltd.
Shephard B (1986). Showbiz imperialism: the case of Peter Lobengula. In JM MacKenzie (Ed). *Imperialism and popular culture* (pp94-112). Manchester: Manchester University Press.
Simons J (2012). *The tiger that swallowed the boy: exotic animals in Victorian England*. Farringdon, UK: Libri Press.
Slout WL (1998). *Olympians of the sawdust circle: a biographical dictionary*. San Bernardino, CA: The Borgo Press.
Slout WL (2006a). En route to the Great Eastern: part one. *Bandwagon*, March-April: 28-36.

Slout WL (2006b). En route to the Great Eastern: part four. *Bandwagon*, September–October: 17–25.
Speaight G (1980). *A history of the circus.* London: The Tantivy Press.
Springhall J (1986). 'Up guards and at them!' British imperialism and popular art, 1880–1914. In JM MacKenzie (Ed). *Imperialism and popular culture* (pp49–72). Manchester: Manchester University Press.
Sramek J (2006). 'Face him like a Briton': tiger hunting, imperialism, and British masculinity in colonial India, 1800–1875. *Victorian Studies*, 48(4): 659–80.
Stark M & Orr G (1940). *Hold that tiger.* Caldwell, ID: The Caxton Printers Ltd.
Stepan NL (2000). Race, gender, science and citizenship. In C Hall (Ed). *Cultures of empire: a reader* (pp61–86). New York: Routledge.
Storey W (1991). Big cats and imperialism: lion and tiger hunting in Kenya and northern India, 1898–1930. *Journal of World History*, 2(2): 135–73.
Streible D (1989). A history of the boxing film, 1894–1915. *Film History* 3(3): 235–57.
Sturtevant CG (1925). Circus menageries. *The Billboard*, 13 June: 76.
Sully J (1892). *The human mind: a text-book of psychology.* Vol. 1. New York: D Appleton & Co.
Summerfield P (1986). Patriotism and empire: music-hall entertainment 1870–1914. In JM MacKenzie (Ed). *Imperialism and popular culture* (pp17–48). Manchester: Manchester University Press.
Tait P (2003). 'The Australian Marvels': wire-walkers Ella Zuila and George Loyal and geographies of aerial gender body identity. In E Schafer & S Bradley Smith (Eds). *Playing Australia* (pp80–92). Amsterdam: Rodopi.
Tait P (2005). *Circus bodies: cultural identity in aerial performance.* London: Routledge.
Tait P (2009). Controversy about a human–animal big cat stunt in Fillis' circus. *Early Popular Visual Culture*, 7(2): 199–211.
Tait P (2011). Emotions in menagerie acts. *PAN: Philosophy Activism Nature*, 8. Retrieved on 7 September 2015 from http://arrow.monash.edu.au/hdl/1959.1/523020 (Minding Animals 2009 Conference publication).
Tait P (2012). *Wild and dangerous performances: animals, emotions, circus.* Basingstoke, UK: Palgrave Macmillan.
Tait P (2015). Acrobatic circus horses: military training to natural wildness. In J Parker-Starbuck & L Orozco (Eds). *Performing animality: animals in performance practices* (pp97–113). London: Palgrave Macmillan.
Tait P (forthcoming). Dressing for war and unnatural poses in human–animal acts. *Humanities Australia*, 7.
Tester K (1991). *Animals and society: the humanity of animal rights.* London: Routledge.

Works cited

Thayer S (2005). *The performers: a history of circus acts*. Seattle, WA: Dauven & Thayer.

Thayer S (2006). The oldest of showmen: the career of Benjamin E Brown of Somers, New York. *Bandwagon*, September–October: 10–16.

Thétard H (1947). *La merveilleuse histoire du cirque* (2 vols). Paris: Prisma.

Thomas K (1984). *Man and the natural world: changing attitudes in England 1500–1800*. London: Penguin Books.

Thomas NJ (2006). Mary Curzon: 'American Queen of India'. In D Lambert & A Lester (Eds). *Colonial lives across the British Empire: imperial careering in the long nineteenth century* (pp285–308). Cambridge: Cambridge University Press.

Thompson JL (2010). *Theodore Roosevelt abroad: nature, empire and the journey of an American president*. Basingstoke, UK: Palgrave Macmillan.

Thompson RW (1934). *Wild animal man*. London: Duckworth.

Turner A (2013). *Taxidermy*. London: Thames & Hudson.

Turner J (1995). *Victorian arena: the performers. A dictionary of British circus biography*. Vol. 1. Formby, UK: Lingdales Press.

Turner J (2000). *Victorian arena: the performers. A dictionary of British circus biography*. Vol. 2. Formby, UK: Lingdales Press.

van der Merwe F (2007). *Frank Fillis: the story of a circus legend*. Stellenbosch, South Africa: FJG Publikasies.

Van Hare G (1893). *Fifty years of a showman's life: the life and travels of Van Hare, by himself*. London: Sampson Low, Marston & Co.

Veltre T (1996). Menageries, metaphors and meanings. In RJ Hoage & WA Deiss (Eds). *New worlds, new animals: from menageries to zoological park in the nineteenth century* (pp19–29). Baltimore, MD: The Johns Hopkins University Press.

Velvin E (1906). *Behind the scenes with wild animals*. New York: Moffat Yard & Co.

Verney P (1978). *Here comes the circus*. New York: Paddington Press.

Wallace AR (1898). *The wonderful century: its successes and its failures*. London: Swan Sonnenschein & Co.

Watts E (pseudonym for RH Horne) (1838). *The life of Van Amburgh: the brute-tamer, with anecdotes of his extraordinary pupils*. Cheapside, UK: Robert Tyas.

Wemmer C & Christen CA (Eds) (2008). *Elephants and ethics*. Baltimore, MD: The Johns Hopkins University Press.

Werner MR (1923). *PT Barnum*. London: Jonathan Cape.

Werry M (2011). *The tourist state: performing leisure, liberalism and race in New Zealand*. Minneapolis, MN: University of Minnesota Press.

Wheeler S (2007). *Too close to the sun*. London: Vintage.

Wickham G (2002). *Early English stages, 1300 to 1660: Vol. Two, 1576 to 1660, Part I*. London: Routledge.

Wilson D (2015). *The welfare of performing animals: a historical perspective*. Berlin: Springer.

Wilson K (2004). Empire, gender, and modernity in the eighteenth century. In P Levine (Ed). *Gender and empire* (pp14–45). Oxford: Oxford University Press.

Wirth G (1925). *Round the world with a circus*. Melbourne: Troedel & Cooper Pty Ltd.

Wirth P (no date). *The life of Philip Wirth*. Melbourne: Troedel & Cooper Pty Ltd.

Wittmann M (2012). The transnational history of the early American circus. In S Weber, KL Ames & M Wittmann (Eds). *The American circus* (pp54–85). New York/New Haven, CT: Bard Graduate Center and Yale University Press.

Woollacott A (2006). *Gender and empire*. Basingstoke, UK: Palgrave Macmillan.

Wroth W & Wroth A (1896). *The London pleasure gardens of the eighteenth century*. London: Macmillan.

Wykes A (1977). *Circus!* London: Jupiter Books Ltd.

Youatt W (1839). *The obligation and extent of humanity to brutes*. London: Longman, Orme, Brown, Green & Longman.

Young Lee P (2010). The curious affair of Monsieur Martin the bear. *Journal for Eighteenth-Century Studies*, 33(4): 615–29.

Younger RM (1988). *Kangaroo images through the ages*. Melbourne: Hutchinson.

Ziter E (2003). *The orient on the Victorian stage*. Cambridge: Cambridge University Press.

Index

adventure narratives 74, 98–102, 161
Akeley, Carl 127, 241
Altick, Richard 43
Amato, Sarah 129
Anglo–Boer War re-enactment 191, 213, 216–217
animal abuse xvii–xviii, 50, 103, 106; *see also* animal handling: physical coercion in
animal handlers and tamers 8–33; *see also* female tamers
  adopting the title of 'professor' 119
  as a hunter 68–72, 81, 250
  first tamers 8–32
  gender identity and 28–32
animal handling 13, 18–19, 22–23
  Christian values in 44
  physical coercion in 9, 150
animal shows xvii; *see also* exotic animal acts, feeding displays, head-in-the-mouth stunts
  advertising of 96–97
  aggression and xvi; *see also* audience misbehaviour
  as emblem of nationalism xiii, xviii–xix, 39–42, 190–192, 209–210, 242–244
  biblical themes in 10, 16, 20, 24, 26, 67, 83
  cage acts 8–35, 70–71, 151–154, 157
  colonial themes in 188–192, 208–210, 213–219
  'combined travelling show' 87
  commercial aspects of xvi, 88–90
  criminal business practices and 114–119
  educational aspects of 83, 119–122, 206, 235
  fatalities in 30–31, 70–73, 156
  Greco-Roman themes in 16, 20, 185
  'the kiss of fraternity' lamb to lion 149
  in Australia and New Zealand 157–163
  orientalist themes in 20, 22, 38, 40, 93
  perception of 18–19, 105–111, 146–149, 168–170
  pre-show parade 87, 91
  spectators' responses to 103–112, 171–172

animal trainers 192–202, 213–215
  as a military hero *see* military hero
  women as 221–235
animal training 244–247
  improved methods in 195–198, 244–245
  perception of 245–247
  quasi-military elements in 193–194, 200–202
animals *see also* trade in animals
  attitude to 51–54; *see also* kindness
  'cage paralysis' in 90
  celebrity 122–133
  in visual art 59–63
  women and 52; *see also* female tamers
anti-cruelty movement xv, 24, 50, 151, 195, 198
Aristotle 59
Assael, Brenda 39
Astley, John 38, 46
Astley, Philip 6, 38, 44, 49
Astley's Circus 6–7, 38–42, 47, 56–58
audience misbehaviour xii–xiii, 250
  examples of 104–112, 162–165
  reasons for 104, 106
  societal conflict and 113
Aurora, Mademoiselle 228

Bain, Alexander 26, 51–53, 59
Baker, Samuel 75
Bakhtin, Mikhail xii
Ballantyne, RM 98
Barnum and Bailey Circus The Greatest Show on Earth 95, 99, 115, 181, 205–212
  behaviour guidelines for spectators 207
Barnum, PT 82–84, 88, 91–99, 122–132
  Animal stories 98–101
  white elephant 'show warfare' 128–132

Batty, Thomas 'Baddy' 111
bear-baiting 2
bears, individuals in menageries
  Monsieur Martin Brown 6
bears, training of 196, 228, 233
Bébé, Tilly 233–235
Bennett, Tony 236
Bentham, Jeremy 51
Bidel, François 148–149
Bishop, Charlotte *see* Pianka, Madame
Blight (Bright), Ellen Eliza 30–31
Bonavita, Captain Jack 198–200, 224–225, 230, 241
Boone, Daniel 77
Bostock, Edward 11, 110, 127, 148, 151, 184–185
Bostock, Frank 9, 151, 185, 192, 198, 201, 222, 245
Bratton, Jacqueline S 39, 42, 98, 183
Bridgeman, Thomas 148
Britannia 33–34
Britannia (performance) 65
British Association for the Advancement of Science 77
Buckland, Frank 7, 182
Bugeja, Salvator 174

Carlyle, Thomas 43, 48
Carter, James [John] 21
Cartmill, Matt 73
Casanova, Lorenzo 79
Castang, Reuben 213–215, 219
Chambers, Paul 75, 122, 210
Chapman, Ellen 28–34
Churchill, Winston 238
circus
  Greco-Roman association with 20
  horse acts in 7, 37–42, 49–50, 160
  in Australia 158–162, 165
  in New Zealand 158–159, 162, 165–173

Index

in the USA 87–94
military heroism in 38, 44, 179, 192–193, 198–201
modernist 247
nationalism and xviii, 38–43
Clarke, John 246
Cochran, Charles 115, 117, 218
Cole's circus 89, 91, 152
colonial conflict xx–xxi, 48–49, 65, 73, 162–165, 177, 180–188
colonialism *see also* animal shows: colonial themes in
  indigenous peoples and xix, 48–49, 65, 75–76, 82–83, 94, 99, 101, 160, 163–165, 181
  masculinist culture and 175
Conklin, George xiv, 105, 108, 116–117, 151–156, 195
  elephant training and 203–205
  Pomp and 152–154
Cook, Erika 80
Cooper, Courtney Ryley 195, 201
Cooper, John 57
costumes 27, 29, 56–58, 71, 92, 94, 99
  female 222, 225–226, 231
  formal 131, 192, 194
  military 40, 42, 112, 179, 192–193, 198, 201, 209
  'native' 32, 58, 99, 163, 187–188
  orientalist/fantasy 12, 197, 209
  Roman style 16, 20, 71, 153
Coup, William xiv, 73, 75, 88, 104–105, 114, 180
Cox, John 166–172
Craven, Stuart [Stewart] 85–86, 203
Crimean War re-enactments 42
Crockett, James 32–33
Crockett, William 185
Cumming, Roualeyn Gordon 68, 77, 99
Curzon, Lady Mary 209

Daniell, Samuel 61
Darwin, Charles 26, 51, 53, 128, 155
Davis, Janet 82, 114, 180
Davis, Jim 110
de Vere, Madame Pauline *see* Chapman, Ellen
Devere, William 110
Disher, Maurice Willson 21, 40–41
Donald, Diana 52, 60
Ducrow, Andrew 7, 17, 40–42, 45
'The Durbar of Delhi' procession 39, 208–210

Edison, Thomas 212
Eipper, Paul 245–246, 252–253
elephants 100, 202–210
  acts with 57–58, 86–87, 94–95, 171, 177, 202–203
  as symbols of colonial rule 37, 48
  attitudes to 9, 37, 216
  etiquette 214
  hunting of 75, 81
  (mis)management of 45–48, 85, 210–212
  significance of 48–49, 131
  training of 155, 202–205
  whitewashed 128–132
elephants, individuals in menageries
  Alice 127
  Chuny 46–47, 214
  Djeck 46–48
  Fritz 211
  Ghuni Sah (Gunnesah) 177
  Julius Caesar 91
  Jumbo 84, 122–128
  Juno 203
  Lallah Rookh 85, 204
  'Light of Asia' 131
  Lizzie 109–110
  Mandarin 212
  Old Bet 84

Old Romeo 85, 104–105
Patsy 216
Queen Annie 203–204
Titania 159
Tom Thumb 127, 204
Topsy 212
Toung Taloung 128–131
Elwood, Robert 91
Emeljanow, Victor 110
equestrian acts *see* horse acts
ethnographic shows *see also* Zulu warriors: with Farini's
  from Africa 188–190
  with animals 180–181
  with Indigenous Australian groups 180
  with peoples from remote regions 185–186
Evelyn, John 2
exotic animal acts *see also* elephants: acts with, lion acts, monkeys
  nationalism and xvii
  themes in xv
exotic animals *see also* elephants
  early exhibiting of 1–4
  imperialism and xii, xx
  paintings of 60–61
  trade in 3; *see also* trade in animals
  violence and xiii; *see also* animal handling: physical coercion in
Eyre, Edward John 48

Farini [William Hunt] 101–102, 181–184, 239
Farini, Lulu [Sam Hunt] 101
feeding displays 146–149
female tamers 28–32, 166, 170; *see also* lion queen
  colonial anxieties and 173, 175–176, 178
female trainers 221–235

marriage and 228, 233–234
perceptions of 222–224
fighting acts *see also* hunting: acts
  educational value of 119–122
  human 159–165, 184
  lion and dog fights 10
  representations in art of 59–63
  significance of x, xii, 43
  with domesticated animals 11
Fillis' circus 165–167, 173–176, 188–191, 213
Fillis, Frank 111, 165–172, 188, 191, 213, 216–217
Forepaugh, Charlie 152
Forepaugh's circus 91, 109, 129, 131
Foucault, Michel xx
Fox, Charles Philip 87, 94
Frost, Thomas 10, 20, 28, 30

Gentner, John *see* Bonavita, Captain Jack
geographical imagination of historians xxii
Golby, JM 107
Goodall, Jane R 27
Gould, Marty 49

Hagenbeck, Carl 78–79, 83, 93, 186, 213, 252
Hagenbeck, Gustav Senior 78
Hagenbeck, Lorenz 79, 186, 242–243
Hagenbeck's 74, 83, 180, 185–187, 194, 213–215, 243
Haggard, Rider 98
Hall, Catherine xix
Ham, Jennifer 78
Hancocks, David 5
Harding, Les 126
Harkaway, Jack 161
Hatton, Denys Finch 251

Index

Haumann (Huth), Klara *see* Heliot, Claire
head-in-the-mouth stunts 15, 29, 150, 152–153, 166–167, 168, 177
Heliot, Claire xxiv, 229–233, 244
Henty, GA 98
Herman, Daniel 77
Hervieu, Paul 112, 150
Hilton, Miss (Polly) 28
hippodrome *see* horse acts
Hone, William 8–9
Horne, RH *see* Watts, Ephraim
horse 'actors' 37, 41
   lying down as if dead 38, 216–217
horse acts 38–45
   circus 6, 38–39
horses, training of 44–45, 50
Hume, David 50, 59
Hunt, Sam 101
Hunt, William *see* Farini
hunter
   as a professional scientist 237, 240
   as an ideal of masculinity 73, 75, 237
   figure in shows 68–71, 81, 184, 250
hunting *see also* safari hunter
   acts 67, 69, 111
   as a sport 68, 77, 97
   by indigenous peoples 74–76, 81, 101
   collecting and 97
   colonial 74–77, 81, 96
   commercial versus sport 76
   definitions of 72–73
   in Africa 75, 206, 251
   in India 237
   in literature 98; *see also* adventure narratives
   military training and 73
   natural history and 77

imperialism xii, xix, 67–102

psychology of 'popular imperialism' xx

Jack, Manchester 10, 22
Johnson, (Professor) GW 159
Joys, Joanne 22

kangaroos 7, 74
Kete, Kathleen xii
kindness x, xv, 24–25, 31, 49–54, 82, 229, 232–233, 235, 250
   royal 55–59
King James I 10
King's Tableaux 58

La Belle Selica 227
Lambert, David xviii, xxi, 74
Landseer, Edwin 17, 62
Le Roux, Hugues 111, 147–148
Lester, Alan xviii, xxi–xxi, 74
Levine, Philippa 175
Lewis, Captain Arthur Waldo 216
lion acts 1–35
   anti-cruelty concerns and 10, 35, 90
   cage in 26
   dance display 154
   jumping display 151
   'lion hunt' 68–72, 184–185
   lion riding a horse act 61
lion attacking a horse, in art 60–61, 135, 138
Lion Jack 97
lion king 12–23, 69
lion queen 28–32
lions, individuals in menageries
   August 231
   George 155–156
   Nero 10
   Pomp 152–154
   Sicchi 229–230, 232
   Wallace 10, 148

Livingstone, David 76
Lobengula, Peter 191

Maccomo, Martini 68–69, 70
MacKenzie, Callum 237
MacKenzie, John 61–63, 72, 76–77, 97, 181
Madame Tussaud's Museum 39
Manders' menagerie 70, 150
Mangan, James Anthony 237
Martin, Henri 11–12, 20, 22
Massarti *see* McCarthy, Thomas
Matabele wars, re-enactment of 188–189
Mathews, Dick 160–161
Matthies, Rudolf 197, 244, 245
McCarthy, Thomas 70–72
Melman, Billie xviii, xx, 113
Menges, Joseph 186, 242
militarisation of British society 39, 193
military dramas 38, 42
military hero 42–44, 98, 182–183, 189, 198–200
military iconography 64, 200, 250
military training 38
  hunting as a form of 73
Mill, John Stuart 25–26, 51
monkeys 27, 155, 166
  riding a horse 27–28
Morelli, Madame Louise 222–225
Mrozek, Donald 200
Munby, Arthur 105

Napoleon, imitation of 40, 56
Napoleonic wars re-enactments 38, 40–41
nationalism 39–43, 130
  animal training and 244
Nietzsche, Friedrich 78

Parkinson, Sydney 7

Parkinson, Tom 87, 94
Peacock, Shane 101
Pepys, Samuel 2
Peters, Willy 196
Pianka, Madame 225–227
Pidcock, Gilbert 3
Plumb, Christopher xiii
Poliquin, Rachel 63
Proske, Roman 234
Purdue, AW 107
Putnam, Walter 5

Queen Adelaide 41
Queen Victoria 17, 29, 33–34, 55–56, 58–59, 94, 124, 146
Queen's Tableau 34

Rhodes, Cecil 173
Ritvo, Harriet xii, xv, xx, 4, 35, 50, 72
Rix, Albert 196
Robbins, Louise xii
Rogers, Joseph 117
Roosevelt, Theodore 198, 214, 238–242
Roth, Louis 201
Rothfels, Nigel 78, 187
Rousseil, Roselia 149
Royal Society for the Prevention of Cruelty to Animals 24, 126, 197
Royal Zoological Society 5, 122, 124, 236
Ruhe, Paul *see* Tuhe, Paul
Russell, Gillian 39

safari hunter 67, 76, 96, 186–187, 235–242
Salt, Henry 237
Sanger, George 28–34, 55, 57, 92, 109
  circus 32–33, 57–59
Sawade, Richard 197, 219, 243–244
Saxon, AH 82, 94, 98
Scheherazade, Madame Jasia 173, 175

Index

Scott, Matthew 122, 125
Scrutator 168–170
seals and sea lions 196
Seeth, Julius 192–193, 200
Simons, John 4
Society for the Preservation of the Wild Fauna of the Empire 251
soldier figure *see* military hero
Somerset, CA 48
Spencer, Herbert 51
Springhall, John 63, 190
Sramek, Joseph 237
St Leon, Mark 158
Stanley, Henry Morton 76
Stepan, Nancy Leys 77
Storey, William 238
Stratton, Charles *see* Thumb, General Tom
Stubbs, George 7, 60–61
Sturtevant, CG 90, 94
Sully, James 232
Summerfield, Penny 63, 190

Tar, Jack 42, 97
taxidermy 56, 63, 97, 127, 236
Thayer, Stuart 88
theatre 38, 41–42, 46, 47
  as public education 63
  audience behaviour in 110
  Drury Lane 11, 17, 41
  war in 37, 39, 42, 48–49, 63–65
Thomas, Keith 50, 53
Thomas, Nicola 209
Thompson, Ephraim 86
Thumb, General Tom 55, 82
Tiebor, John 196
trade in animals 73, 78–80, 242–243
  animal fairs 79
  traders of animals 3; *see also* Hagenbeck's
    Reiche brothers 74–75

travelling menageries 4, 8, 23, 67–102, 174; *see also* Barnum, PT, Cole's circus, Forepaugh's circus
  as organised leisure 107
  cultural significance of xviii
  development of x, 3–5, 246
  in the USA 87–94
  mistreatment of animals in 25
  scale of xi
  violence and x–xiii, 103–114, 250
Tuhe, Paul 75

Van Amburgh, Isaac A 12–23, 62, 146, 153
van der Merwe, Floris 165–166, 217
Van Hare, G 81–82
Velvin, Ellen xiv, 226, 231
Verne, Jules 215
Verney, Peter 110
Verreaux, Jules 63

Wallace, Alfred Russel 193
war 37–42
  in art works 190
  on other animal species x, 73, 101, 249–253
  public understanding of 64
  re-enactments; see also Crimean war, Matabele wars, Napoleonic wars 38, 41, 48–49, 56, 162–165, 190, 213
war narratives, symbolic centrality of animals in 64
Ward, Henry 127
Ward, Rowland 97
Waterloo, The battle of (performance) 40–42
Watts, Ephraim 14
White, Professor C 92
whitewashed elephants *see* elephants: whitewashed

Whittle, Joseph 155–157
Wild West shows 82, 162–163, 187, 189, 215
Williams, Arthur *see* Maccomo, Martini
Wirth, John 159
Wirth, George 159–165
Wirth's Circus 159–165, 176–177
   fighting act 159–164
Wombwell, George 3, 4, 9–11, 148
Wombwell's Menagerie 4, 8, 28–30, 55, 70, 80, 109, 127–128, 146–148
Woodward, Captain Joseph 196

Youatt, W 24–25
Young Lee, Paula 6

Ziter, Edward 8
zoo xi, xiii–xiv, xvii, 67, 72–73, 77, 106, 126, 187, 221, 245; *see also* travelling menageries
   animal show versus xiv, 83, 124, 229, 235
   as rational recreation 105, 119
   Victorian xii, 157
Zoological Gardens, London 105, 123
Zoological Institute (USA) 84
Zulu warriors 181–184, 190, 191
   with Farini's 181–184
   with Fillis' 166
   with Wirth's 163, 187

www.ingramcontent.com/pod-product-compliance
Lightning Source LLC
Chambersburg PA
CBHW062001220426
43662CB00010B/1195